Acknowledgements

The publishers would like to thank the

Telegraph Colour Library
for permission to reproduce

Cover image:
Tom Van Sant / Geosphere Project, Santa Monica,
Science Photo Library.

The illustrations are by Chapman Bounford,
Hard Lines, and Gary Hinks.

The page design is by Adrian Smith.

Oil spillage data is from
*Oil Pollution Survey around the Coast
of the United Kingdom, 1995*
by kind permission of the publishers,
ACOPS (Advisory Committee on Protection of the Sea).

THE
OXFORD
Practical
ATLAS

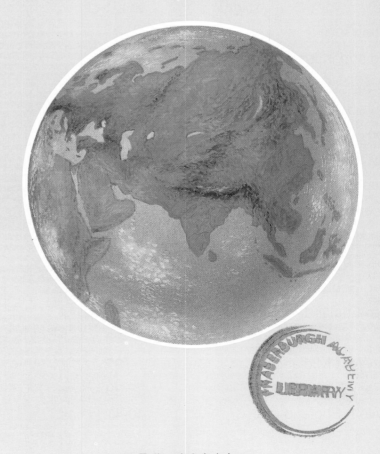

© Oxford University Press, 1997

© Maps copyright Oxford University Press

Oxford University Press, Great Clarendon Street, Oxford OX2 6DP

Oxford New York
Athens Auckland Bangkok Bombay
Calcutta Cape Town Dar es Salaam Delhi
Florence Hong Kong Istanbul Karachi
Kuala Lumpur Madras Madrid Melbourne
Mexico City Nairobi Paris Singapore
Taipei Tokyo Toronto

and associated companies in
Berlin Ibadan

Oxford is a trade mark of Oxford University Press

First published 1997.
Reprinted with corrections, December 1997

ISBN 0 19 831835 9 (paperback)   ISBN 0 19 831836 7 (hardback)

Printed in Italy by G. Canale & C. S.p.A. - Borgaro T.se - Turin

Editorial Adviser

Patrick Wiegand

Oxford University Press

2 **Contents** The World, The British Isles

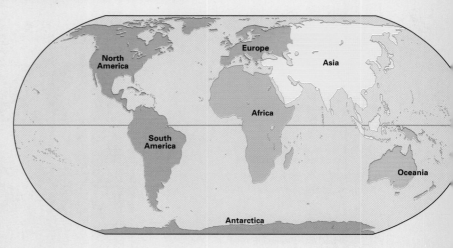

The World

Countries	4-5
Land and water	6-7
Climate and ecosystems	8-9
Earthquakes and volcanoes	10-11
Population	12-13
Development and interdependence	14-15
Environment and pollution	16-17

The British Isles

Countries	18
Land and water	19
Climate	20-21
Population	22
Farming and industry	23
Energy	24
Communications	25
Pollution	26
Scenery and conservation	27
Topographic map	28
Orkney and Shetland Islands	29
Scottish Highlands and Islands	30-31
Northern Ireland	32
Southern Scotland	33
Northern England	34-35
Wales	36
English West Midlands	37
South East England	38-39
South West England	40-41

Maps that show general features of regions, countries or continents are called **topographic maps.**
These maps are shown with a light band of colour in the contents list.

For example:

South West England

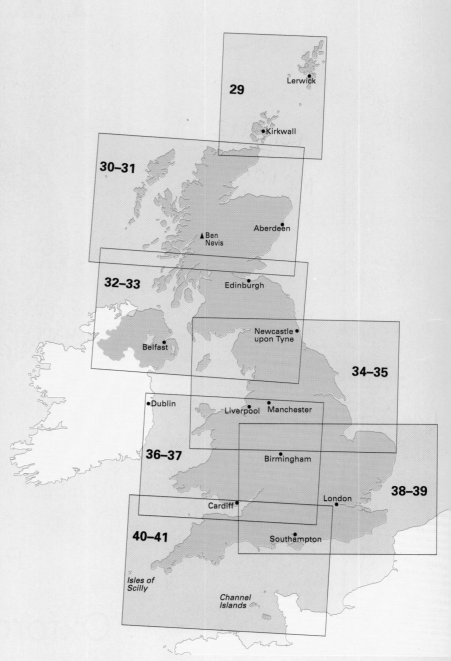

© Oxford University Press

Contents   Continents and Poles 3

Europe

Topographic map	42-43
European Union	43
Wealth	43
Climate and ecosystems	44
Farming, energy, and minerals	45
Industry and environmental issues	46
Population	47
France	48
Benelux, Germany, Alps	49
Spain and Portugal	50
Italy	51

Asia

Countries, land and water	52
Climate and ecosystems	53
Farming, energy, minerals, and industry	54
Population and environmental issues	55
Commonwealth of Independent States	56-57
Southern Asia	58
China and Japan	59
South East Asia	60
The Middle East and North Africa	61

Africa

Countries, land and water	62
Climate and ecosystems	63
Farming, energy, minerals, and industry	64
Population and environmental issues	65
North and West Africa	66
South and East Africa	67

Oceania

Countries, land and water	68
Climate and ecosystems	69
Farming, energy, minerals, and industry	70
Population and environmental issues	71
Australia	72
New Zealand	73

North America

Countries, land and water	74
Climate and ecosystems	75
Farming, energy, minerals, and industry	76
Population and environmental issues	77
Canada, Greenland, USA, Mexico and the Caribbean	78-79

South America

Countries, land and water	80
Climate and ecosystems	81
Farming, energy, minerals, and industry	82
Population and environmental issues	83
South America	84-85

The Poles

The Arctic Ocean	86
Antarctica	86

Index   87-96

Key

CANADA   Country name

   Country area

A	ALBANIA
AR	ARMENIA
AU	AUSTRIA
AZ	AZERBAIJAN
B	BELGIUM
BD	BRUNEI DARUSSALAM
BE	BENIN
BH	BOSNIA-HERZEGOVINA
BU	BURKINA
C	CROATIA
CAR	CENTRAL AFRICAN REPUBLIC
CZ	CZECH REPUBLIC
G	THE GAMBIA
G-B	GUINEA-BISSAU
H	HUNGARY
IS	ISRAEL
L	LEBANON
LI	LITHUANIA
LU	LUXEMBOURG
M	FORMER YUGOSLAV REPUBLIC OF MACEDONIA
N	NETHERLANDS
Q	QATAR
R	ROMANIA
S	SLOVAKIA
SL	SLOVENIA
SW	SWITZERLAND
T	TAJIKISTAN
TU	TURKMENISTAN
U	UGANDA
UAE	UNITED ARAB EMIRATES
Y	YUGOSLAVIA
ZIM	ZIMBABWE

Scale

1: 105 000 000

One centimetre on the map represents
1050 kilometres on the ground.

0   1050   2100   3150   4200 km

Making a world map

There are many ways of
showing the spherical Earth on
a flat map. Each map projection
uses a different grid pattern.

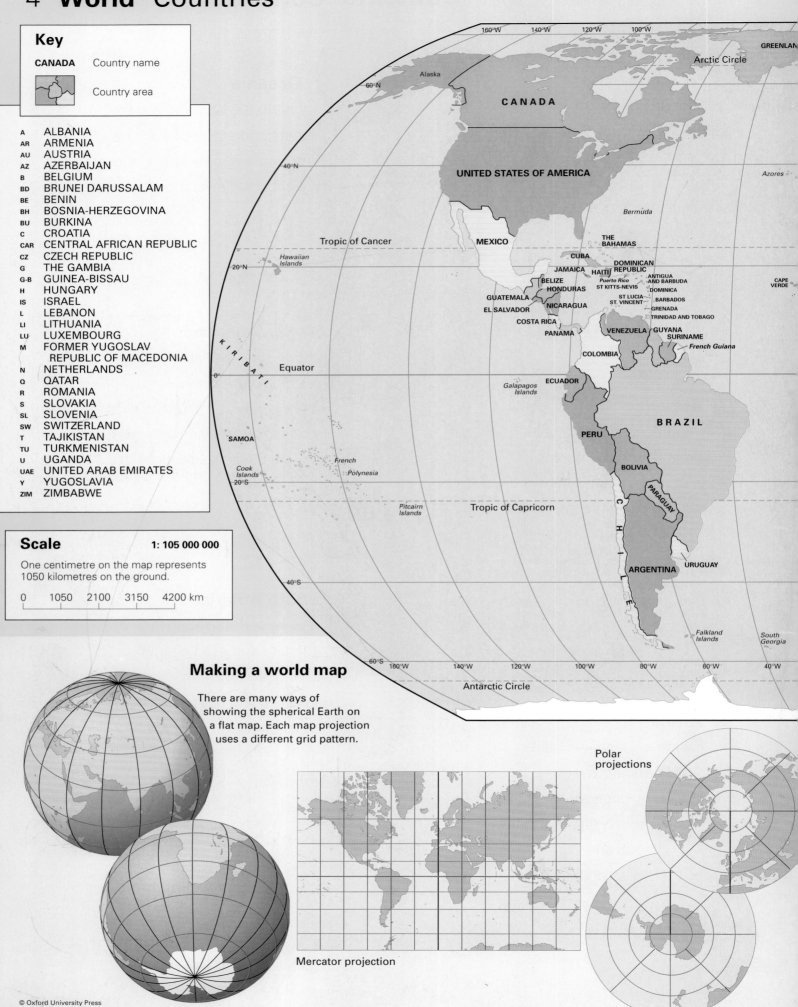

Polar
projections

Mercator projection

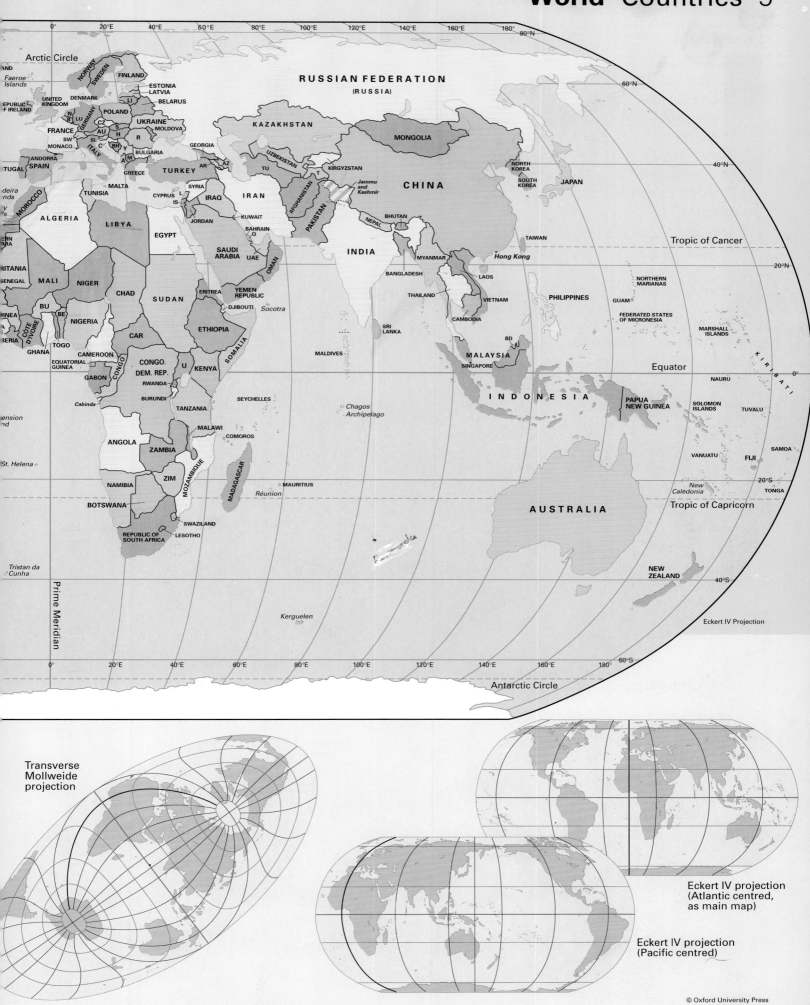

Arctic Circle

80°N

0° 20°E 40°E 60°E 80°E 100°E 120°E 140°E 160°E 180°

RUSSIAN FEDERATION
(RUSSIA)

60°N

Faeroe
Islands

NORWAY
SWEDEN
FINLAND

ESTONIA
LATVIA

REPUBLIC
OF IRELAND

UNITED
KINGDOM

DENMARK

BELARUS

KAZAKHSTAN

MONGOLIA

N
LU
B

GERMANY

POLAND

NORTH
KOREA

40°N

FRANCE

CZ
AU
S
SL
H
R

UKRAINE

MOLDOVA

UZBEKISTAN

KIRGYZSTAN

CHINA

SOUTH
KOREA

JAPAN

MONACO

ITALY

M

BULGARIA

GEORGIA

AR
AZ
TU

T

SW

A
BH

GREECE

ANDORRA

SPAIN

TURKEY

IRAN

Jammu
and
Kashmir

SYRIA

AFGHANISTAN

PAKISTAN

TUGAL

MALTA

TUNISIA

CYPRUS

L
IS

IRAQ

JORDAN

KUWAIT

NEPAL

BHUTAN

Tropic of Cancer

40°N

ds

MOROCCO

ALGERIA

LIBYA

EGYPT

SAUDI
ARABIA

BAHRAIN
Q
UAE

OMAN

INDIA

MYANMAR

Hong Kong

20°N

ERN

RITANIA

MALI

NIGER

CHAD

SUDAN

ERITREA

YEMEN
REPUBLIC

DJIBOUTI

BANGLADESH

THAILAND

LAOS

VIETNAM

PHILIPPINES

GUAM

NORTHERN
MARIANAS

FEDERATED STATES
OF MICRONESIA

MARSHALL
ISLANDS

SENEGAL

BU

GUINEA

NIGERIA

COTE
D'IVOIRE

TOGO

GHANA

CAMEROON

EQUATORIAL
GUINEA

CAR

CONGO
DEM. REP.

Socotra

ETHIOPIA

SOMALIA

MALDIVES

SRI
LANKA

CAMBODIA

MALAYSIA

SINGAPORE

BD

Equator

NAURU

KIRIBATI

0°

GABON

U

KENYA

RWANDA

Cabinda

BURUNDI

TANZANIA

SEYCHELLES

Chagos
Archipelago

INDONESIA

PAPUA
NEW GUINEA

SOLOMON
ISLANDS

TUVALU

ANGOLA

ZAMBIA

MALAWI

COMOROS

MADAGASCAR

MOZAMBIQUE

VANUATU

FIJI

SAMOA

St. Helena

ension
nd

NAMIBIA

ZIM

MAURITIUS

Réunion

New
Caledonia

20°S

TONGA

BOTSWANA

SWAZILAND

AUSTRALIA

Tropic of Capricorn

REPUBLIC OF
SOUTH AFRICA

LESOTHO

Tristan da
Cunha

NEW
ZEALAND

40°S

Prime Meridian

Kerguelen

Eckert IV Projection

0° 20°E 40°E 60°E 80°E 100°E 120°E 140°E 160°E 180°

60°S

Antarctic Circle

Transverse
Mollweide
projection

Eckert IV projection
(Atlantic centred,
as main map)

Eckert IV projection
(Pacific centred)

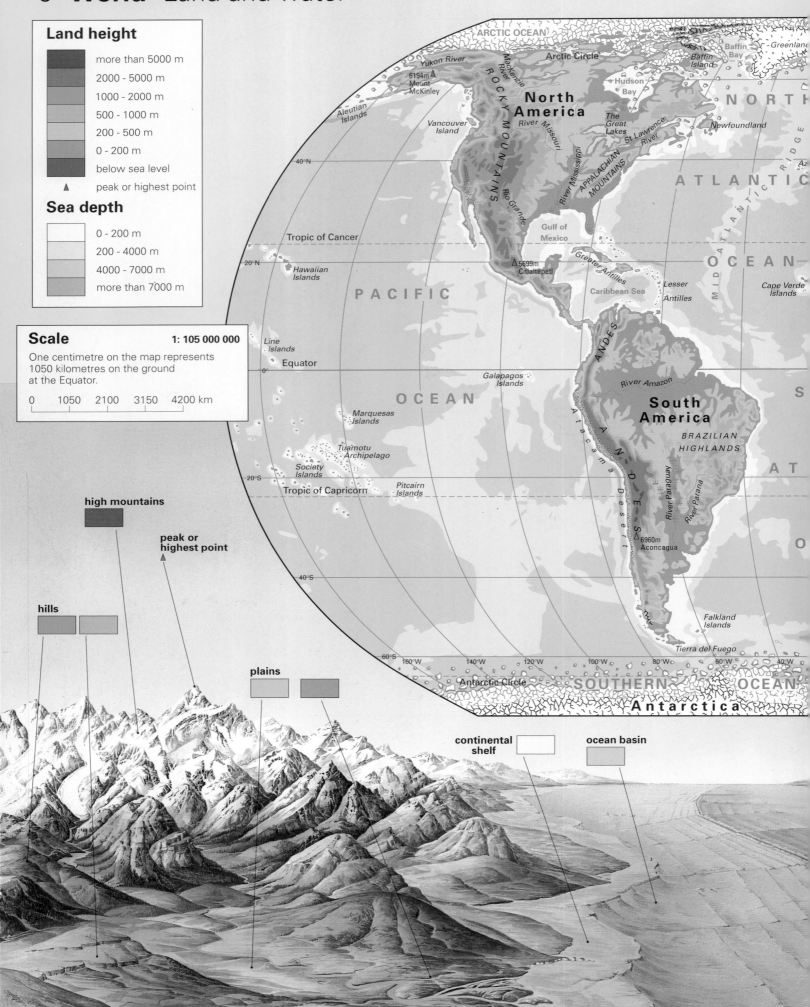

Land height

- more than 5000 m
- 2000 - 5000 m
- 1000 - 2000 m
- 500 - 1000 m
- 200 - 500 m
- 0 - 200 m
- below sea level
- ▲ peak or highest point

Sea depth

- 0 - 200 m
- 200 - 4000 m
- 4000 - 7000 m
- more than 7000 m

Scale   1: 105 000 000

One centimetre on the map represents
1050 kilometres on the ground
at the Equator.

0   1050   2100   3150   4200 km

high mountains

peak or
highest point
▲

hills

plains

continental
shelf

ocean basin

ARCTIC OCEAN
Arctic Circle
Baffin
Bay
Greenland
Baffin
Island
NORTH
Yukon River
6194m
Mount
McKinley
Mackenzie
River
ROCKY MOUNTAINS
North
America
Hudson
Bay
Aleutian
Islands
Vancouver
Island
River Missouri
The
Great
Lakes
St Lawrence
River
Newfoundland
ATLANTIC
40°N
River Mississippi
APPALACHIAN
MOUNTAINS
Az
20°N
Tropic of Cancer
Rio Grande
Gulf of
Mexico
△5699m
Citlaltépetl
Greater Antilles
OCEAN
MID-ATLANTIC RIDGE
Hawaiian
Islands
PACIFIC
Caribbean Sea
Lesser
Antilles
Cape Verde
Islands
Line
Islands
Equator
OCEAN
Galapagos
Islands
River Amazon
South
America
AT
Marquesas
Islands
BRAZILIAN
HIGHLANDS
Tuamotu
Archipelago
ANDES
Society
Islands
20°S
Tropic of Capricorn
Pitcairn
Islands
Atacama Desert
River Paraguay
River Paraná
O
40°S
△6960m
Aconcagua
Falkland
Islands
Tierra del Fuego
60°S 160°W 140°W 120°W 100°W 80°W 60°W 40°W
Antarctic Circle
SOUTHERN
OCEAN
Antarctica

Eckert IV Projection
© Oxford University Press

Europe

Asia

Africa

Oceania

Antarctica

ARCTIC OCEAN

Arctic Circle

Barents
Sea

North
Sea

British
Isles

R. Rhine

ALPS
4807m
Mont
Blanc

River Danube

River Volga

URAL MOUNTAINS

Pripet
Marshes

Mount
Elbrus
5642m

CAUCASUS

Black Sea

TAURUS
MOUNTAINS

Aral
Sea

Caspian
Sea

River Ob

Yenisey River

River Irtysh

River Lena

ALTAI MOUNTAINS

Lake
Baykal

Sea of
Okhotsk

Bering Sea

60°N

Aleutian Trench

Kuril Trench

Honshu

Gobi Desert

Hwang-Ho
River

Communism
Peak
7495m

8611m
K2

TIBETAN
PLATEAU

HIMALAYAS

8848m
Mount Everest

River Ganges

DECCAN

River Yangtze

Mekong River

40°N

East
China
Sea

Ryukyu Trench

Tropic of Cancer

PACIFIC

OCEAN

20°N

Sahara Desert

ATLAS MOUNTAINS

Mediterranean Sea

Madeira
Islands

River Nile

Red Sea

ZAGROS MOUNTAINS

Arabian
Sea

Bay of
Bengal

Andaman
Islands

Nicobar
Islands

South
China
Sea

Philippines

Philippine Trench

Marianas
Islands

Yap
Islands

Mariana Trench

Caroline Islands

Marshall
Islands

River Niger

Lake
Chad

Lake
Victoria

5895m
Mount
Kilimanjaro

River Congo

Lake
Tanganyika

Seychelles

Aldabra
Islands

Lake
Nyasa
(Malawi)

Comoro
Archipelago

Maldive
Archipelago

INDIAN

OCEAN

Sumatra

Borneo

Java

New
Guinea

4508m
Mount
Wilhelm

Solomon
Islands

Espiritu
Santo

Equator

Gilbert
Islands

Phoenix
Islands

Samoa
Islands

Fiji
Islands

0°

River Zambezi

Namib Desert

Okavango
Swamp

Kalahari
Desert

Madagascar

Mauritius

Réunion

Great Sandy
Desert

Great Victoria
Desert

NULLARBOR PLAIN

River Darling

GREAT DIVIDING RANGE

Murray R.

New
Caledonia

Tonga
Islands

Tropic of Capricorn

Prime Meridian

Kerguelen
Islands

SOUTHERN OCEAN

Tasmania

Tasman
Sea

North
Island

3764m
Mount
Cook

South
Island

40°S

ATLANTIC

RIDGE

20°E   40°E   60°E   80°E   100°E   120°E   140°E   160°E   180°

high plateau

low plateau

**ocean
trench**

continental shelf

ocean ridge

8 **World** Climate and Ecosystems

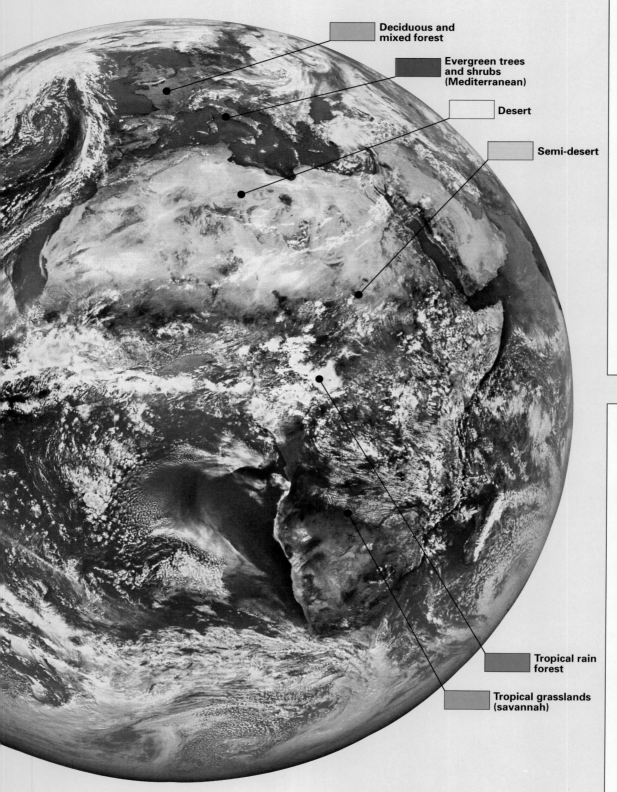

Deciduous and mixed forest

Evergreen trees and shrubs (Mediterranean)

Desert

Semi-desert

Tropical rain forest

Tropical grasslands (savannah)

A Meteosat view of
the Earth recorded
by a geostationary satellite
positioned 36 000 km above
the intersection of the
Prime Meridian and the Equator

Climatic regions

Hot tropical rainy

rain all year

monsoon

dry in winter

Very dry

with no reliable rain

with a little rain

Influenced by the sea: warm summers, mild winters

with dry summers (Mediterranean type)

with dry winters

with no dry season

Cool

with dry winters

rain all year

Cold polar

no warm season and fairly dry

Mountain

height of the land strongly affects the climate

Ecosystems

Vegetation types are those which would occur naturally without interference by people

Coniferous forest

cone bearing trees

Deciduous and mixed forest

leaf shedding and coniferous tress

Tropical rain forest

many species of lush, tall trees

Tropical grasslands (savannah)

tall grass parkland with scattered trees

Thorn forest

low trees and shrubs with spines or thorns

Evergreen trees and shrubs

plants and small trees with leathery leaves

Temperate grasslands

prairies, steppes, pampas and veld

Semi-desert

short grasses and drought-resistant scrub

Desert

sand and stones, very little vegetation

Tundra

moss and lichen, with few trees

Ice

no vegetation

Mountains

thin soils, steep slopes and high altitude affects type of vegetation

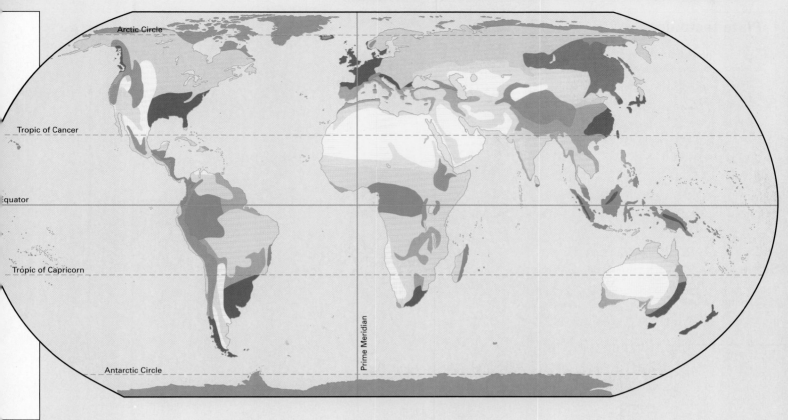

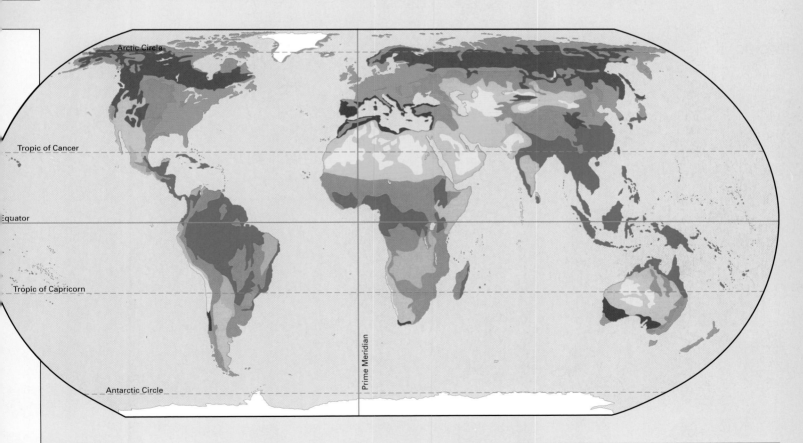

Eckert IV Projection

© Oxford University Press

Scale　　　　　　　　　**1: 190 000 000**

One centimetre on the map represents
1900 kilometres on the ground
at the Equator.

0　　　1900　　3800　　5700 km

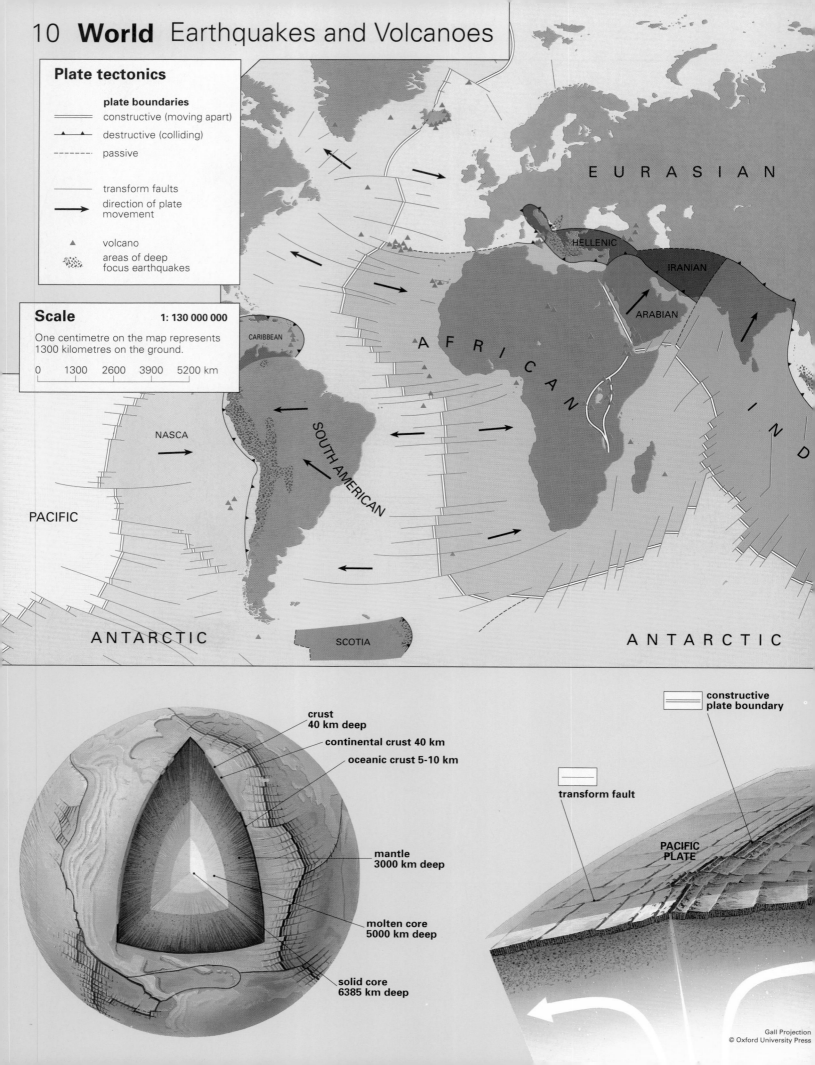

Plate tectonics

plate boundaries

constructive (moving apart)

destructive (colliding)

passive

transform faults

direction of plate movement

▲ volcano

areas of deep focus earthquakes

Scale

1: 130 000 000

One centimetre on the map represents 1300 kilometres on the ground.

0   1300   2600   3900   5200 km

EURASIAN

HELLENIC

IRANIAN

ARABIAN

A F R I C A N

CARIBBEAN

NASCA

SOUTH AMERICAN

PACIFIC

I N D

ANTARCTIC

ANTARCTIC

SCOTIA

crust
40 km deep

continental crust 40 km

oceanic crust 5-10 km

mantle
3000 km deep

molten core
5000 km deep

solid core
6385 km deep

constructive
plate boundary

transform fault

PACIFIC
PLATE

Gall Projection
© Oxford University Press

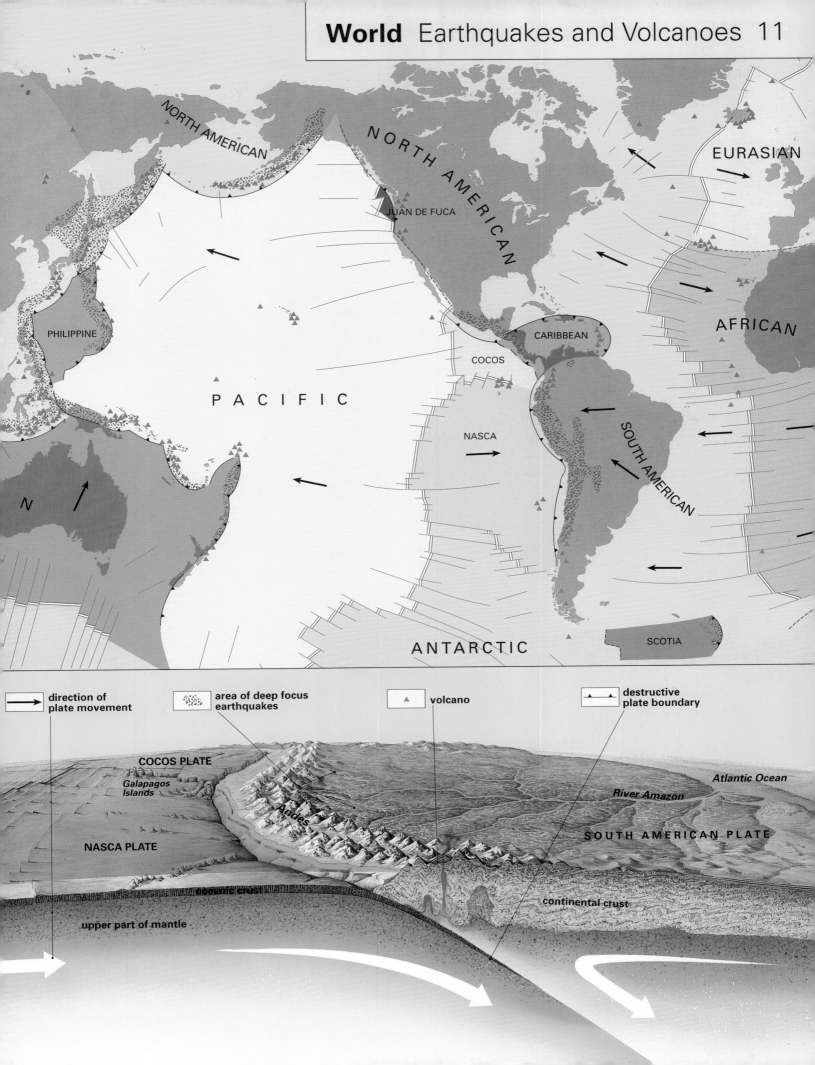

NORTH AMERICAN

NORTH AMERICAN

EURASIAN

JUAN DE FUCA

PHILIPPINE

CARIBBEAN

COCOS

AFRICAN

PACIFIC

NASCA

SOUTH AMERICAN

N

ANTARCTIC

SCOTIA

direction of plate movement

area of deep focus earthquakes

volcano

destructive plate boundary

COCOS PLATE

Galapagos Islands

Atlantic Ocean

River Amazon

Andes

SOUTH AMERICAN PLATE

NASCA PLATE

oceanic crust

continental crust

upper part of mantle

Population density

number of people
per square kilometre

high		more than 50
moderate		6 - 49
sparse		1 - 5
very low		less than 1

○ major cities and built up
areas of at least 3 000 000
people

—— international boundary

Scale   1: 105 000 000

One centimetre on the map represents
1050 kilometres on the ground
at the Equator.

0   1050   2100   3150   4200 km

World population growth
AD1 to 1994

thousand
million
people

1AD 100 200 300 400 500 600 700 800 900 1000 1100 1200 1300 1400 1500 1600 1700 1800 1900 1994

Black Death

Agricultural and Industrial Revolutions

Revolution in Health Care

World population growth
Twentieth century and the future

| | economically developing countries |
| | economically developed countries |

12 thousand
million
people

1900 1920 1940 1960 1980 2000 2020 2040 2060 2080 2100 2120 2140

projected

In 1995 the total world population was
approximately 5 700 000 000.

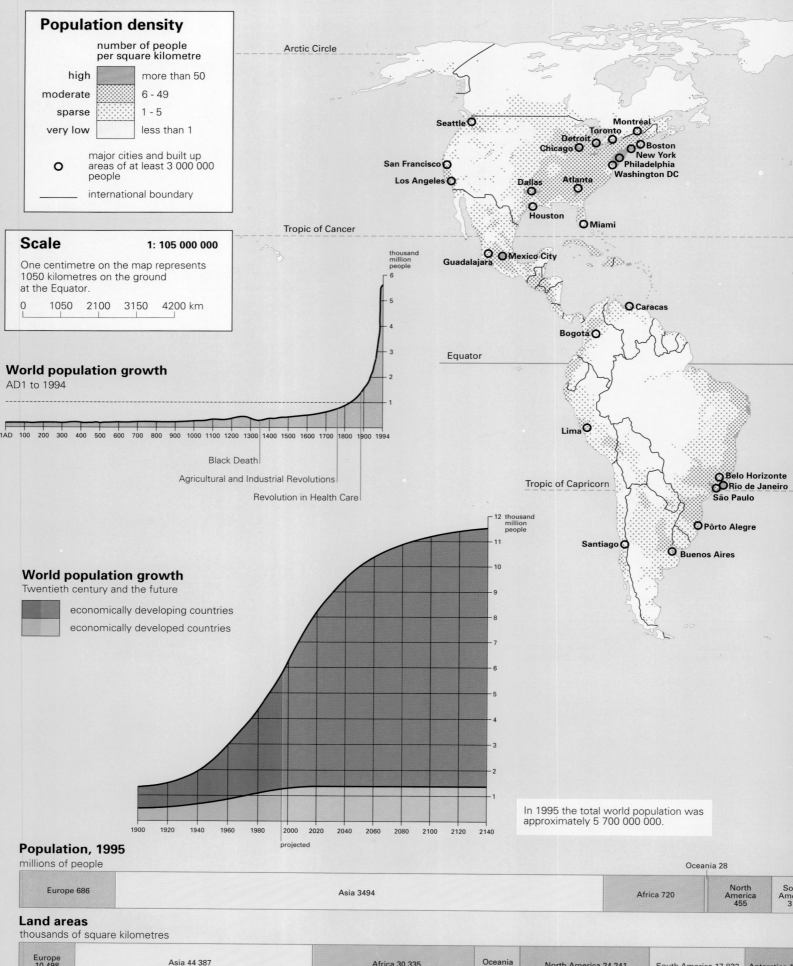

Arctic Circle

Seattle

Montréal
Toronto
Detroit
Chicago   Boston
                 New York
San Francisco   Philadelphia
                 Washington DC
Los Angeles
Dallas   Atlanta

Houston
        Miami

Tropic of Cancer

Guadalajara   Mexico City

Caracas

Bogotá

Equator

Lima

Tropic of Capricorn

Belo Horizonte
Rio de Janeiro
São Paulo

Pôrto Alegre

Santiago
Buenos Aires

Population, 1995
millions of people

Oceania 28

| Europe 686 | Asia 3494 | Africa 720 | North America 455 | Sou... Amer... 319 |

Land areas
thousands of square kilometres

| Europe 10 498 | Asia 44 387 | Africa 30 335 | Oceania 8503 | North America 24 241 | South America 17 832 | Antarctica 13... |

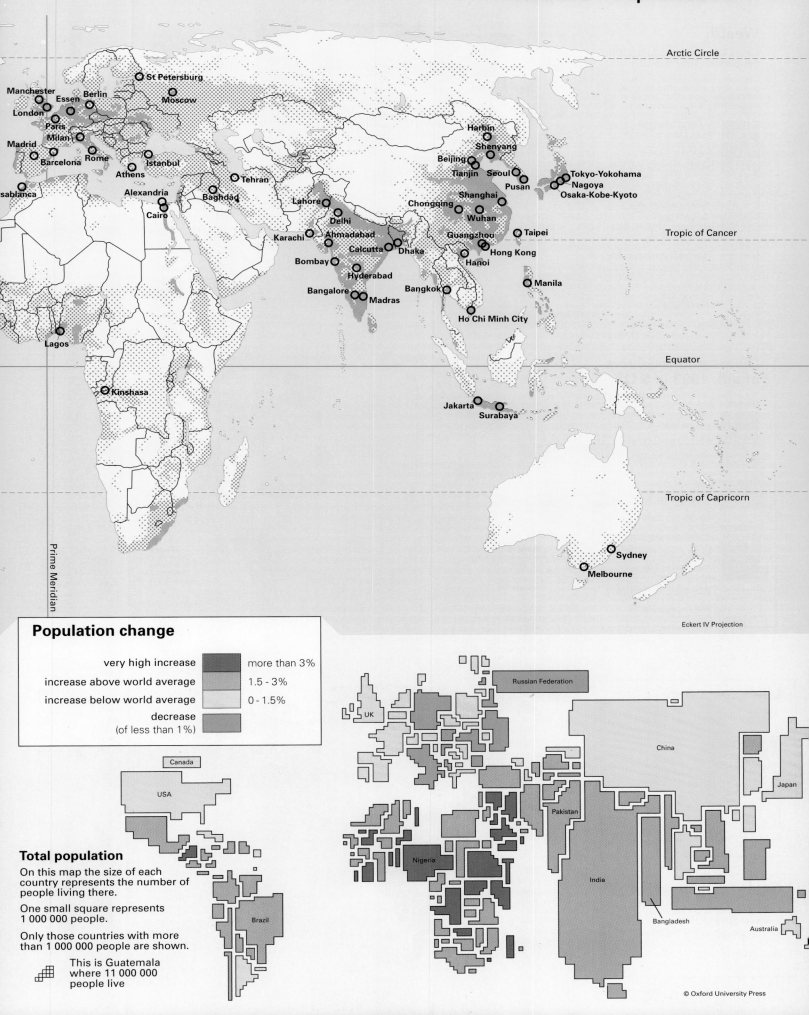

Arctic Circle

Manchester
Essen   Berlin
London   Moscow
Paris
Madrid   Milan
Barcelona Rome
          Athens   Istanbul
sablanca   Alexandria   Tehran
          Cairo   Baghdad
St Petersburg

Harbin
Shenyang
Beijing
Tianjin   Seoul
          Pusan
Chongqing   Shanghai
          Wuhan
Guangzhou
Hong Kong   Taipei

Tokyo-Yokohama
Nagoya
Osaka-Kobe-Kyoto

Tropic of Cancer

Lahore
Karachi   Delhi
       Ahmadabad
       Calcutta   Dhaka
Bombay
       Hyderabad   Hanoi
Bangalore   Bangkok
       Madras
          Ho Chi Minh City

Manila

Lagos

Kinshasa

Equator

Jakarta
Surabaya

Tropic of Capricorn

Eckert IV Projection

Sydney
Melbourne

Population change

very high increase		more than 3%
increase above world average		1.5 - 3%
increase below world average		0 - 1.5%
decrease (of less than 1%)		

Total population

On this map the size of each
country represents the number of
people living there.

One small square represents
1 000 000 people.

Only those countries with more
than 1 000 000 people are shown.

This is Guatemala
where 11 000 000
people live

Russian Federation
UK
China
Japan
Canada
USA
Pakistan
Nigeria
India
Brazil
Bangladesh
Australia

Wealth

Gross Domestic Product (GDP) per person, 1992 in $ US

The annual total value of all the goods and services produced in a country, divided by the number of people living in that country.

15 000–24 000 (the top 25 in the world)

10 000–15 000

5000–10 000
— World average

3000–5000

1000–3000

under 1000 (the bottom 22 in the world)

— international boundary

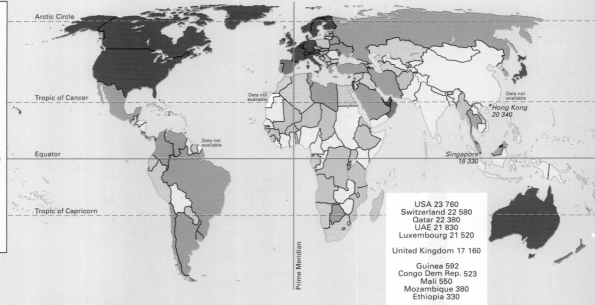

Hong Kong 20 340

Singapore 18 330

Data not available

USA 23 760
Switzerland 22 580
Qatar 22 380
UAE 21 830
Luxembourg 21 520

United Kingdom 17 160

Guinea 592
Congo Dem Rep. 523
Mali 550
Mozambique 380
Ethiopia 330

Givers and receivers of aid, 1993 in $ US

Givers

more than 100 per person

50-100 per person

25-50 per person

Receivers

0-10 per person

10-25 per person

25-50 per person

50-100 per person

more than 100 per person

— international boundary

data not available

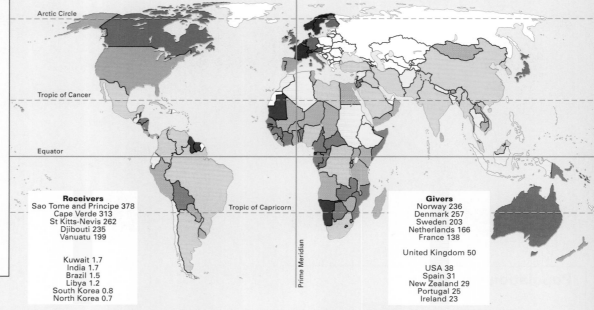

Receivers
Sao Tome and Principe 378
Cape Verde 313
St Kitts-Nevis 262
Djibouti 235
Vanuatu 199

Kuwait 1.7
India 1.7
Brazil 1.5
Libya 1.2
South Korea 0.8
North Korea 0.7

Givers
Norway 236
Denmark 257
Sweden 203
Netherlands 166
France 138

United Kingdom 50

USA 38
Spain 31
New Zealand 29
Portugal 25
Ireland 23

Life expectancy

Average number of years a baby

70 years and over

65-70 years

55-65 years

45-55 years

35-45 years

— international boundary

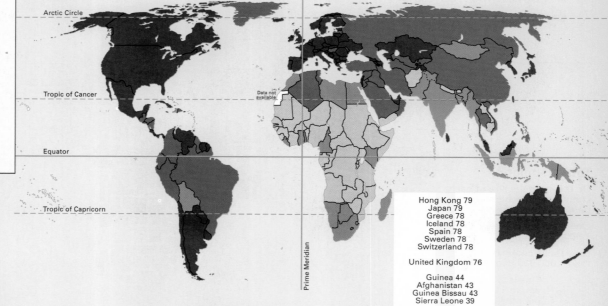

Data not available

Hong Kong 79
Japan 79
Greece 78
Iceland 78
Spain 78
Sweden 78
Switzerland 78

United Kingdom 76

Guinea 44
Afghanistan 43
Guinea Bissau 43
Sierra Leone 39

Scale

1: 235 000 000

One centimetre on the map represents 2350 kilometres on the ground at the Equator.

0   2350   4700   7050 km

Eckert IV Projection

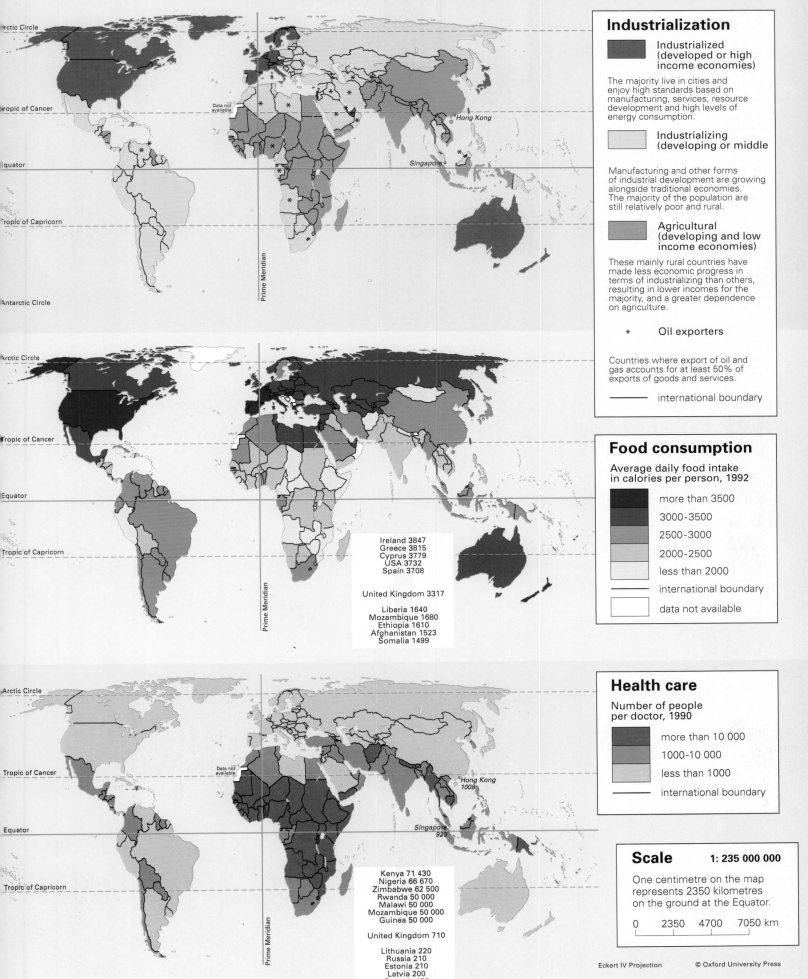

Industrialization

**Industrialized
(developed or high
income economies)**

The majority live in cities and
enjoy high standards based on
manufacturing, services, resource
development and high levels of
energy consumption.

**Industrializing
(developing or middle**

Manufacturing and other forms
of industrial development are growing
alongside traditional economies.
The majority of the population are
still relatively poor and rural.

**Agricultural
(developing and low
income economies)**

These mainly rural countries have
made less economic progress in
terms of industrializing than others,
resulting in lower incomes for the
majority, and a greater dependence
on agriculture.

* Oil exporters

Countries where export of oil and
gas accounts for at least 50% of
exports of goods and services.

—— international boundary

Food consumption

**Average daily food intake
in calories per person, 1992**

more than 3500
3000-3500
2500-3000
2000-2500
less than 2000
—— international boundary
data not available

Ireland 3847
Greece 3815
Cyprus 3779
USA 3732
Spain 3708

United Kingdom 3317

Liberia 1640
Mozambique 1680
Ethiopia 1610
Afghanistan 1523
Somalia 1499

Health care

**Number of people
per doctor, 1990**

more than 10 000
1000-10 000
less than 1000
—— international boundary

Kenya 71 430
Nigeria 66 670
Zimbabwe 62 500
Rwanda 50 000
Malawi 50 000
Mozambique 50 000
Guinea 50 000

United Kingdom 710

Lithuania 220
Russia 210
Estonia 210
Latvia 200
Georgia 170

Scale 1: 235 000 000

One centimetre on the map
represents 2350 kilometres
on the ground at the Equator.

0   2350   4700   7050 km

Hong Kong
Singapore
Data not available
Hong Kong 1008
Singapore 920

Arctic Circle
Tropic of Cancer
Equator
Tropic of Capricorn
Antarctic Circle
Prime Meridian

Eckert IV Projection   © Oxford University Press

Water

Surplus

Enough water to support vegetation and crops without irrigation

- large surplus
- surplus

Deficiency

Not enough water to support vegetation and crops without irrigation. After long periods of deficiency, these areas may lose their natural vegetation.

- deficiency
- chronic deficiency
- international boundary

Map labels: Arctic Circle, Scandinavia, Siberia, North European Plain, Prairies, Great Plains, Gobi Desert, South West USA Desert, Tibetan Plateau, Tropic of Cancer, Himalayas, Sahara Desert, Western Ghats, Sahel, Equator, Congo Basin, Amazonia, Atacama, Tropic of Capricorn, Namib Desert, Kalahari Desert, Great Victoria Desert, Great Dividing Range, Patagonia, Prime Meridian

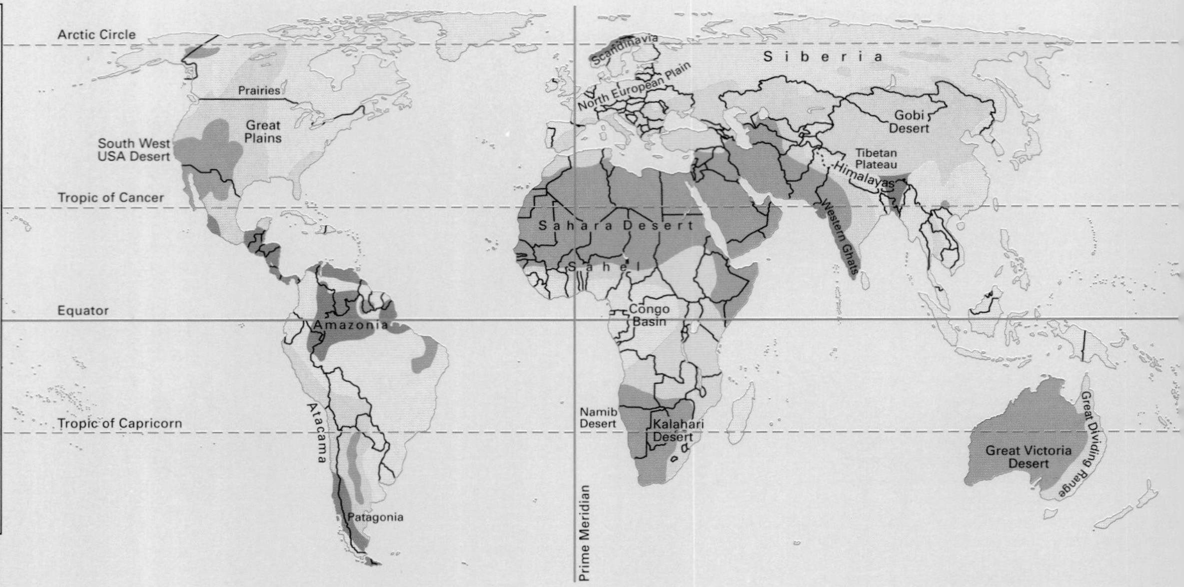

Desertification

- existing areas of desert
- areas with a high risk of desertification
- areas with a moderate risk of desertification
- international boundary

Map labels: Arctic Circle, South West USA Desert, Turkestan Desert, Gobi Desert, Tropic of Cancer, Sahara Desert, Thar Desert, Arabian Desert, Sahel, Somali Desert, Equator, Atacama, Namib Desert, Kalahari Desert, Tropic of Capricorn, Great Victoria Desert, Patagonian Desert, Prime Meridian

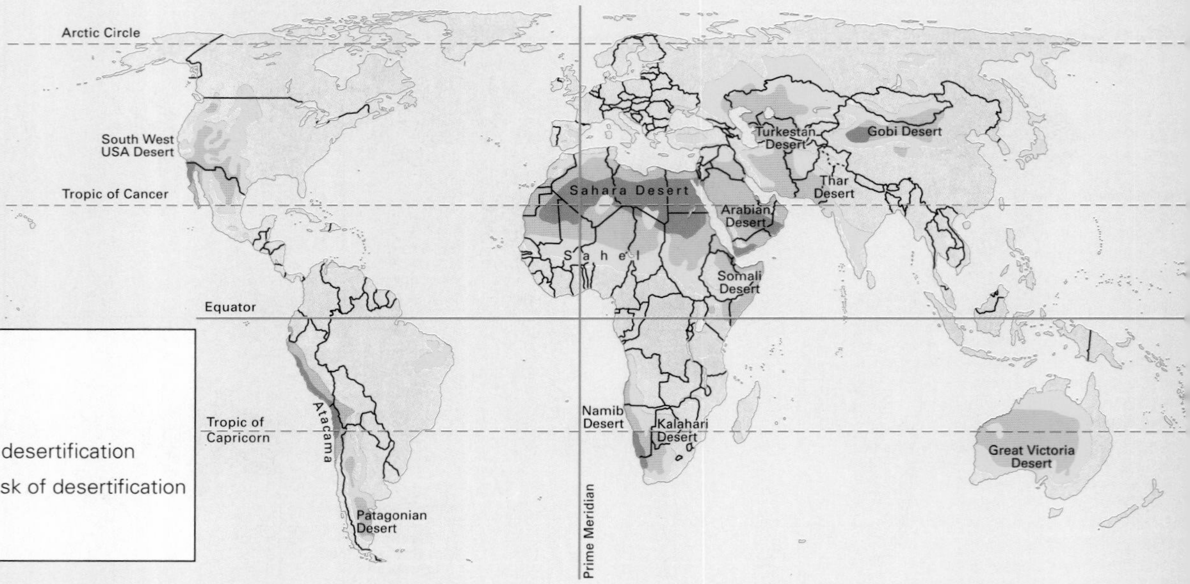

Tropical deforestation

- existing areas of rainforest
- former areas of rainforest
- international boundary

Map labels: Arctic Circle, Tropic of Cancer, Caribbean, Northern India, Assam, South East China, Western India, Burma, Vietnam, Philippines, Sri Lanka, Cambodia, West Africa, Congo Basin, Thailand, Malaya, Equator, Sumatra, Borneo, Amazonia, New Guinea, Eastern Brazil, Mozambique, Tropic of Capricorn, Madagascar, Queensland, Prime Meridian

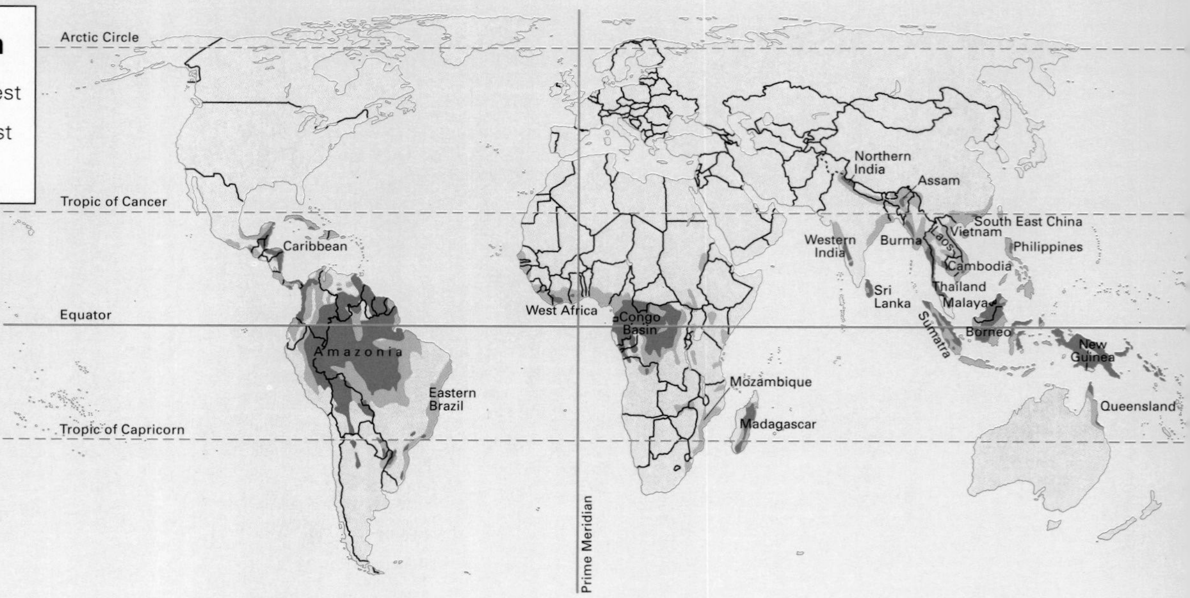

Scale

1: 235 000 000

One centimetre on the map measures 2350 kilometres on the ground at the Equator.

0   2350   4700   7050 km

Eckert IV Projection
© Oxford University Press

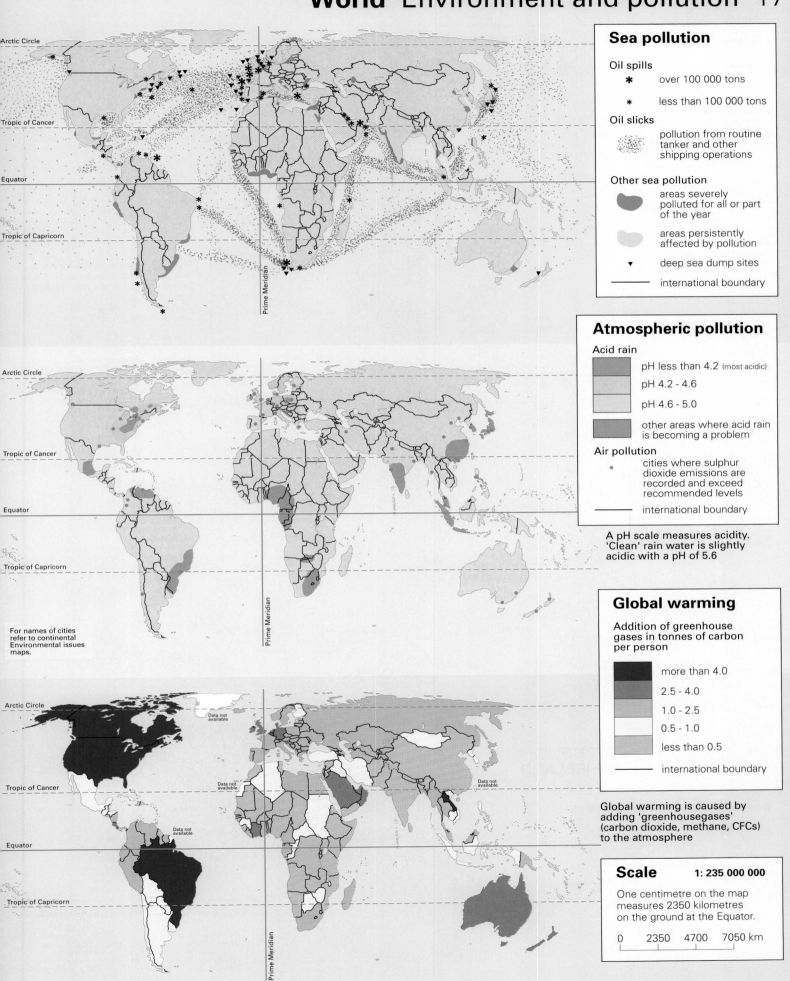

Sea pollution

Oil spills

*   over 100 000 tons

*   less than 100 000 tons

Oil slicks

pollution from routine tanker and other shipping operations

Other sea pollution

areas severely polluted for all or part of the year

areas persistently affected by pollution

▼   deep sea dump sites

——   international boundary

Atmospheric pollution

Acid rain

pH less than 4.2 (most acidic)

pH 4.2 - 4.6

pH 4.6 - 5.0

other areas where acid rain is becoming a problem

Air pollution

•   cities where sulphur dioxide emissions are recorded and exceed recommended levels

——   international boundary

A pH scale measures acidity. 'Clean' rain water is slightly acidic with a pH of 5.6

For names of cities refer to continental Environmental issues maps.

Global warming

Addition of greenhouse gases in tonnes of carbon per person

more than 4.0

2.5 - 4.0

1.0 - 2.5

0.5 - 1.0

less than 0.5

——   international boundary

Global warming is caused by adding 'greenhousegases' (carbon dioxide, methane, CFCs) to the atmosphere

Scale   1: 235 000 000

One centimetre on the map measures 2350 kilometres on the ground at the Equator.

0   2350   4700   7050 km

Eckert IV Projection

© Oxford University Press

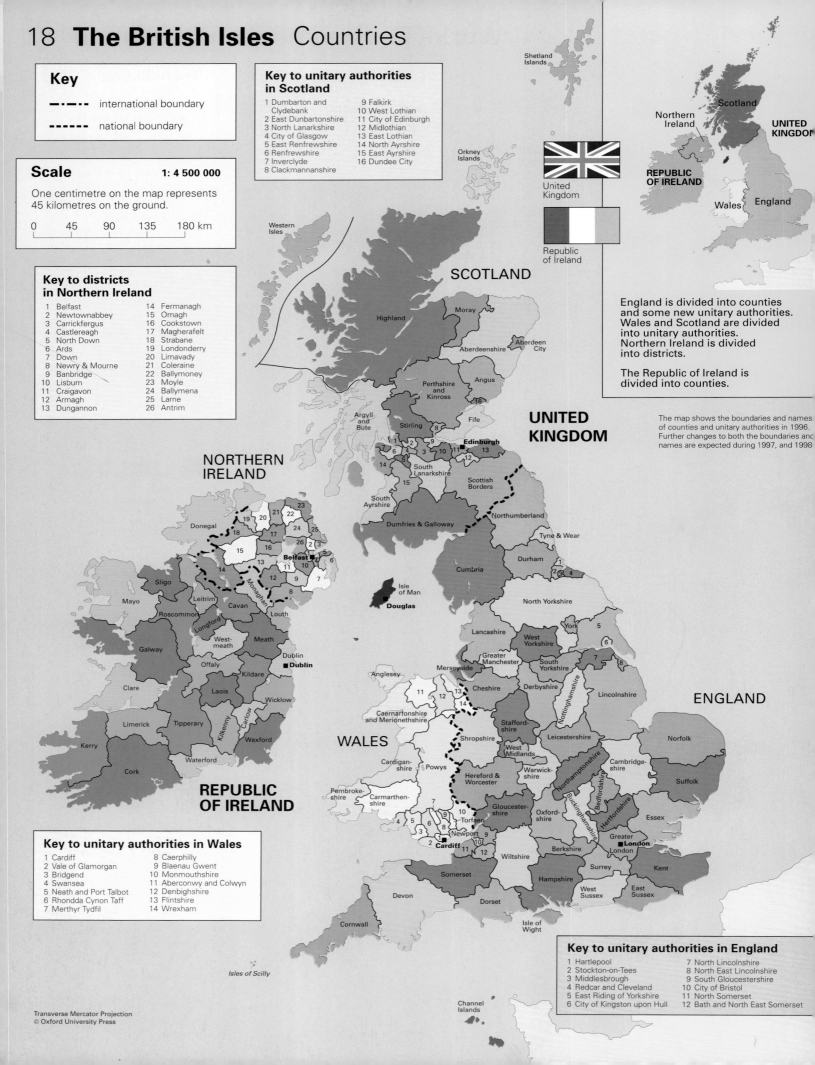

Key

- —·—·— international boundary
- ------ national boundary

Scale

1 : 4 500 000

One centimetre on the map represents 45 kilometres on the ground.

0   45   90   135   180 km

Key to unitary authorities in Scotland

1 Dumbarton and Clydebank
2 East Dunbartonshire
3 North Lanarkshire
4 City of Glasgow
5 East Renfrewshire
6 Renfrewshire
7 Inverclyde
8 Clackmannanshire
9 Falkirk
10 West Lothian
11 City of Edinburgh
12 Midlothian
13 East Lothian
14 North Ayrshire
15 East Ayrshire
16 Dundee City

Key to districts in Northern Ireland

1 Belfast
2 Newtownabbey
3 Carrickfergus
4 Castlereagh
5 North Down
6 Ards
7 Down
8 Newry & Mourne
9 Banbridge
10 Lisburn
11 Craigavon
12 Armagh
13 Dungannon
14 Fermanagh
15 Omagh
16 Cookstown
17 Magherafelt
18 Strabane
19 Londonderry
20 Limavady
21 Coleraine
22 Ballymoney
23 Moyle
24 Ballymena
25 Larne
26 Antrim

England is divided into counties and some new unitary authorities. Wales and Scotland are divided into unitary authorities. Northern Ireland is divided into districts.

The Republic of Ireland is divided into counties.

The map shows the boundaries and names of counties and unitary authorities in 1996. Further changes to both the boundaries and names are expected during 1997, and 1998

United Kingdom

Republic of Ireland

Key to unitary authorities in Wales

1 Cardiff
2 Vale of Glamorgan
3 Bridgend
4 Swansea
5 Neath and Port Talbot
6 Rhondda Cynon Taff
7 Merthyr Tydfil
8 Caerphilly
9 Blaenau Gwent
10 Monmouthshire
11 Aberconwy and Colwyn
12 Denbighshire
13 Flintshire
14 Wrexham

Key to unitary authorities in England

1 Hartlepool
2 Stockton-on-Tees
3 Middlesbrough
4 Redcar and Cleveland
5 East Riding of Yorkshire
6 City of Kingston upon Hull
7 North Lincolnshire
8 North East Lincolnshire
9 South Gloucestershire
10 City of Bristol
11 North Somerset
12 Bath and North East Somerset

Transverse Mercator Projection
© Oxford University Press

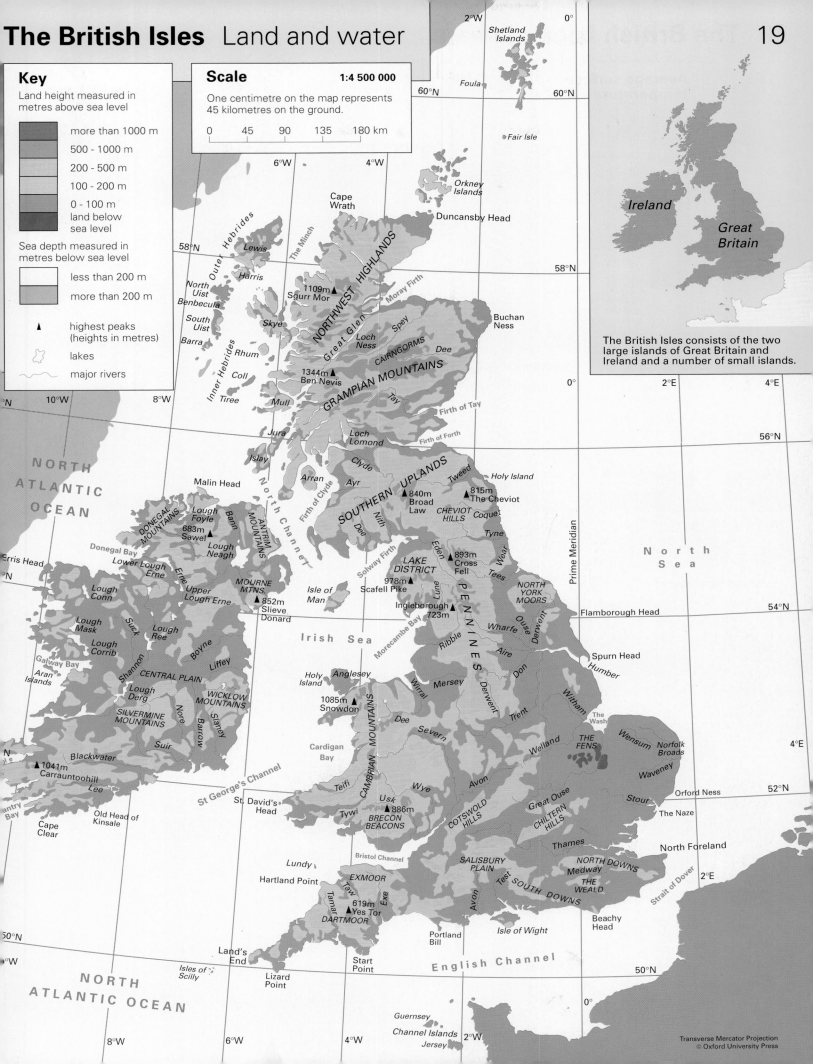

Key

Land height measured in metres above sea level

- more than 1000 m
- 500 - 1000 m
- 200 - 500 m
- 100 - 200 m
- 0 - 100 m
  land below sea level

Sea depth measured in metres below sea level

- less than 200 m
- more than 200 m

- ▲ highest peaks (heights in metres)
- lakes
- major rivers

Scale

1:4 500 000

One centimetre on the map represents 45 kilometres on the ground.

0   45   90   135   180 km

The British Isles consists of the two large islands of Great Britain and Ireland and a number of small islands.

Ireland

Great Britain

Transverse Mercator Projection
© Oxford University Press

Map labels:

Shetland Islands
Foula
Fair Isle
Orkney Islands
Cape Wrath
Duncansby Head
Outer Hebrides
Lewis
The Minch
NORTHWEST HIGHLANDS
Harris
North Uist
Benbecula
South Uist
Barra
1109m Sgurr Mor
Skye
Loch Ness
Great Glen
Moray Firth
Spey
Buchan Ness
CAIRNGORMS
Dee
Rhum
Coll
1344m Ben Nevis
GRAMPIAN MOUNTAINS
Inner Hebrides
Tiree
Mull
Tay
Firth of Tay
Jura
Loch Lomond
Firth of Forth
Islay
Clyde
Arran
Ayr
Firth of Clyde
SOUTHERN UPLANDS
Tweed
Holy Island
Malin Head
840m Broad Law
815m The Cheviot
NORTH CHANNEL
Nith
Dee
CHEVIOT HILLS
Coquet
DONEGAL MOUNTAINS
Lough Foyle
Bann
ANTRIM MOUNTAINS
683m Sawel
Lough Neagh
Tyne
Donegal Bay
Lower Lough Erne
Erne
Eden
893m Cross Fell
Wear
Erris Head
Upper Lough Erne
MOURNE MTNS.
Solway Firth
LAKE DISTRICT
Tees
NORTH YORK MOORS
Lough Conn
852m Slieve Donard
Isle of Man
978m Scafell Pike
PENNINES
Lough Mask
Lough Ree
Suck
Lough Corrib
Boyne
Ingleborough 723m
Wharfe
Ouse
Derwent
Flamborough Head
Galway Bay
Liffey
Irish Sea
Ribble
Aire
Spurn Head
Aran Islands
Shannon
CENTRAL PLAIN
Morecambe Bay
Holy Island
Anglesey
Mersey
Don
Humber
Lough Derg
WICKLOW MOUNTAINS
Wirral
Derwent
Trent
Witham
SILVERMINE MOUNTAINS
Nore
Barrow
Slaney
1085m Snowdon
CAMBRIAN MOUNTAINS
Dee
The Wash
1041m Carrauntoohill
Blackwater
Lee
Suir
Cardigan Bay
Severn
Welland
THE FENS
Wensum
Norfolk Broads
Teifi
Wye
Avon
COTSWOLD HILLS
Great Ouse
CHILTERN HILLS
Waveney
Cape Clear
Old Head of Kinsale
St George's Channel
St. David's Head
Tywi
Usk
886m BRECON BEACONS
Stour
Orford Ness
The Naze
Lundy
Bristol Channel
SALISBURY PLAIN
Thames
NORTH DOWNS
North Foreland
Hartland Point
EXMOOR
Taw
Exe
Avon
Test
SOUTH DOWNS
Medway
THE WEALD
619m Yes Tor
DARTMOOR
Tamar
Portland Bill
Isle of Wight
Beachy Head
Strait of Dover
Land's End
Isles of Scilly
Lizard Point
Start Point
English Channel
Guernsey
Channel Islands
Jersey

NORTH ATLANTIC OCEAN
NORTH SEA

Coordinate labels:
2°W, 0°, 60°N, 58°N, 56°N, 54°N, 52°N, 50°N
10°W, 8°W, 6°W, 4°W, 2°W
Prime Meridian
0°, 2°E, 4°E

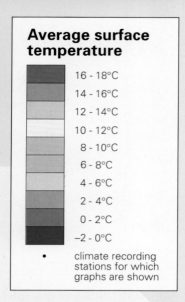

Average surface temperature

	16 - 18°C
	14 - 16°C
	12 - 14°C
	10 - 12°C
	8 - 10°C
	6 - 8°C
	4 - 6°C
	2 - 4°C
	0 - 2°C
	−2 - 0°C
•	climate recording stations for which graphs are shown

Scale   1: 8 000 000

One centimetre on the map represents 80 kilometres on the ground.

0   80   160   240 km

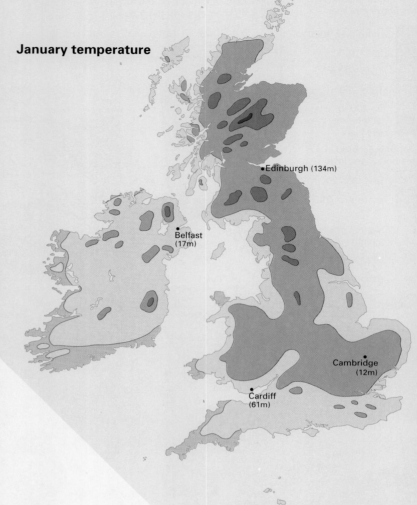

January temperature

Edinburgh (134m)

Belfast (17m)

Cambridge (12m)

Cardiff (61m)

July temperature

Edinburgh (134m)

Belfast (17m)

Cambridge (12m)

Cardiff (61m)

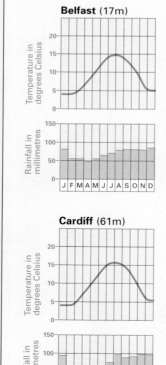

Belfast (17m)

Temperature in degrees Celsius

Rainfall in millimetres

J F M A M J J A S O N D

Edinburgh (134m)

Temperature in degrees Celsius

Rainfall in millimetres

J F M A M J J A S O N D

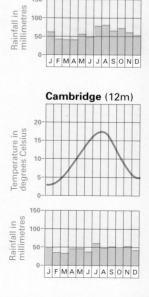

Cardiff (61m)

Temperature in degrees Celsius

Rainfall in millimetres

J F M A M J J A S O N D

Cambridge (12m)

Temperature in degrees Celsius

Rainfall in millimetres

J F M A M J J A S O N D

Transverse Mercator Projection
© Oxford University Press

Average annual rainfall

- more than 2400 millimetres
- 1200 - 2400 millimetres
- 800 - 1200 millimetres
- less than 800 millimetres
- • climate recording stations for which graphs are shown

Scale   1: 8 000 000

One centimetre on the map measures 80 kilometres on the ground.

0   80   160   240 km

Drought and flood

- inland areas in regular danger of flooding
- coastal areas in regular danger of flooding
- areas in regular danger of drought

Edinburgh (134m)

•Belfast (17m)

Cambridge (12m)

Cardiff (61m)

Scale   1: 16 000 000

One centimetre on the map represents 160 kilometres on the ground.

0   160   320   480 km

e water cycle

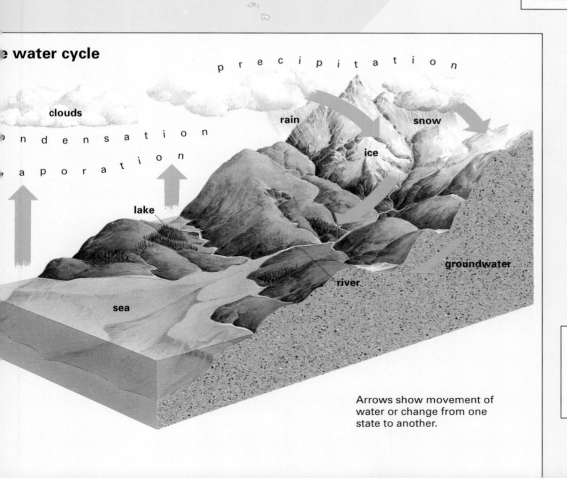

p r e c i p i t a t i o n

clouds

ondensation

aporation

rain

snow

ice

lake

river

groundwater

sea

Arrows show movement of water or change from one state to another.

Cold winters, cool summers

Mild winters, cool summers

Cool winters, warm summers

Mild winters, warm summers

Climate regions

- - - - - average January temperature (4°C)
- ———— average July temperature (16°C)

Transverse Mercator Projection
© Oxford University Press

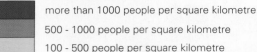

Population structure of the United Kingdom

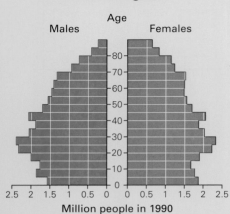

Age

Males   Females

- 80
- 70
- 60
- 50
- 40
- 30
- 20
- 10
- 0

2.5 2 1.5 1 0.5 0   0 0.5 1 1.5 2 2.5

Million people in 1990

Population density

- more than 1000 people per square kilometre
- 500 - 1000 people per square kilometre
- 100 - 500 people per square kilometre
- less than 100 person per square kilometre

- - - - international boundary

———— national boundary

———— county, region, or district boundary

Major cities

- ● with more than 6 million people
- ● with 1 million people
- • with between 500 000 and 1 million people
- · with between 100 000 and 500 000 people

Scale   1: 8 000 000

One centimetre on the map represents 80 kilometres on the ground.

0   80   160   240 km

British Isles population data

United Kingdom	Overall population density 241 people per square kilometre
Republic of Ireland	Overall population density 52 people per square kilometre

Total population 1995
England	48.7 million people
Wales	2.9 million people
Scotland	5.1 million people
Northern Ireland	1.6 million people
United Kingdom	58.4 million people
Republic of Ireland	3.6 million people

Population change

Change in population in each county, region or district, 1981 - 1991

very large increase	(more than 10%)
large increase	(5 - 10%)
small increase	(less than 5%)
small decrease	(less than 5%)
large decrease	(more than 5%)

- - - - international boundary

———— national boundary

———— county, region, or district boundary

Transverse Mercator Projection
© Oxford University Press

Farming, forestry and fishing

mostly livestock farms (cattle are kept for meat)

mostly hill farms (sheep are kept for meat and wool)

mostly dairy farms (cows are kept for milk)

mostly arable farms (crops are grown)

Many farms in Britain are mixed farms. Farmers grow crops and keep animals.

forestry (trees are planted for wood)

market gardening (fruit and vegetables are grown)

no farming (built-up areas)

fishing port

main fishing grounds

- - - - international boundary

Scale   1: 8 000 000

One centimetre on the map represents 80 kilometres on the ground.

0   80   160   240 km

United Kingdom employment structure

The number of people employed in each activity , 1995

Primary activity
agriculture, farming, fishing, mining, and quarrying

Secondary activity
manufacturing industry

Tertiary activity
energy and water supply, construction, transport and other services

Quaternary activity
information services

0 1 2 3 4 5 6 7 8 9 10 11 12 13
million people

Industry and business

major industrial area

• office and business centre

─── national boundary

- - - - international boundary

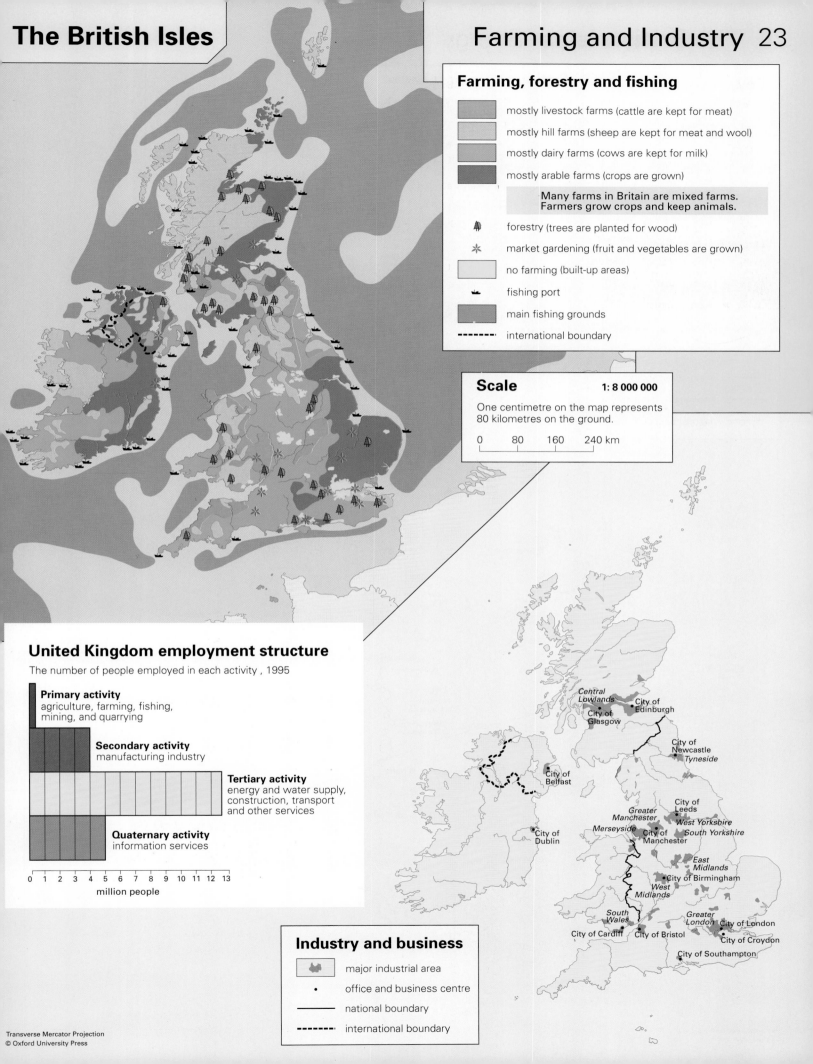

Central Lowlands
City of Glasgow
City of Edinburgh
City of Newcastle
Tyneside
City of Belfast
City of Dublin
Greater Manchester
Merseyside
City of Manchester
City of Leeds
West Yorkshire
South Yorkshire
East Midlands
City of Birmingham
West Midlands
South Wales
Greater London
City of London
City of Cardiff
City of Bristol
City of Croydon
City of Southampton

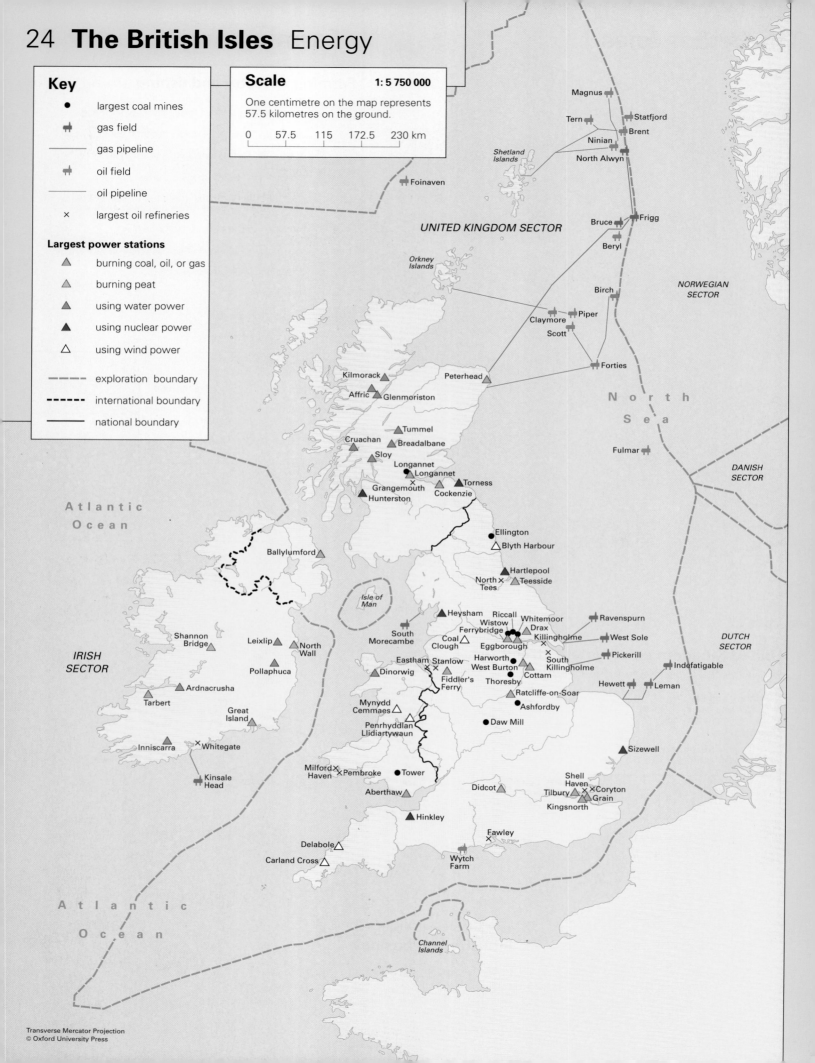

Key

- ● largest coal mines
- ⊥ gas field
- — gas pipeline
- ⊥ oil field
- — oil pipeline
- × largest oil refineries

Largest power stations

- ▲ burning coal, oil, or gas
- ▲ burning peat
- ▲ using water power
- ▲ using nuclear power
- △ using wind power

- — · — exploration boundary
- — — — international boundary
- ——— national boundary

Scale   1: 5 750 000

One centimetre on the map represents
57.5 kilometres on the ground.

| 0 | 57.5 | 115 | 172.5 | 230 km |

Magnus
Tern
Statfjord
Brent
Ninian
North Alwyn
Shetland Islands
Foinaven

UNITED KINGDOM SECTOR

Bruce
Frigg
Beryl

NORWEGIAN SECTOR

Orkney Islands

Birch

Claymore
Piper
Scott

Forties

N o r t h
S e a

Fulmar

DANISH SECTOR

Kilmorack
Affric
Glenmoriston
Peterhead

Tummel
Cruachan
Breadalbane
Sloy
Longannet
Longannet
Grangemouth
Hunterston
Cockenzie
Torness

A t l a n t i c
O c e a n

Ellington
Blyth Harbour

Ballylumford

Hartlepool
North × Teesside
Tees

Isle of Man

Heysham
Riccall
Whitemoor
Ravenspurn

South Morecambe
Wistow
Ferrybridge
Drax
Killingholme
West Sole

Shannon Bridge
Leixlip
North Wall
Coal Clough
Eggborough
South Killingholme
Pickerill

IRISH SECTOR

Pollaphuca
Eastham
Stanlow
Harworth
West Burton
Cottam
Hewett
Leman
Indefatigable

Dinorwig
Fiddler's Ferry
Thoresby

DUTCH SECTOR

Ardnacrusha
Tarbert
Ratcliffe-on-Soar
Ashfordby

Mynydd Cemmaes
Great Island
Daw Mill

Inniscarra
× Whitegate
Penrhyddlan Llidiartywaun
Sizewell

Kinsale Head
Milford × Pembroke
Haven
Tower
Shell Haven
Tilbury × Coryton
Grain
Kingsnorth

Delabole
Aberthaw
Didcot
Fawley

Carland Cross
Hinkley
Wytch Farm

A t l a n t i c
O c e a n

Channel Islands

The British Isles

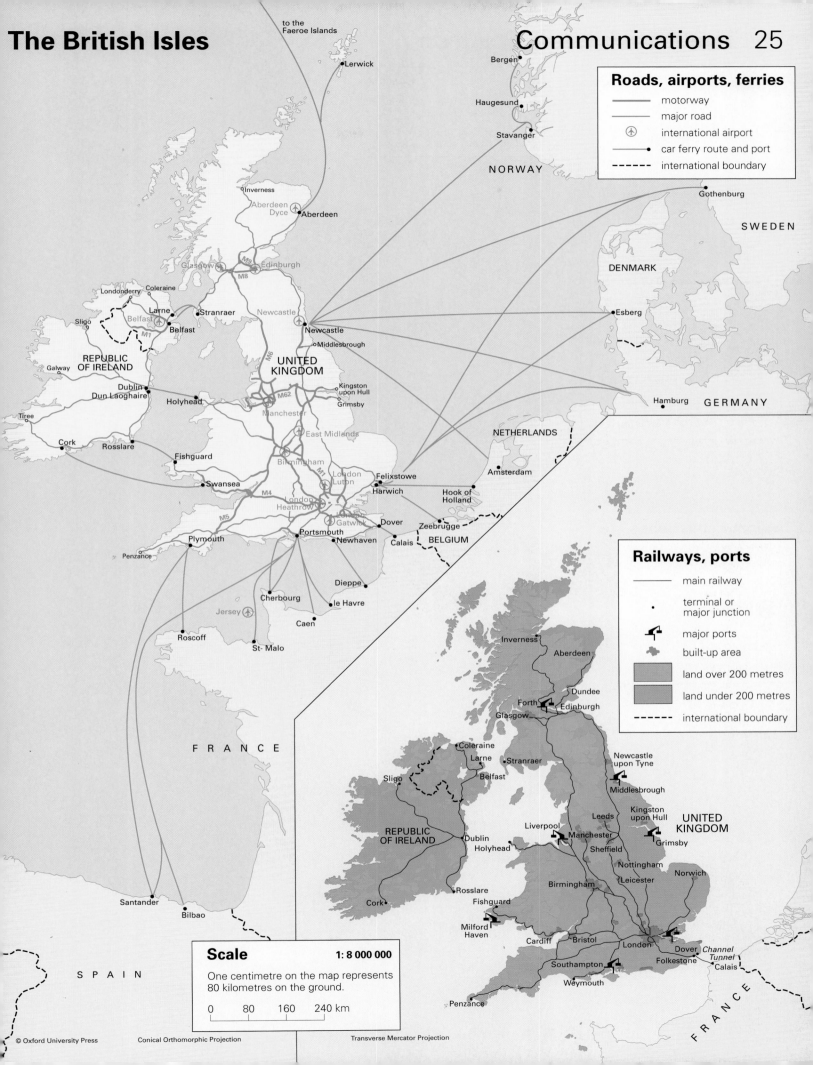

to the Faeroe Islands

Lerwick

Roads, airports, ferries

⎯⎯⎯	motorway
⎯⎯⎯	major road
✈	international airport
⎯⎯●	car ferry route and port
– – –	international boundary

Bergen

Haugesund

Stavanger

NORWAY

Gothenburg

SWEDEN

DENMARK

Esberg

Inverness

Aberdeen Dyce ✈ Aberdeen

Hamburg   GERMANY

Glasgow ✈ M9 Edinburgh
M8

Londonderry   Coleraine
Larne   Stranraer   Newcastle
Belfast ✈
Belfast   Newcastle
M1   Middlesbrough

Sligo

REPUBLIC OF IRELAND

UNITED KINGDOM

M6

Galway

NETHERLANDS

Dublin   Kingston upon Hull
Dun Laoghaire   Holyhead   M62   Grimsby
Manchester

Tiree

Amsterdam

Cork   East Midlands ✈

Rosslare   Fishguard   Birmingham   Felixstowe
Swansea   M1   London   Harwich   Hook of
M4   Luton   Holland
M5   London
Heathrow
London   Dover   Zeebrugge
Gatwick   BELGIUM
Plymouth   Portsmouth   Newhaven   Calais
Penzance   Dieppe

Cherbourg   le Havre
Jersey ✈   Caen
Roscoff
St- Malo

FRANCE

Railways, ports

⎯⎯⎯	main railway
●	terminal or major junction
⚓	major ports
▨	built-up area
▨	land over 200 metres
▨	land under 200 metres
– – –	international boundary

Inverness

Aberdeen

Forth   Dundee
Glasgow   Edinburgh

Coleraine
Larne   Newcastle
Stranraer   upon Tyne
Sligo   Belfast
Middlesbrough

REPUBLIC OF IRELAND   Leeds   Kingston upon Hull
Liverpool   Manchester   UNITED
Dublin   Sheffield   Grimsby   KINGDOM
Holyhead   Nottingham
Birmingham   Leicester   Norwich
Rosslare
Fishguard
Milford   Cardiff   Bristol   London
Haven   Dover   Channel
Folkestone   Tunnel
Southampton   Calais
Cork   Weymouth
Penzance

FRANCE

Santander

Bilbao

SPAIN

Scale   1: 8 000 000

One centimetre on the map represents
80 kilometres on the ground.

0   80   160   240 km

FRANCE

Conical Orthomorphic Projection   Transverse Mercator Projection

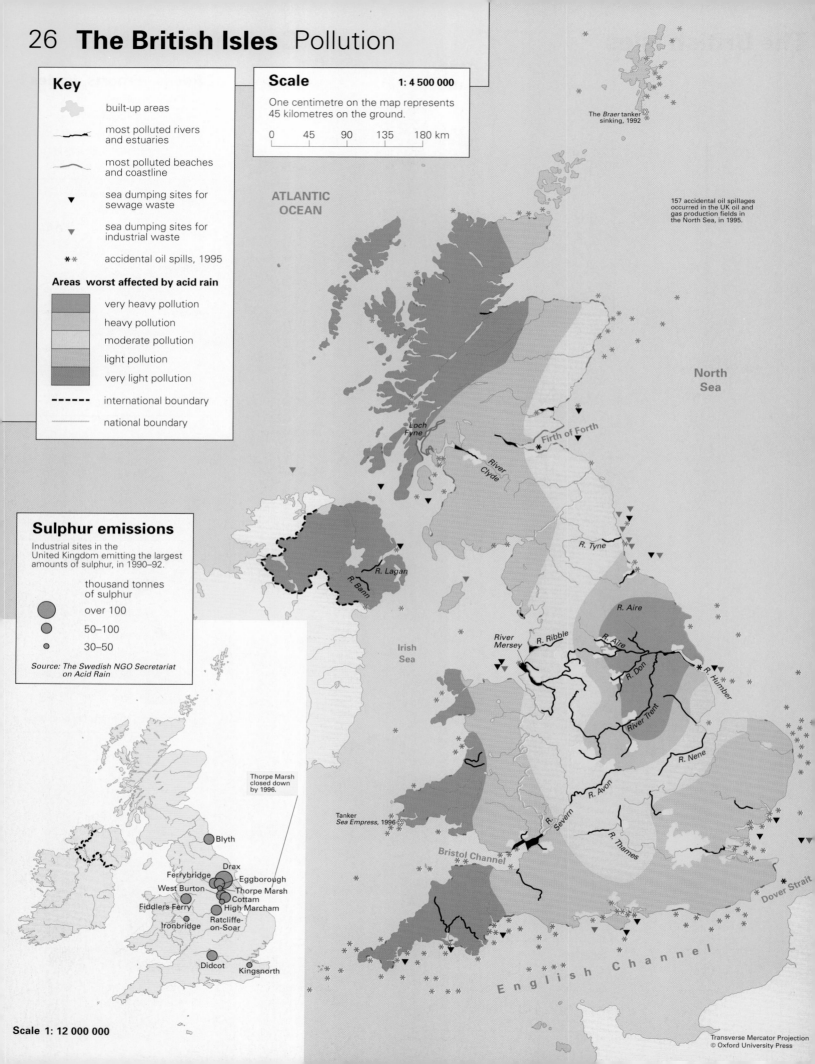

Key

- built-up areas
- most polluted rivers and estuaries
- most polluted beaches and coastline
- ▼ sea dumping sites for sewage waste
- ▽ sea dumping sites for industrial waste
- ＊＊ accidental oil spills, 1995

Areas worst affected by acid rain

- very heavy pollution
- heavy pollution
- moderate pollution
- light pollution
- very light pollution
- - - - international boundary
- ——— national boundary

Scale

1 : 4 500 000

One centimetre on the map represents 45 kilometres on the ground.

0   45   90   135   180 km

Sulphur emissions

Industrial sites in the United Kingdom emitting the largest amounts of sulphur, in 1990–92.

thousand tonnes of sulphur
- over 100
- 50–100
- 30–50

Source: The Swedish NGO Secretariat on Acid Rain

Scale 1 : 12 000 000

Blyth
Ferrybridge
Drax
Eggborough
West Burton
Thorpe Marsh
Cottam
Fiddlers Ferry
High Marcham
Ironbridge
Ratcliffe-on-Soar
Didcot
Kingsnorth

Thorpe Marsh closed down by 1996.

ATLANTIC OCEAN

The *Braer* tanker sinking, 1992

157 accidental oil spillages occurred in the UK oil and gas production fields in the North Sea, in 1995.

North Sea

Loch Fyne
River Clyde
Firth of Forth
R. Tyne

R. Lagan
R. Bann

Irish Sea

R. Aire
River Mersey
R. Ribble
R. Aire
R. Don
R. Humber
River Trent
R. Nene
R. Avon
R. Severn
R. Thames

Tanker *Sea Empress*, 1996

Bristol Channel

Dover Strait

English Channel

Transverse Mercator Projection
© Oxford University Press

The British Isles

National Parks

- National Park
- land over 200 metres
- land under 200 metres
- major built-up area
- national boundary
- --- international boundary

World Heritage Sites

Sites and monuments of world-wide natural (★) and cultural heritage (★), considered to be of such exceptional interest and value that their protection is agreed by international cooperation.

Aberdeen

Dundee

Glasgow

Edinburgh

Glenveagh

Belfast

Northumberland

Newcastle upon Tyne

Middlesbrough

Connemara

Dublin

Lake District

Yorkshire Dales

North York Moors

Leeds

Kingston upon Hull

Manchester

Liverpool

Sheffield

Peak District

Snowdonia

Nottingham

Killarney

Leicester

Birmingham

Norwich

Pembrokeshire Coast

Brecon Beacons

London

Cardiff

Bristol

Exmoor

Southampton

Dartmoor

St Kilda ★

Giant's Causeway ★

Hadrian's Wall ★
Durham Castle/ ★
Cathedral

Fountain's Abbey/ ★
Studley Royal Park

Castles/Town Walls of King Edward

Ironbridge Gorge ★

Blenheim Palace ★

Westminster Palace/Abbey ★

Bath ★

Stonehenge/ ★
Avebury

Scale   1 : 8 000 000

One centimetre on the map represents 80 kilometres on the ground.

0   80   160   240 km

Other protected areas

- Areas of Outstanding Natural Beauty (England, Wales, Northern Ireland); National Scenic Areas (Scotland)
- Heritage Coast (England and Wales); Coastal Conservation Zones (Scotland); Conservation designated coast (Northern Ireland);
- major built-up area
- national boundary
- --- international boundary

South Lewis, Harris and North Uist

Wester Ross

Cairngorm Mountains

Ben Nevis and Glen Coe

Jura

Loch Lomond

Upper Tweeddale

Antrim Coast and Glens

Sperrin

North Pennines

Mourne

Nidderdale

Forest of Bowland

Anglesey

Lincolnshire Wolds

Clwydian Range

Norfolk Coast

LLeyn

Shropshire Hills

The Broads Authority

Wye Valley

Suffolk Coast and Heaths

Gower

Cotswolds

North Wessex Downs

Chilterns

Surrey Hills

High Weald

Kent Downs

Bodmin Moor

Blackdown Hills

Cranbourne Chase

New Forest

Sussex Downs

Dorset

Isle of Wight

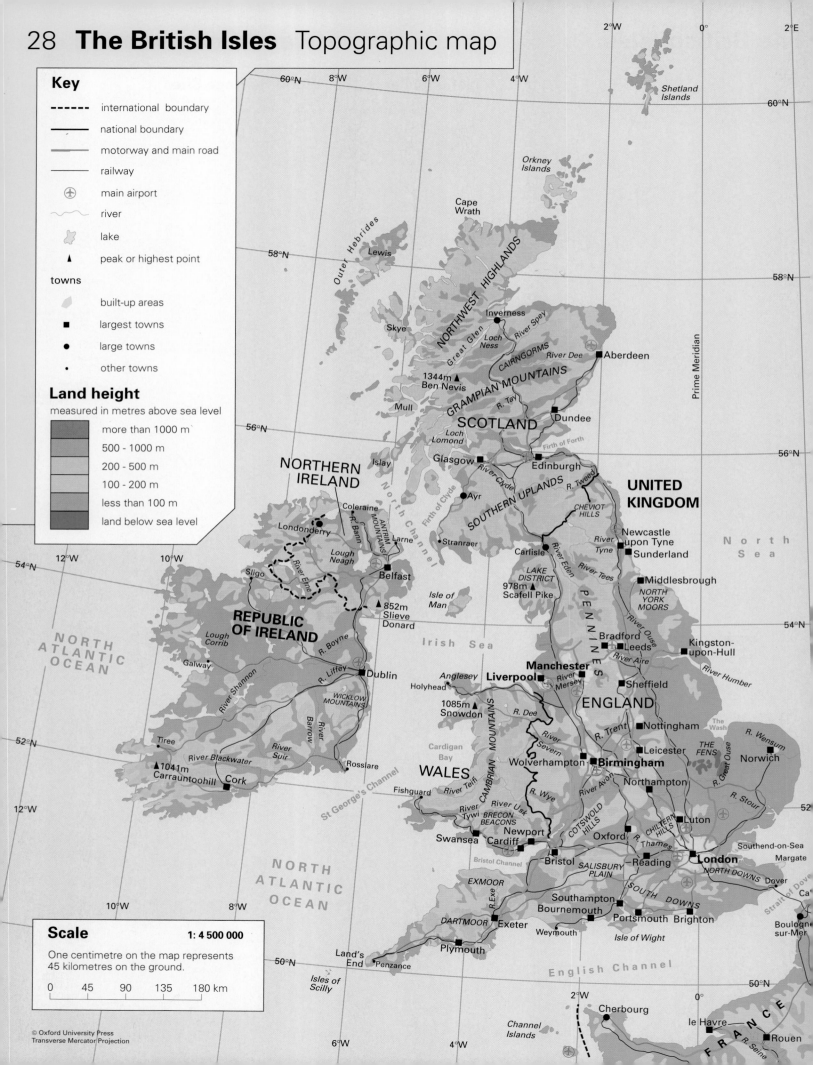

Key

- – – – – international boundary
- ——— national boundary
- ——— motorway and main road
- ——— railway
- ✈ main airport
- ～～ river
- 🦴 lake
- ▲ peak or highest point

towns

- built-up areas
- ■ largest towns
- ● large towns
- • other towns

Land height

measured in metres above sea level

- more than 1000 m
- 500 - 1000 m
- 200 - 500 m
- 100 - 200 m
- less than 100 m
- land below sea level

Scale

1: 4 500 000

One centimetre on the map represents 45 kilometres on the ground.

0   45   90   135   180 km

Shetland Islands

Orkney Islands

Outer Hebrides

Cape Wrath

Lewis

Skye

NORTHWEST HIGHLANDS

Inverness

Great Glen

Loch Ness

River Spey

CAIRNGORMS

River Dee

Aberdeen

1344m ▲ Ben Nevis

GRAMPIAN MOUNTAINS

R. Tay

Mull

SCOTLAND

Dundee

Loch Lomond

Firth of Forth

NORTHERN IRELAND

Islay

Glasgow

Edinburgh

River Clyde

Ayr

SOUTHERN UPLANDS

R. Tweed

UNITED KINGDOM

Stranraer

CHEVIOT HILLS

Coleraine

R. Bann

ANTRIM MOUNTAINS

Larne

Carlisle

Newcastle upon Tyne

River Tyne

Sunderland

NORTH Sea

Londonderry

Lough Neagh

Belfast

North Channel

Firth of Clyde

River Eden

River Tees

Middlesbrough

Sligo

River Erne

852m ▲ Slieve Donard

Isle of Man

978m ▲ Scafell Pike

LAKE DISTRICT

NORTH YORK MOORS

REPUBLIC OF IRELAND

Lough Corrib

R. Boyne

Irish Sea

PENNINES

River Ouse

Bradford

Leeds

Kingston-upon-Hull

NORTH ATLANTIC OCEAN

Galway

River Shannon

R. Liffey

Dublin

WICKLOW MOUNTAINS

River Aire

Manchester

Liverpool

River Mersey

Sheffield

River Humber

Anglesey

Holyhead

ENGLAND

Tiree

River Blackwater

River Suir

River Barrow

River

Rosslare

1085m ▲ Snowdon

Cardigan Bay

R. Dee

Nottingham

The Wash

R. Wensum

Norwich

1041m ▲ Carrauntoohill

Cork

St George's Channel

Fishguard

CAMBRIAN MOUNTAINS

River Teifi

R. Severn

Leicester

R. Trent

THE FENS

R. Great Ouse

R. Stour

Wolverhampton

Birmingham

WALES

River Tywi

River Usk

BRECON BEACONS

R. Wye

River Avon

Northampton

NORTH ATLANTIC OCEAN

Swansea

Cardiff

Newport

COTSWOLD HILLS

Oxford

CHILTERN HILLS

Luton

R. Thames

Southend-on-Sea

EXMOOR

Bristol

SALISBURY PLAIN

Reading

London

Margate

Bristol Channel

SOUTH DOWNS

NORTH DOWNS

Dover

R. Exe

Southampton

Bournemouth

Portsmouth

Brighton

Strait of Dover

DARTMOOR

Exeter

Weymouth

Isle of Wight

Boulogne-sur-Mer

Land's End

Penzance

Plymouth

English Channel

Isles of Scilly

Cherbourg

Channel Islands

le Havre

FRANCE

Rouen

R. Seine

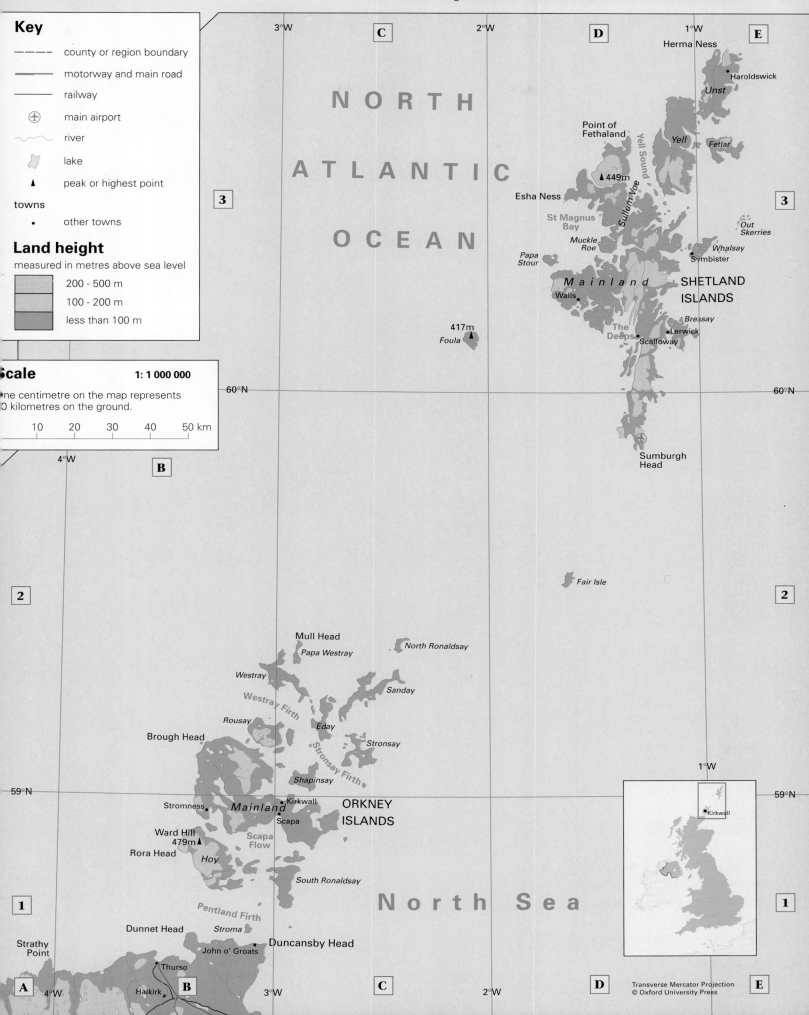

Key

- – – – county or region boundary
- —— motorway and main road
- —— railway
- ✈ main airport
- ∿ river
- 🌣 lake
- ▲ peak or highest point

towns

- • other towns

Land height

measured in metres above sea level

- 200 - 500 m
- 100 - 200 m
- less than 100 m

Scale

1: 1 000 000

ne centimetre on the map represents
0 kilometres on the ground.

10   20   30   40   50 km

NORTH
ATLANTIC
OCEAN

Herma Ness
Haroldswick
Unst
Point of
Fethaland
Yell Sound
Yell
Fetlar
▲ 449m
Esha Ness
St Magnus
Bay
Muckle
Roe
Out
Skerries
Papa
Stour
Whalsay
Symbister
Mainland
SHETLAND
ISLANDS
Walls
Bressay
Lerwick
The
Deeps
Scalloway

417m
Foula ▲

60°N   60°N

Sumburgh
Head

Fair Isle

Mull Head
Papa Westray
North Ronaldsay
Westray
Sanday
Westray Firth
Rousay
Eday
Brough Head
Stronsay
Stronsay Firth
Shapinsay

59°N   59°N

Stromness
Mainland
Kirkwall
ORKNEY
ISLANDS
Scapa
Ward Hill
479m ▲
Scapa
Flow
Rora Head
Hoy
South Ronaldsay

North Sea

Strathy
Point
Pentland Firth
Stroma
Dunnet Head
Duncansby Head
John o' Groats
Thurso
Halkirk

Kirkwall

Transverse Mercator Projection
© Oxford University Press

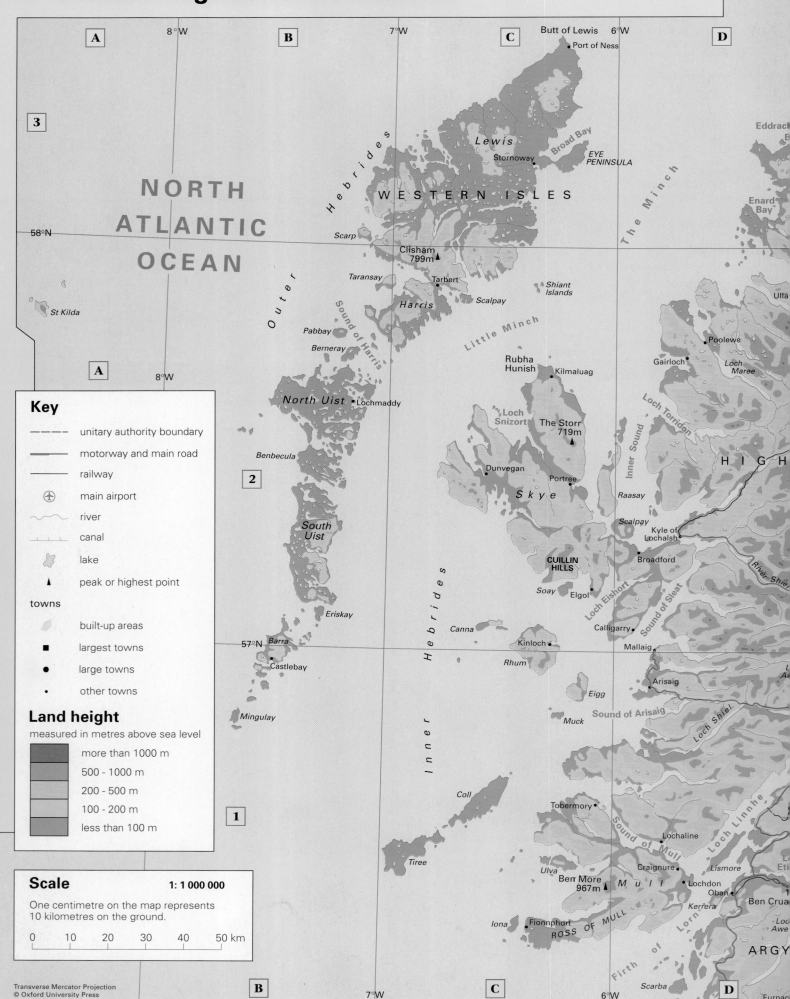

A   8°W   B   7°W   C   Butt of Lewis   6°W   D

3

Port of Ness

NORTH ATLANTIC OCEAN

Lewis

Stornoway   Broad Bay

EYE PENINSULA

Eddrach

Hebrides

WESTERN ISLES

The Minch

58°N

Scarp

Enard Bay

Clisham 799m▲

Taransay   Tarbert

Harris   *Scalpay*

Shiant Islands

Ulfa

Outer

Sound of Harris

Little Minch

Poolewe

Pabbay

Rubha Hunish   Kilmaluag

Gairloch   *Loch Maree*

Berneray

Loch Torridon

A   8°W

North Uist • Lochmaddy

Loch Snizort

The Storr 719m▲

HIGH

Benbecula

Dunvegan   Portree

Inner Sound

Raasay

2

Skye

Scalpay

Kyle of Lochalsh

South Uist

CUILLIN HILLS

Broadford

River Shiel

Soay   Elgol

Loch Eishort

Sound of Sleat

Eriskay

Hebrides

Canna

Calligarry

57°N   *Barra*

Kinloch

Mallaig

Castlebay

Rhum

Arisaig

Eigg

Mingulay

Muck

Sound of Arisaig

Loch Shiel

Inner

Coll

Tobermory

Loch Linnhe

1

Lochaline

Ulva   Ben More 967m   Craignure   *Lismore*

Tiree   *Mull*

Lochdon   Oban

Kerrera   Ben Crua

Iona   Fionnphort   *ROSS OF MULL*

Firth of Lorn

Loch Awe

ARGY

Scarba

B   7°W   C   6°W   D

Key

— — — unitary authority boundary

═══ motorway and main road

——— railway

⊕ main airport

〜 river

━┿━ canal

lake

▲ peak or highest point

towns

built-up areas

■ largest towns

● large towns

• other towns

Land height

measured in metres above sea level

more than 1000 m

500 - 1000 m

200 - 500 m

100 - 200 m

less than 100 m

Scale   1: 1 000 000

One centimetre on the map represents 10 kilometres on the ground.

0   10   20   30   40   50 km

Transverse Mercator Projection
© Oxford University Press

North
Sea

E
F
Dunnet
Head
Stroma
3°W
4°W
Strathy
Point
John o'
Groats
Thurso
Halkirk
G
Cape Wrath
Loch Eriboll
HIGHLANDS
Ben
Hope
927m ▲
Wick
961m ▲
Ben
Klibreck
Loch
nan
Clar
Kinbrace
Morven
705m ▲
Lybster
River Thurso
7m
nisp
998m ▲
Ben More
Assynt
River Helmsdale
Loch Shin
Helmsdale
Lairg
Brora
Bonar Bridge
Dornoch
58°N
H
Beinn Dearg
1081m ▲
Dornoch Firth
Tarbat Ness
Tain
109m
Sgurr Mór
1046m ▲
Ben
Wyvis
Invergordon
Cromarty
Firth
Cromarty
Moray Firth
Branderburgh
Lossiemouth
Burghead
Portknockie
Portsoy
Banff
Rosehearty
Fraserburgh
River Meig
Dingwall
Nairn
Elgin
Buckie
Cullen
Macduff
2
Forres
R. Spey
Fochabers
Aberchirder
Turriff
Peterhead
Buchan Ness
D
Inverness
R. Beauly
River Nairn
Rothes
Keith
Huntly
River Deveron
Loch
rdoch
Drumnadrochit
Charlestown
of Aberlour
Ellon
Eige
m
Loch
Ness
Dufftown
River
Spey
Oldmeldrum
Inverurie
Invermoriston
Grantown-
on-Spey
MORAY
River Don
River Don
Dyce ⊕
ABERDEEN
CITY
Fort
Augustus
Aviemore
ABERDEENSHIRE
Aberdeen
MONADHLIATH
MOUNTAINS
Invergarry
Kingussie
Newtonmore
CAIRNGORMS
1244m ▲
Cairn Gorm
Aboyne
Banchory
River Dee
57°N
Loch
Lochy
Braemar
Ballater
1155m ▲
Lochnagar
Stonehaven
Ben Alder
1148m ▲
GRAMPIAN
MOUNTAINS
River North Esk
illiam
344m
Ben Nevis
Loch
Ericht
PERTHSHIRE
River Isla
ANGUS
Laurencekirk
Inverbervie
Blackwater
Reservoir
AND
Pitlochry
River South Esk
Milton Ness
KINROSS
Kirriemuir
Brechin
Montrose
Loch
Rannoch
River Tay
Aberfeldy
Blairgowrie
Rattray
Alyth
Forfar
Arbroath
Ben Lawers
1214m ▲
Loch
Tay
River Tay
Coupar
Angus
SIDLAW HILLS
DUNDEE
CITY
Carnoustie
1
Tyndrum
Perth
Dundee
almaly
Crianlarich
Ben More
1174m ▲
Crieff
River Earn
Newburgh
St Andrews
aray
Loch
Earn
Auchterarder
Auchtermuchty
Cupar
Crail
SCOTLAND
Callander
OCHIL HILLS
Kinross
FIFE
Loch
Katrine
M90
Glenrothes
Anstruther
BUTE
Ben Lomond
974m ▲
Dunblane
CLACKMANNAN
SHIRE
Loch Leven
Buckhaven
E
STIRLING
F
G
H
Tarbet
Loch
Lomond
River Forth
4°W
3°W
2°W

3

2°W
58°N
Ben
Nevis ▲
Aberdeen

Key

- –·–·– international boundary
- – – – national boundary
- –·–·– county, district or unitary authority boundary
- motorway and main road
- railway
- main airport
- river
- canal
- lake
- ▲ peak or highest point

towns

- built-up areas
- ■ largest towns
- ● large towns
- • other towns

Land height

measured in metres above sea level

- more than 1000 m
- 500 - 1000 m
- 200 - 500 m
- 100 - 200 m
- less than 100 m

Transverse Mercator Projection
© Oxford University Press

REPUBLIC OF IRELAND

NORTHERN IRELAND

Scale 1: 1 000 000

One centimetre on the map represents 10 kilometres on the ground.

0 10 20 30 40 50 km

North Sea

Irish Sea

E

F

G

H

4

3

2

1

▲1174m Ben More
Loch Earn
4°W
Crieff
River Earn
Perth
Newburgh
3°W
Cupar
St Andrews
Crail
Auchterarder
Auchtermuchty
2°W
Loch Katrine
Callander
Dunblane
Kinross
FIFE
Glenrothes
Anstruther
Ben Lomond 974m
OCHIL HILLS
CLACKMANNAN-SHIRE
Loch Leven
St Abb's Head
STIRLING
River Forth
Alloa
Buckhaven
Loch Lomond
Stirling
Dunfermline
Kirkcaldy
North Berwick
Dunbar
56°N
DUMBARTON & CLYDEBANK
CAMPSIE FELLS
FALKIRK
Grangemouth
Bo'ness
Inverkeithing
Firth of Forth
Alexandria
EAST DUNBARTONSHIRE
Falkirk
Linlithgow
Edinburgh
Musselburgh
EAST LOTHIAN
St Abb's Head
LAMMERMUIR HILLS
Eyemouth
Dumbarton
Cumbernauld
Bathgate
CITY OF EDINBURGH
MIDLOTHIAN
Duns
Berwick-upon-Tweed
enock
Clydebank
Bearsden
Kirkintilloch
Airdrie
WEST LOTHIAN
Livingston
Penicuik
Whiteadder Water
Port
Glasgow
NORTH LANARKSHIRE
PENTLAND HILLS
River Tweed
Coldstream
Holy Island
gow
Paisley
CITY OF GLASGOW
Motherwell
Peebles
Innerleithen
Galashiels
Kelso
Leader Water
Bamburgh
Johnstone
Hamilton
Wishaw
Lanark
Melrose
Wooler
REFREWSHIRE
EAST RENFREWSHIRE
East Kilbride
Biggar
SCOTTISH
Selkirk
CHEVIOT HILLS
▲815m The Cheviot
River
S
Kilmarnock
SOUTH LANARKSHIRE
SCOTLAND
Broad Law ▲840m
Yarrow Water
BORDERS
Jedburgh
River Aln
Alnwick
tcoats
Darvel
UPLANDS
St Mary's Loch
River Teviot
Hawick
ne
EAST AYRSHIRE
Cumnock
LOWTHER
Daer Reservoir
Amble
oon
New Cumnock
HILLS
Sanquhar
Moffat
602m Peel Fell ▲
River Rede
River Coquet
stwick
Ayr
River Ayr
River Doon
Thornhill
R. Annan
River Esk
Kielder Water
NORTHUMBERLAND
Ashington
Maybole
Loch Doon
SOUTH
DUMFRIES AND GALLOWAY
Lockerbie
Langholm
Liddel Water
River Wansbeck
Blyth
Stinchar
AYRSHIRE
St John's Town of Dalry
Lochmaben
Cramlington
River Blyth
Whitley Bay
Newton Stewart
New Galloway
Loch Ken
Dumfries
River Nith
River Annan
Newcastle upon Tyne
55°N
R. Cree
Castle Douglas
Dalbeattie
Kirkbean
Annan
River Irthing
Haltwhistle
Hexham
River Tyne
Gateshead
Washington
nluce
Wigtown
Gatehouse of Fleet
River Dee
Kirkcudbright
Solway Firth
Carlisle
River Eden
Brampton
PENNINES
Consett
Chester-le-Street
Whithorn
Wigtown Bay
Wigton
Cross Fell ▲893m
River Derwent
Durham
Spennymoor
r I s h
Maryport
River Ellen
Cockermouth
Skiddaw ▲931m
Penrith
River Wear
DURHAM
Bishop Auckland
S e a
Point of Ayre
Workington
R. Derwent
Keswick
Derwent Water
Ullswater
Appleby-in-Westmorland
790m Mickle Fell ▲
Brough
Barnard Castle
Newton Aycliffe
Darlington
Whitehaven
CUMBRIA
Helvellyn ▲950m
Kirkby Stephen
Snaefell 620m ▲
Ramsey
St Bees Head
Scafell Pike ▲978m
Ambleside
LAKE DISTRICT
Windermere
E N G L A N D
River Swale
Richmond
Kirk Michael
Seascale
Windermere
River Ure
Leyburn
Peel
South Barrule 483m ▲
Coniston Water
Kendal
River Lune
Whernside ▲737m
Ingleborough ▲723m
Pen-y-Ghent 693m ▲
704m Great Whernside ▲
NORTH YORKSHIRE
Ripon
ISLE OF MAN
Douglas
Dalton-in-Furness
Whernside
R. Greta
River Wharfe
River Nidd
stleton
Barrow-in-Furness
Morecambe Bay
Carnforth
560m Ward's Stone ▲
River Aire
Skipton
Morecambe
Heysham
Lancaster
4°W
3°W
2°W
54°N

© Oxford University Press

A · B · C · D
4

Lockerbie 3°W C 2°W D

NORTHUMBERLAND

55°N Annan Newcastle upon Tyne

River Irthing Haltwhistle R. Tyne Gateshead

A Brampton Hexham Washing

Newton Stewart Castle Kirkbean Carlisle Consett Chester-
Douglas le-Street

Glenluce Gatehouse Dalbeattie River Eden Durham

Wigtown of Fleet Kirkcudbright Wigton Cross Fell River Wear DURHAM Spennymoo

Luce Maryport R. Derwent 893m Bishop Newton
Bay Wigtown Cockermouth Penrith Mickle Fell Auckland Aycliff
Bay River Ellen 931m 790m Darlingto

Mull of Workington Skiddaw Appleby-in- Barnard
Galloway Keswick CUMBRIA Westmorland Castle

3 Whitehaven Derwent Ullswater Brough Richmond
Water Helvellyn LAKE Kirkby

St Bees Head 950m Stephen River Swale

Point of Ayre 978m DISTRICT Ambleside River Ure Leyburn

Ramsey Scafell Pike Windermere NORTH YORKSHIRE

Kirk Snaefell Seascale Coniston Windermere Whernside River Wharfe
Michael 620m Water 737m

Peel ISLE OF MAN Kendal Pen-y-Ghent River Nidd

South Douglas Dalton-in- 693m Great Whernside
Barrule Furness 723m 704m Ri
483m Barrow-in- Morecambe Ingleborough

Castletown Furness Bay Carnforth River
54°N Morecambe Lancaster Skipton Harroga
Heysham 560m Nidd
Ward's Stone FOREST OF
BOWLAND River Aire

Fleetwood Barnoldswick Ilkley Keighley

River Wyre Clitheroe Colne
LANCASHIRE Nelson

Irish Sea Blackpool River Ribble Burnley **Bradford** Lee

Carmel Amlwch **Preston** Blackburn Halifax WEST
Head Lytham Brighouse

Holyhead St Anne's Leyland Chorley **Huddersfield** Dewsb
YORKSHIRE

Holy Southport Bury **Rochdale**
Island ANGLESEY Formby **Bolton** **Oldham**

2 Skelmersdale Wigan GREATER
Wallasey Kirkby MERSEYSIDE MANCHESTER **Manchester**

Carnarfon Llandudno Bootle St Helens **Salford**
Bay Conwy Rhyl **Birkenhead** **Liverpool** Sale **Stockport**

Bangor Colwyn River Dee Widnes **Warrington** Cheadle The Peak
Bay 636m

Bethesda R. Conwy FLINTSHIRE Runcorn
Caernarfon Flint R. Mersey Macclesfield Buxton

Snowdon ABERCONWY Denbigh Ellesmere Northwich
1085m Port CHESHIRE

AND River Clwyd Chester Winsford Bakewell DERBYSH
COLWYN Mold River Dove Matloc

53°N DENBIGHSHIRE Crewe Kidsgrove
Blaenau Newcastle- **Stoke-on-Trent**
Ffestiniog Wrexham under-Lyme

Portmadog River Dee WREXHAM **ENGLAND**
Harlech Llangollen Whitchurch

Pwllheli Market Uttoxeter
Drayton

CAERNARFONSHIRE AND Bala Oswestry Burton upon
MERIONETHSHIRE Lake Stafford Trent

Barmouth Vyrnwy CAMBRIAN Newport Rugeley
Dolgellau Bala MOUNTAINS STAFFORDSHIRE
1 Cardigan Cader Idris Lake POWYS R. Vyrnwy 407m Cannock Lichfield
Bay 892m Vyrnwy The Wrekin

Welshpool **Telford**
Shrewsbury

© Oxford University Press WALES R. Dyfi Machynlleth SHROPSHIRE **Wolverhampton** Tamworth
4°W A B 3°W C 2°W D

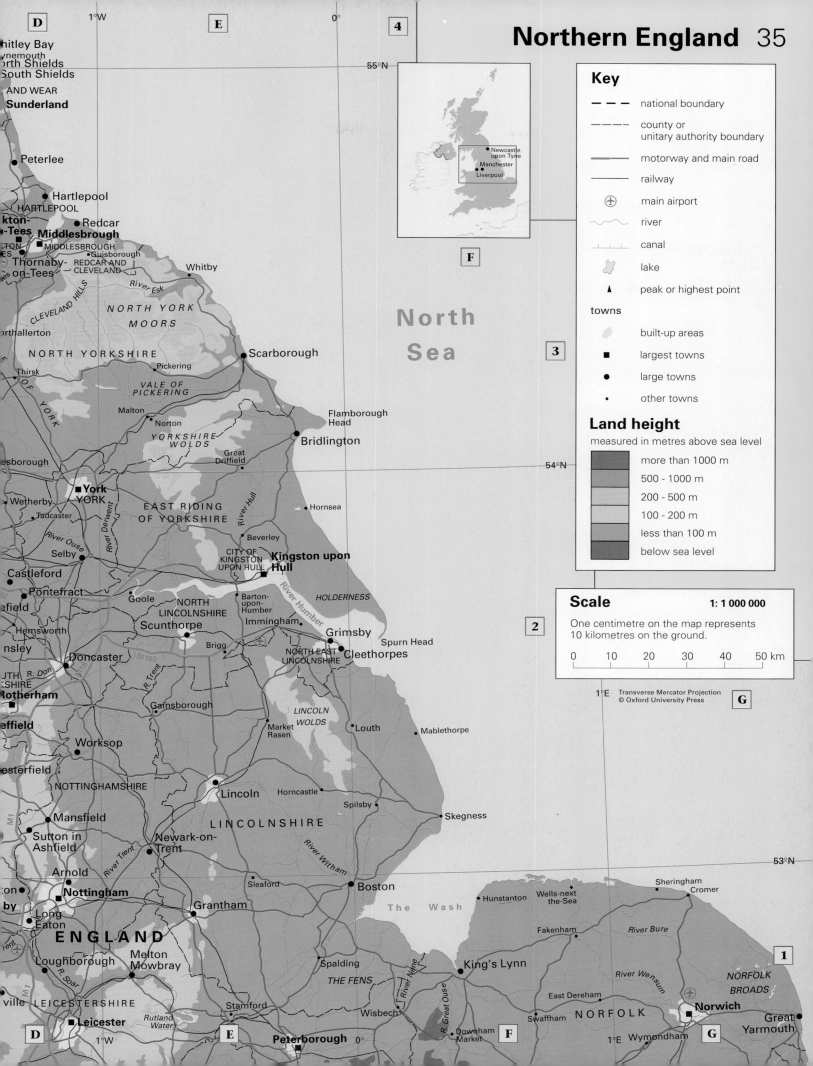

Key

- – – – national boundary
- – · – · county or unitary authority boundary
- motorway and main road
- railway
- ⊕ main airport
- ∿ river
- ⊢ canal
- lake
- ▲ peak or highest point

towns

- built-up areas
- ■ largest towns
- ● large towns
- · other towns

Land height

measured in metres above sea level

- more than 1000 m
- 500 - 1000 m
- 200 - 500 m
- 100 - 200 m
- less than 100 m
- below sea level

Scale   1: 1 000 000

One centimetre on the map represents
10 kilometres on the ground.

0   10   20   30   40   50 km

Transverse Mercator Projection
© Oxford University Press

North Sea

D · Whitley Bay
·ynemouth
·rth Shields
·South Shields
·AND WEAR
● **Sunderland**
● Peterlee
● Hartlepool
HARTLEPOOL
·kton-
·n-Tees
·es ■ **Middlesbrough**
·on ● Redcar
·on-Tees MIDDLESBROUGH
Thornaby- ● Guisborough
on-Tees REDCAR AND
CLEVELAND
CLEVELAND HILLS
River Esk
Whitby
NORTH YORK MOORS
·rthallerton
·esborough
NORTH YORKSHIRE
Thirsk
·OF YORK
Pickering
● Scarborough
VALE OF PICKERING
Malton
Norton
YORKSHIRE WOLDS
Flamborough Head
Great Driffield
● Bridlington
·Wetherby
■ **York**
YORK
Tadcaster
River Derwent
EAST RIDING OF YORKSHIRE
River Hull
● Hornsea
Beverley
River Ouse
Selby
CITY OF KINGSTON UPON HULL
■ **Kingston upon Hull**
● Castleford
● Pontefract
·field
Goole
NORTH LINCOLNSHIRE
Barton-upon-Humber
River Humber
HOLDERNESS
·Hemsworth
Scunthorpe
Immingham
● Grimsby
Spurn Head
·nsley
● Doncaster
M180
Brigg
NORTH EAST LINCOLNSHIRE
● Cleethorpes
·UTH
·KSHIRE
■ **Rotherham**
R. Don
R. Trent
Gainsborough
LINCOLN WOLDS
● Louth
Mablethorpe
·effield
● Worksop
Market Rasen
·esterfield
·NOTTINGHAMSHIRE
Horncastle
Spilsby
● Lincoln
· Skegness
LINCOLNSHIRE
● Mansfield
● Sutton in Ashfield
Newark-on-Trent
River Trent
Sleaford
River Witham
Arnold
·ton
■ **Nottingham**
·by
Long Eaton
ENGLAND
● Grantham
Boston
·Loughborough
Melton Mowbray
Spalding
R. Soar
·ville LEICESTERSHIRE
Rutland Water
Stamford
THE FENS
■ **Leicester**
Peterborough
·Trent

The Wash
Hunstanton
Wells-next-the-Sea
Sheringham
Cromer
Fakenham
River Bure
NORFOLK BROADS
King's Lynn
East Dereham
River Wensum
NORFOLK
Swaffham
■ **Norwich**
Wisbech
R. Great Ouse
River Nene
Downham Market
Wymondham
● Great Yarmouth

1°W   0°   55°N   54°N   53°N   1°E

D   E   4   F   3   2   G   1

A 6°W

B

5°W

C

4°W

D

Irish Sea

Formby

MERSEYSIDE

Bootle

Wallasey

Liverpool

Birkenhead

Malahide

Howth

Carmel Head

Amlwch

Holyhead

Holy Island

ANGLESEY

Llandudno

Conwy

Rhyl

3

Dublin

Dún Laoghaire

Bangor

Colwyn Bay

FLINTSHIRE

Flint

Bethesda

Caernarfon

R. Conwy

ABERCONWY

Denbigh

Mold

REPUBLIC OF IRELAND

Caernarfon Bay

Snowdon 1085m

AND COLWYN

DENBIGHSHIRE

Wrexham

WREX

Bray

53°N

Wicklow

Blaenau Ffestiniog

Bala

River Dee

Llangollen

LLEYN PENINSULA

Porthmadog

Pwllheli

Harlech

CAERNARFONSHIRE AND MERIONETHSHIRE

905m Aran Fawddy

Bala Lake

Lake Vyrnwy

Oswestry

Irish Sea

Barmouth

Dolgellau

Cader Idris 892m

R. Dyfi

R. Vyrnwy

Welshpool

WALES

Machynlleth

R. Severn

Montgo

2

Cardigan Bay

752m Plynlimon

Llanidloes

Newtown

SHROPS

Aberystwyth

Rhayader

Knightor

CARDIGANSHIRE

Aberaeron

New Quay

Llandrindod Wells

POWYS

Kin

Cemaes Head

River Teifi

Builth Wells

Lampeter

MYNYDD EPPYNT

R. Wye

Hay-on

Cardigan

River Teifi

Strumble Head

Newcastle Emlyn

Llandovery

BLAC

52°N

Fishguard

MYNYDD PRESELI

R. Tywi

River Usk

Brecon

811m

MOUNTA

St David's Head

CARMARTHENSHIRE

St David's PEMBROKESHIRE

Carmarthen

Llandeilo

BRECON

886m BEACONS

Abergavenn

Haverfordwest

St Brides Bay

R. Tywi

Ammanford

Merthyr Tydfil

Ebbw Val

BLAENAU GWENT

TORF

Kidwelly

Pontardulais

Aberdare

MERTHYR TYDFIL

Abertillery

Milford Haven

Burry Port

RHONDDA

Pontypool

1

Pembroke

Tenby

Carmarthen Bay

Llanelli

SWANSEA

NEATH AND PORT TALBOT

Neath

CYNON

Rhondda

TAFF

CAERPHILLY

Cwmbra

Pontypridd

Newpo

Swansea

Port Talbot

BRIDGEND

Caerphilly

NEW

NORTH

Worms Head

GOWER

Bridgend

CARDIFF

Cardiff

VALE OF GLAMORGAN

ATLANTIC

Barry

Weston-super-Mare

OCEAN

Bristol Channel

Bridgwater Bay

St George's Channel

Lynton

Dunkery Beacon

Minehead

Lundy

Ilfracombe

DEVON

EXMOOR 519m

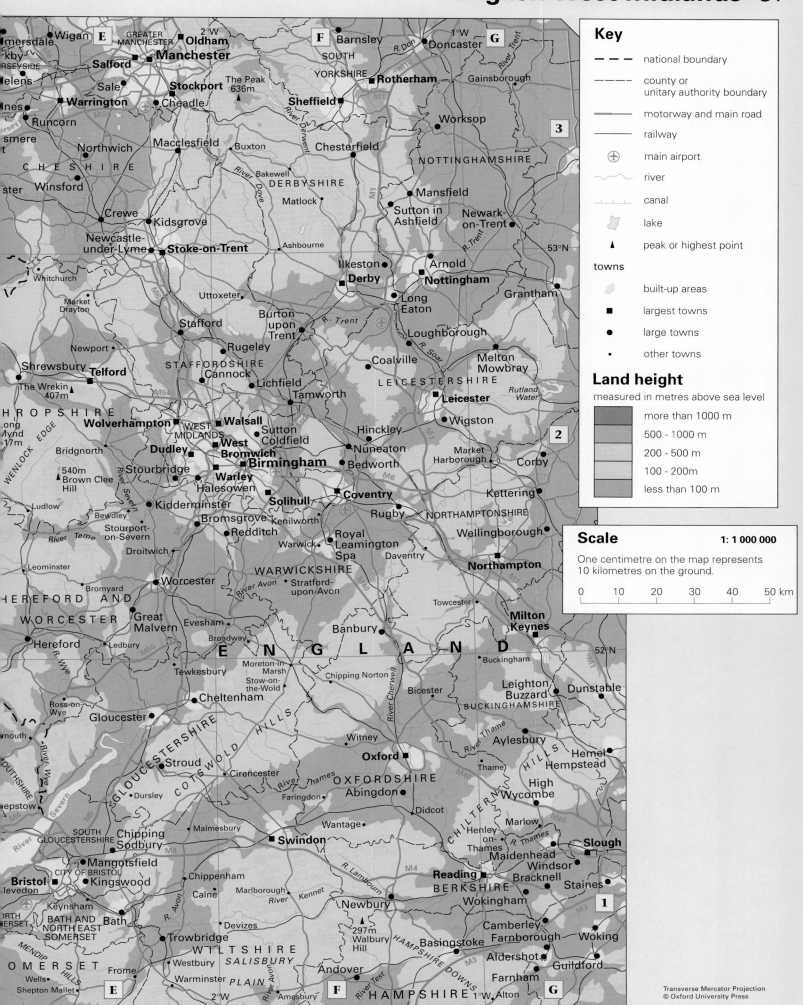

Key

– – –	national boundary
–·–·–	county or unitary authority boundary
━━━	motorway and main road
───	railway
⊕	main airport
～	river
┿	canal
◠	lake
▲	peak or highest point

towns

	built-up areas
■	largest towns
●	large towns
•	other towns

Land height

measured in metres above sea level

	more than 1000 m
	500 - 1000 m
	200 - 500 m
	100 - 200m
	less than 100 m

Scale   1: 1 000 000

One centimetre on the map represents 10 kilometres on the ground.

0	10	20	30	40	50 km

Transverse Mercator Projection
© Oxford University Press

A 3°W •Oswestry
Market
Drayton   B
407m
Welshpool   The Wrekin ▲
Shrewsbury   Telford
Montgomery   SHROPSHIRE
Newport   Long
Mynd
517m
Wolverhampton
3   Bridgnorth
540m
▲ Brown Clee
Hill
Knighton   Ludlow   Stourbridge   Dudley
Kidderminster
Kington   Bewdley
Leominster   Stourport-on-Severn
Bromsgrove
Droitwich
Redditch
Bromyard
HEREFORD AND
WORCESTER   Worcester
Hereford   Great
Malvern   R. Avon
Ledbury
52°N
BLACK   Broadway
MOUNTAINS   Tewkesbury
Ross-on-Wye   Moreton-in-Marsh
Stow-on-the-Wold
Abergavenny   Cheltenham
Monmouth   Gloucester
MONMOUTHSHIRE
Pontypool   Stroud   Cirencester
TORFAEN   Cwmbran   GLOUCESTERSHIRE   COTSWOLD HILLS
Chepstow
Newport   Chipping
NEWPORT   SOUTH   Sodbury
GLOUCESTERSHIRE
2   Mangotsfield
Clevedon   Bristol   CITY OF BRISTOL
Kingswood
Weston-super-Mare   Keynsham   Chippenham
NORTH   Calne
SOMERSET   BATH AND
NORTH EAST   Bath
SOMERSET
Wells   MENDIP HILLS   R. Avon
Frome
Shepton
Mallet
Bridgwater   Glastonbury
SOMERSET   Trowbridge
R. Parrett   Westbury   SALISBURY
R. Tone   Mere   WILTSHIRE   PLAIN
Wincanton   Warminster
River Yeo   Amesbury
1   Ilchester   Devizes
Chard   Yeovil   Sherborne
Ilminster   Crewkerne   Shaftesbury
Axminster
Lyme   River Axe   Blandford
Regis   Forum   Wimborne
Bridport   Minster   Ringwood
DORSET
Dorchester   River Frome
Poole
Weymouth   Wareham   Christchurch
Bournemouth
Portland
Bill   Swanage
St Alban's
Head
3°W © Oxford University Press   B   2°W

4   1°W   R. Trent   D   LINCOLNSHIRE   R. Witham
53°N   C   Arnold   Sleaford   Boston
Ilkeston   Nottingham   Spald
Derby   Long Eaton   Grantham   THE
Burton upon   Loughborough   R. Soar   Melton
Trent   Mowbray   Stamford
Rugeley   STAFFORDSHIRE   Coalville   LEICESTERSHIRE   Rutland
Cannock   Lichfield   Water
Stafford   Tamworth   Leicester   Peterboro
Walsall   Hinckley   Wigston
WEST   Sutton   Nuneaton   Market
MIDLANDS   Coldfield   Harborough   Corby
West   Bedworth   Oundle   CAMBRIDGESHI
Bromwich   Birmingham   Coventry   Kettering   Hunting
Warley   Halesowen   Rugby   St Ive
Solihull   Kenilworth   NORTHAMPTONSHIRE   Wellingborough
Warwick   Royal   Northampton   St Neots
Leamington   Daventry
WARWICKSHIRE   Spa   Bedford
Stratford-   Towcester   Biggleswade
upon-Avon   Roys
ENGLAND
Banbury   Buckingham   BEDFORDSHIRE   Letchwo
Chipping Norton   Milton   Hitchin
Keynes   Leighton   Stevena
Witney   Bicester   Buzzard   Dunstable   Luton
BUCKINGHAMSHIRE   HERTFORDSH
River Thame   Aylesbury   Welwy
Oxford   Thame   Hemel   Garder
OXFORDSHIRE   Hempstead   St Albans
River Thames   Cheshun
Faringdon   CHILTERN   Watford   Enfie
Abingdon   Didcot   High   Waltham
Wantage   Wycombe   Barnet   Fores
Swindon   Marlow   HILLS   Harrow   GREATE
Maidenhead   Brent   Lon
Henley-on-Thames   Slough   Hillingdon
Chippenham   Reading   Thames   Windsor   Ealing   Greenwi
Marlborough   BERKSHIRE   Bracknell   Hounslow   Richmond
R. Avon   River Kennet   Newbury   Wokingham   Staines   upon Thames   LON
297m   Camberley   Kingston   Merto
▲ Walbury Hill   upon Thames   Sutton
Basingstoke   Woking   SURREY   Cro
HAMPSHIRE DOWNS   Farnborough   Epsom
Andover   Aldershot   Guildford   Reigate
Farnham   Dorking   Redhi
River Test   Alton   294m   M23
Stockbridge   Leith Hill   Crawley
R. Itchen   NORTH DOWNS   Haslemere
Salisbury   Winchester   Haywards
HAMPSHIRE   Horsham   Heath
Romsey   Petersfield
Eastleigh   WEST SUSSEX
Totton   River Meon   SOUTH DOWNS   Lev
Southampton   Waterlooville   R. Arun
River Avon   Havant   Chichester   Worthing   SOU
Fareham   Arundel
Fawley   Gosport   Bognor   Hove
Lymington   Cowes   Portsmouth   Regis   Littlehampton   Brigh
Ryde   Selsey Bill
The Needles   Newport   Sandown
ISLE OF WIGHT   Shanklin
St Catherine's   Point   C   1°W   D

1   51°N
B   2°W   C   D

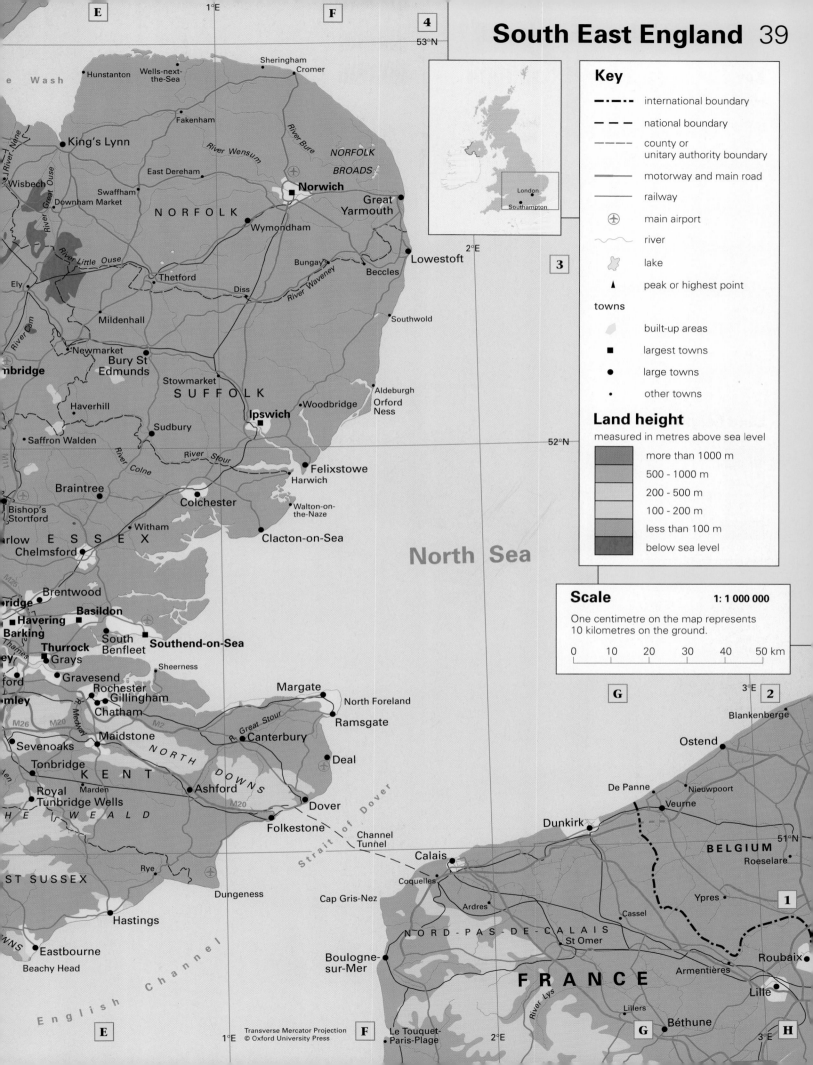

Key

- —·—·— international boundary
- ——— county or unitary authority boundary
- ——— motorway and main road
- ——— railway
- ⊕ main airport
- ⌇ river
- ⊢⊣ canal
- 🗺 lake
- ▲ peak or highest point

towns

- 🮑 built-up areas
- ■ largest towns
- ● large towns
- • other towns

Land height

measured in metres above sea level

- more than 1000 m
- 500 - 1000 m
- 200 - 500 m
- 100 - 200 m
- less than 100 m

NORTH

ATLANTIC

OCEAN

Lundy

Bideford Bay

Hartland Point

Bude Bay

Trevose Head

Ilfracombe

Lynton

Minehead
Dunkery Beacon
▲ 519m

Braunton
Barnstaple

EXMOOR

River Exe

South Molton

Bideford

River Taw

Great Torrington

D E V O N

Tiverton

Cullom

River Torridge

Bude

Holsworthy

Hatherleigh

Crediton

Boscastle

Okehampton

Exeter

Launceston

Brown Willy
▲ 420m

BODMIN MOOR

Yes Tor
619

River Teign

D A R T M O O R

Exmo

Padstow

Wadebridge

River Camel

River Tavy

R. Tamar

Bovey Tracey

Dawlis

Teignmouth

Tavistock

Newton Abbot

Newquay

Bodmin

River Fowey

Liskeard

Buckfastleigh

R. Dart

Torb

CORNWALL

Lostwithiel

Saltash

Totnes

Bri

St Agnes

Truro

River Fal

St Austell

Fowey

Looe

Torpoint

Plymouth

Dartmouth

Kingsbridge

St Ives

Redruth
Camborne

Penryn

Bigbury Bay

Salcombe

Start Bay

Start Poin

St Just
Penzance

Sennen
Land's End

Falmouth

Helston

Mount's Bay

Mullion

Lizard
Lizard Point

50°N
Bryher
St Martin's
Tresco
St Mary's
Hugh Town
Isles of Scilly

NORTH

ATLANTIC

OCEAN

Cardiff

Southampton

Isles of Scilly

Channel Islands

Bristol Channel

VALE GLAMC

Scale

1 : 1 000 000

One centimetre on the map represents 10 kilometres on the ground.

| 0 | 10 | 20 | 30 | 40 | 50 km |

Transverse Mercator Projection
© Oxford University Press

D Cardiff
3°W
Clevedon
Barry

Veston-super-Mare

gwater Bay

CITY OF BRISTOL
Bristol   Kingswood
E
Keynsham
BATH AND
NORTH EAST
SOMERSET
NORTH WEST
SOMERSET
Bath

M4
2°W
Chippenham
Calne
Devizes
Trowbridge
Westbury
Warminster
WILTSHIRE
SALISBURY
PLAIN
F
297m
Walbury
Hill
Andover
Amesbury
Basingstoke
HAMPSHIRE DOWNS
1°W Camberley
Farnborough-
Aldershot
Farnham
Alton
G
Woking Epsom
SURREY
Guildford
Dorking
Haslemere
NORTH DOWNS
4

MENDIP HILLS
Wells
Shepton Mallet
Glastonbury
Frome
River Test
River Itchen
Stockbridge
Winchester
HAMPSHIRE
Romsey
Eastleigh
Petersfield
SOUTH DOWNS
Horsham
WEST SUSSEX
51°N

OMERSET
Taunton
illington
River Tone
Bridgwater
R. Parrett
QUANTOCK HILLS
River Yeo
Ilchester
Wincanton
Mere
Shaftesbury
Salisbury
River Avon
Totton
Southampton
Fawley
Lymington
Fareham
Gosport
Waterlooville
Havant
M27
Portsmouth
Chichester
Arundel
Bognor
Regis
Littlehampton
Worthing
River Arun

DORSET
Yeovil
Sherborne
Ilminster
Crewkerne
Chard
River Axe
Axminster
oniton
Bridport
Lyme Regis
Seaton
Sidmouth
Dorchester
River Frome
Blandford
Forum
River Stour
Wimborne
Minster
Ringwood
Poole
Wareham
Christchurch
Bournemouth
The Needles
Cowes
ISLE OF WIGHT
Newport
The Solent
Ryde
Sandown
Shanklin
Selsey Bill

Weymouth
Swanage
St Alban's
Head
Lyme Bay
St Catherine's
Point

Portland Bill

English Channel

50°N

Cap de la Hague
Auderville
Alderney
Barfleur
Cherbourg
Baie de la Seine
2

Guernsey
St Peter-Port
Sark
CHANNEL
ISLANDS
Valognes
FRANCE
Carteret
Carentan
Isigny-sur-Mer
Bayeux

Jersey
St Helier
Lessay
River Vire
St-Lô
Caen
River Orne

Coutainville
Coutances

D
3°W
E
2°W
© Oxford University Press
F
1°W
G
49°N
1

R
S
T
U
V
9
8
7
6
5
4
3
2
1
N
P
Q
45°E
50°E
55°E
60°E
65°E
60°N
65°N
55°N
50°N
45°N
40°N
35°N
30°N
30°E
35°E
40°E
Pechora
URAL MOUNTAINS
Ukhta
Serov
Syktyvkar
North Dvina
Solikamsk
Berezniki
Nizhniy Tagil
Kotlas
Perm
Yekaterinburg (Sverdlovsk)
Kirov (Vyatka)
Glazov
Izhevsk
Vologda
Nizhnekamsk
Naberezhnye Chelny
Ufa
Rybinsk
Volga
Nizhniy-Novgorod (Gorkiy)
Kazan'
Cheboksary
Ivanovo
Vladimir
Oka
Sterlitamak
Ul'yanovsk (Simbirsk)
Tol'yatti
Samara (Kuybyshev)
Orenburg
Ryazan
Tula
RUSSIAN FEDERATION (RUSSIA)
Penza
Balakovo
Ural'sk
Ural
Tambov
Orel
Lipetsk
Saratov
Engel's
Voronezh
Kursk
Kamyshin
KAZAKHSTAN
Don
Kharkov
Volgograd
Donets
Luhans'k
Tsimlyansk Reservoir
Dnipropetrovsk
Shakhty
Astrakhan
Donetsk
Rostov-on-Don
Zaporizhzhya
Mariupol
Caspian Sea
Stavropol
Kherson
Sea of Azov
Krasnodar
Grozny
Crimea
Maykop
Pyatigorsk
Nalchik
Makhachkala
Mt. Elbrus 5642 m
Vladikavkaz
CAUCASUS
Simferopol
Sochi
Sukhumi
Kutaisi
GEORGIA
Tbilisi
Gyandzha
AZERBAIJAN
Black Sea
Batumi
ARMENIA
Yerevan
Araks
Mt. Ararat 5123 m
IRAN
Samsun
Trabzona
Erzurum
Lake Urmia
Zonguldak
Kizil Irmak
Lake Van
Sivas
Ankara
Kirikkale
Elâziğ
Diyarbakir
TURKEY
Kayseri
Malatya
Firat
Arbil
Lake Tuz
Mosul
Kirkuk
Konya
Gaziantep
Tigris
Adana
Aleppo
Mersin
Antalya
Euphrates
Latakia
Hamah
Nicosia
Homs
SYRIA
CYPRUS
Limassol
Tripoli
LEBANON
Zahlé
Beirut
Damascus
IRAQ
Haifa
ISRAEL
Irbid
Zarqa
Tel Aviv-Jaffa
Amman
Jerusalem
SAUDI ARABIA
Port Said
JORDAN
Beersheba
Jauf
Cairo
Suez
Giza
Aqaba
Mt. Sinai 2641 m
Tabuk

SWEDEN
FINLAND
Stockholm
Helsinki
DENMARK
Copenhagen
Dublin
REPUBLIC OF IRELAND
UNITED KINGDOM
London
NETHERLANDS
Amsterdam
Berlin
Brussels
BELGIUM
GERMANY
Warsaw
POLAND
LUXEMBOURG
Luxembourg
Paris
FRANCE
Bern
SWITZERLAND
Vienna
AUSTRIA
Budapest
HUNGARY
PORTUGAL
Lisbon
Madrid
SPAIN
ITALY
Rome
Ankara
TURKEY
GREECE
Athens
MALTA
Valletta

The European Union

- ---- international boundary
- • national capital
- member country of the European Union
- countries that have applied to join the European Union

Scale

1: 40 000 000

One centimetre on the map represents 400 kilometres on the ground.

0 400 800 1200 km

Wealth

Gross Domestic Product (GDP) per person, 1992

The annual total value of all the goods and services produced in a country divided by the number of people living in that country.

- more than 20 000 — among the top 10 countries of the world
- 15 000 – 20 000 — among the top 25 countries of the world
- 10 000 – 15 000 — among the top 30 countries of the world
- 5000 – 10 000 — among the top 70 countries of the world
- 0 – 5000 — among the top 120 countries of the world

European average wealth per person: 11 963 US dollars

World average wealth per person: 5410 US dollars

Climatic regions

Very dry

with no reliable rain

with a little rain

Influenced by the sea: warm summers, mild winters

with dry summers (Mediterranean type)

with no dry season

Cool

rain all year

Cold polar

no warm season and fairly dry

Mountain

height of the land strongly affects the climate

Ocean currents

→ warm

→ cold

Climate recording stations

• climate recording stations for which graphs are shown

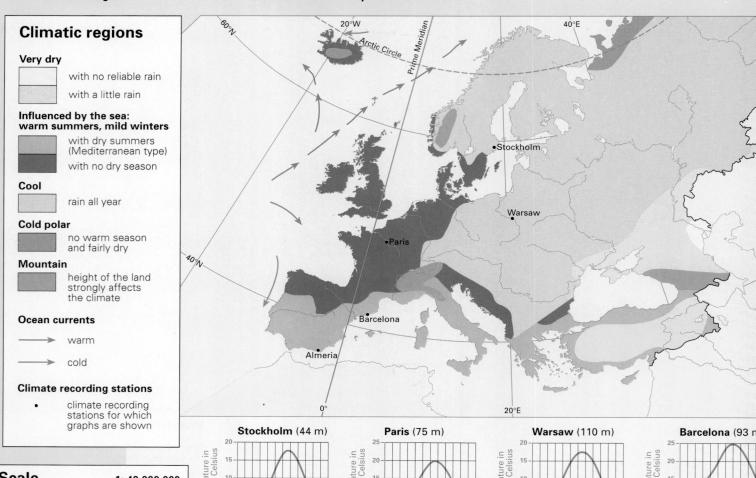

Scale

1: 40 000 000

One centimetre on the map represents 400 kilometres on the ground.

0 400 800 1200 km

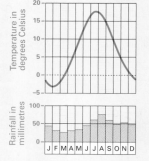

Stockholm (44 m)

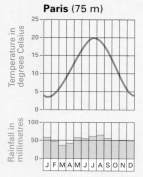

Paris (75 m)

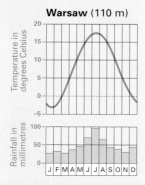

Warsaw (110 m)

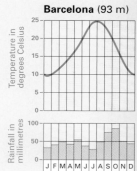

Barcelona (93 m)

Ecosystems

Vegetation types are those which would occur naturally without interference by people.

 coniferous forest

 deciduous and mixed forest

 evergreen trees and shrubs

 temperate grasslands

 semi-desert

 tundra

 ice

 mountains

—— country boundary

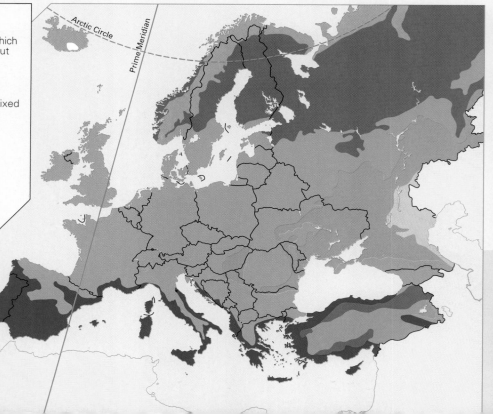

Stockholm
Mean annual rainfall : 524 mm
Mean January temperature : -3.
Mean July temperature : 18.0°C

Paris
Mean annual rainfall : 589 mm
Mean January temperature : 3.5
Mean July temperature : 20.0°C

Warsaw
Mean annual rainfall : 525 mm
Mean January temperature : -3.
Mean July temperature : 19.5°C

Barcelona
Mean annual rainfall : 587 mm
Mean January temperature : 9.5
Mean July temperature : 24.5°C

Almeria
Mean annual rainfall : 233 mm
Mean January temperature : 12.
Mean July temperature : 25.0°C

More information about these ecosystems can be found on page 8.

Conical Orthomorphic Projection

© Oxford University Press

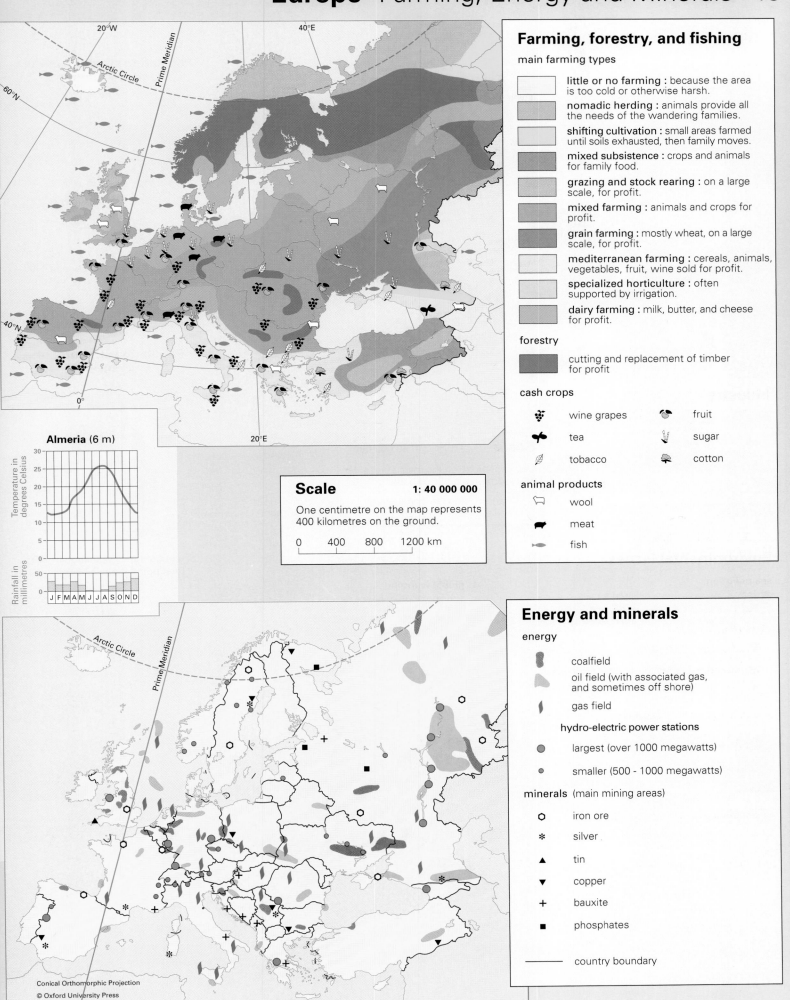

Farming, forestry, and fishing

main farming types

	little or no farming : because the area is too cold or otherwise harsh.
	nomadic herding : animals provide all the needs of the wandering families.
	shifting cultivation : small areas farmed until soils exhausted, then family moves.
	mixed subsistence : crops and animals for family food.
	grazing and stock rearing : on a large scale, for profit.
	mixed farming : animals and crops for profit.
	grain farming : mostly wheat, on a large scale, for profit.
	mediterranean farming : cereals, animals, vegetables, fruit, wine sold for profit.
	specialized horticulture : often supported by irrigation.
	dairy farming : milk, butter, and cheese for profit.

forestry

	cutting and replacement of timber for profit

cash crops

	wine grapes		fruit
	tea		sugar
	tobacco		cotton

animal products

	wool
	meat
	fish

Almeria (6 m)

Temperature in degrees Celsius

Rainfall in millimetres

J F M A M J J A S O N D

Scale   1: 40 000 000

One centimetre on the map represents 400 kilometres on the ground.

0   400   800   1200 km

Energy and minerals

energy

	coalfield
	oil field (with associated gas, and sometimes off shore)
	gas field

hydro-electric power stations

	largest (over 1000 megawatts)
	smaller (500 - 1000 megawatts)

minerals (main mining areas)

○	iron ore
✳	silver
▲	tin
▼	copper
+	bauxite
■	phosphates

——— country boundary

Conical Orthomorphic Projection
© Oxford University Press

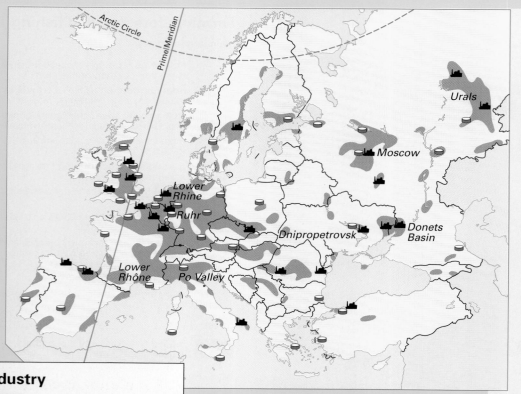

Industry

▓	industrial areas
⚒	iron and steel
⬭	oil refining and petro-chemicals
—	country boundary

Scale

1 : 40 000 000

One centimetre on the map represents 400 kilometres on the ground.

0   400   800   1200 km

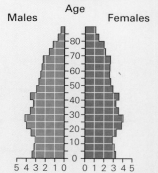

Population structure of the United Kingdom

Age

Males   Females

80
70
60
50
40
30
20
10

5 4 3 2 1 0   0 1 2 3 4 5

percent of total population in 1990
Total population : 57.4 million

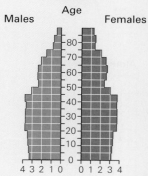

Population structure of France

Age

Males   Females

80
70
60
50
40
30
20
10
0

4 3 2 1 0   0 1 2 3 4

percent of total population in 1993
Total population : 57.5 million

Environmental issues

sea pollution

areas severely polluted for all or part of the year
areas persistently affected by pollution

▼   deep sea dump sites

✳   major oil spills (over 100 000 tonnes)

✲   major oil spills (less than 100 000 tonnes)

acid rain A pH scale measures acidity. Unaffected rain water is slightly acidic with a pH of 5.6

pH less than 4.2 (the most acidic)
pH 4.2 - 4.6
pH 4.6 - 5.0

air pollution

◆   cities where sulphur dioxide emmissions are recorded, and exceed recommended levels

industrial sites emmitting the largest amounts of sulphur, in 1990-92

thousands of tonnes of sulphur

◯ over 200
◯ 100 - 200
◯ 50 - 100
∘ 30 - 50

global warming
addition of greenhouse gases in tonnes of carbon per person (look at the world map on page 17)

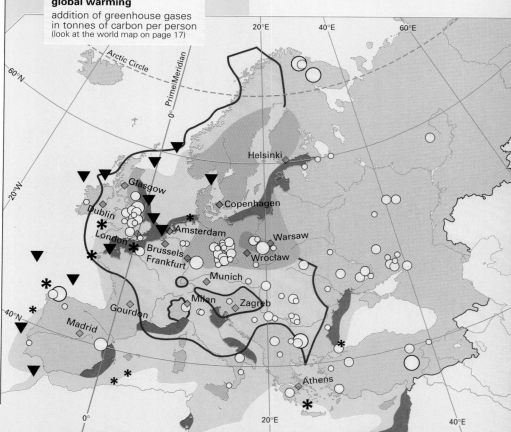

Conical Orthomorphic Projection
© Oxford University Press

Population structure of Germany

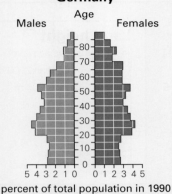

Males — Age — Females

percent of total population in 1990
Total population : 74.4 million

Population structure of Greece

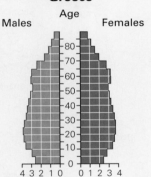

Males — Age — Females

percent of total population in 1993
Total population : 10.4 million

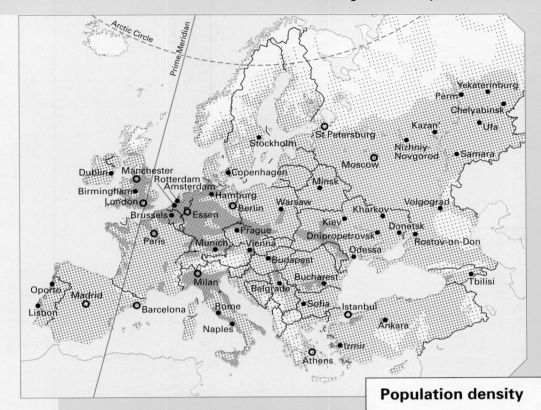

Scale   1: 40 000 000

One centimetre on the map represents
400 kilometres on the ground.

0   400   800   1200 km

Population density

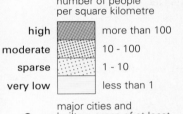

number of people
per square kilometre

high	more than 100
moderate	10 - 100
sparse	1 - 10
very low	less than 1

○ major cities and built up areas of at least 3 million people

• cities with 1 - 3 million people

— country boundary

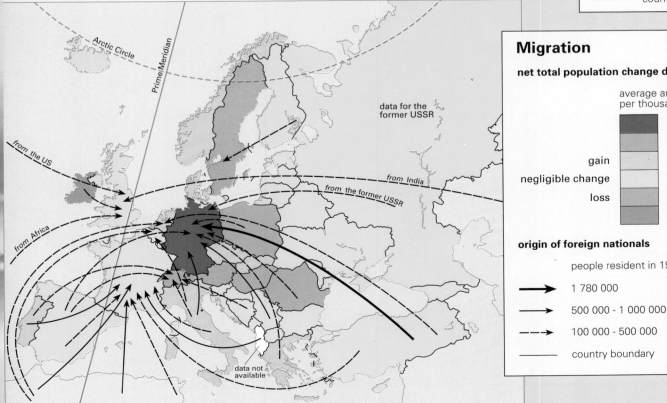

data for the former USSR

from the US

from India

from the former USSR

from Africa

data not available

Migration

net total population change due to migration

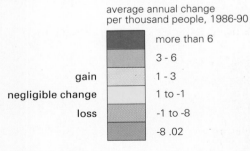

average annual change
per thousand people, 1986-90

	more than 6
	3 - 6
gain	1 - 3
negligible change	1 to -1
loss	-1 to -8
	-8 .02

origin of foreign nationals

people resident in 1990

→ 1 780 000

→ 500 000 - 1 000 000

--→ 100 000 - 500 000

— country boundary

Conical Orthomorphic Projection
© Oxford University Press

48 France

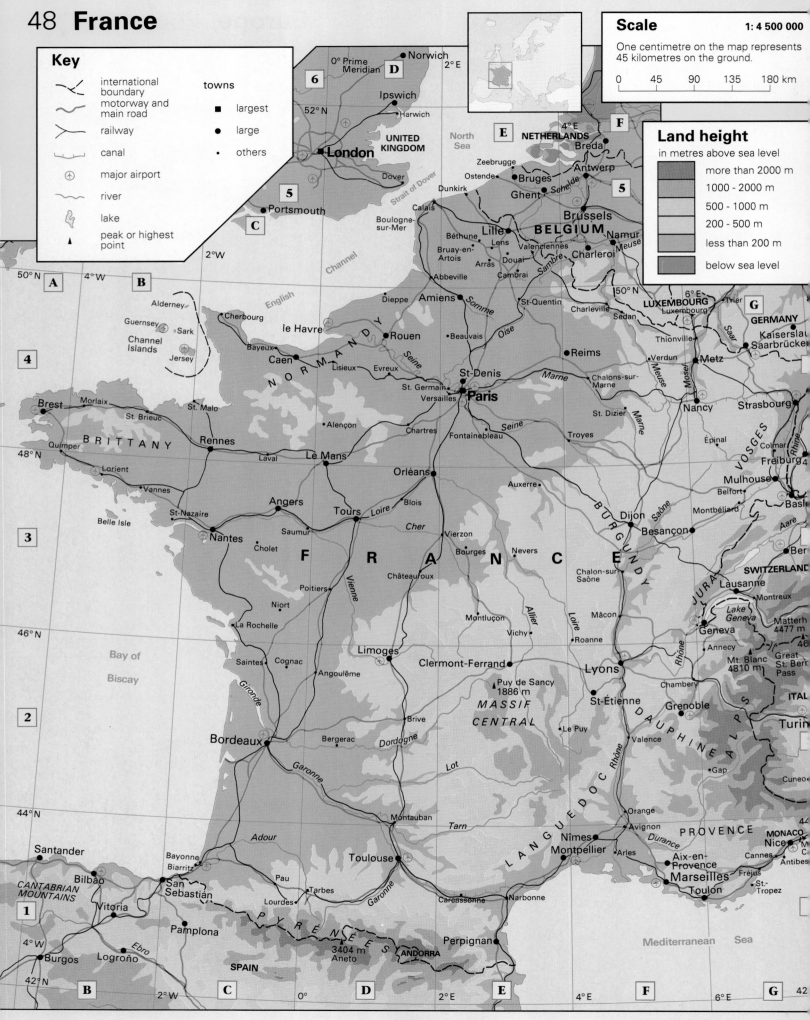

Key

international boundary	towns
motorway and main road	■ largest
railway	● large
canal	• others
✈ major airport	
river	
lake	
▲ peak or highest point	

Land height

in metres above sea level

more than 2000 m
1000 - 2000 m
500 - 1000 m
200 - 500 m
less than 200 m
below sea level

Scale

1: 4 500 000

One centimetre on the map represents 45 kilometres on the ground.

| 0 | 45 | 90 | 135 | 180 km |

SWEDEN
Bornholm

DENMARK
Jutland
Fyn Zealand
Odense
Lolland Falster
Flensburg
Fehmarn
North Friesian Islands
Baltic Sea
Rugen
Kiel
Stralsund
Lübeck
Rostock
Schwerin
Szczecin
Bremerhaven
Hamburg
POLAND
Elbe
Bremen
Wittenberge
Oder
Wolfsburg
Brandenburg Potsdam Berlin
Hannover
Brunswick
Magdeburg
Osnabrück
Bielefeld
Salzgitter
Dessau
Cottbus
HARZ
Paderborn
Göttingen
Halle
Leipzig
Dresden
Kassel
GERMANY
Erfurt
Jena Gera Chemnitz
Siegen
Zwickau
Giessen
Koblenz
Coburg
Cheb
Prague
Frankfurt
Wiesbaden
Main
Bamberg Bayreuth
CZECH REPUBLIC
Mainz
Würzburg
Plzeň
Darmstadt
Erlangen
Ludwigshafen
Mannheim
Nuremberg
Heidelberg
Kaiserslautern
Saarbrücken
Heilbronn
Karlsruhe
Regensburg
Pforzheim
BAVARIA
Danube
Baden-Baden
Stuttgart
Ingolstadt
Linz
Reutlingen Ulm
Augsburg
Inn
Munich
Salzburg
Freiburg
Danube
Lake Constance
Oberammergau
St. Anton
Innsbruck
AUSTRIA
Mulhouse
Winterthur
Rhine
Vaduz
Brenner Pass
3797 m Grossglockner
Mur
Belfort
Montbéliard
Basle
LIECHTENSTEIN
ALPS
Klagenfurt
Dijon
Saône
Zürich
Drava
Besançon
Aare
Lucerne
3899 m Ortles
Bolzano
Sava
SWITZERLAND
Bern
St. Moritz
DOLOMITES
Lausanne
Montreux
4158 m Jungfrau
St. Gotthard Pass
4050 m Bernina
Trento
Udine
Ljubljana
JURA
Lake Geneva
ALPS
Simplon Pass
Lugano
Lake Como
SLOVENIA
Geneva
Rhône
Lake Maggiore
Trieste
Annecy
4477 m Matterhorn
Como
Bergamo
Rijeka
Lyons
4810 m Mt. Blanc
Great St. Bernard Pass
Monza Brescia Vicenza Lake Garda
Verona Padua Venice
Grenoble
Chambery
Novara
Milan
ITALY
CROATIA
Turin
Piacenza
Po
Istria

UNITED KINGDOM
pswich
wich
Ipswich
Dover
Calais
gne-Mer
Boulogne-sur-Mer
North Sea
NETHERLANDS
IJsselmeer
Haarlem
Amsterdam
Apeldoorn
Hengelo
Leiden
Hilversum
The Hague
Utrecht
Enschede
Rotterdam
Rhine
Arnhem
Münster
Dordrecht
Waal
Nijmegen
Breda
Maas
Tilburg
Gelsenkirchen
Recklinghausen
Hamm
Zeebrugge
Ostende
Antwerp
Eindhoven
Duisburg
Bochum
Dortmund
Bruges
Ghent
Schelde
München Gladbach
Krefeld
Essen
Dunkirk
Krefeld
Wuppertal Remscheid
BELGIUM
Düsseldorf
Leverkusen
Lille
Brussels
Maastricht
Aachen
Cologne
Bonn
Lens
Namur
Liège
Béthune
Bruay-en-Artois
Valenciennes
Meuse
Arras
Douai
Charleroi
ARDENNES
Cambrai
Sambre
Abbeville
St-Quentin
LUXEMBOURG
Luxembourg
Trier
Mosel
0°N
Amiens
Somme
Charleville
Sedan
Beauvais
Oise
Thionville
Saar
St-Denis
Germain
Versailles
Paris
St-Germain
Marne
Reims
Verdun
Metz
Chalons-sur-Marne
Seine
Nancy
Strasbourg
Fontainebleau
St. Dizier
Marne
VOSGES
Troyes
Épinal
Colmar
Rhine
BLACK FOREST
FRANCE
Auxerre

West Friesian Islands
East Friesian Islands
Wilhelmshaven
Emden
Groningen
Oldenburg
Mittelland Canal
Ems
Weser
Kiel Canal

ical Orthomorphic Projection   © Oxford University Press

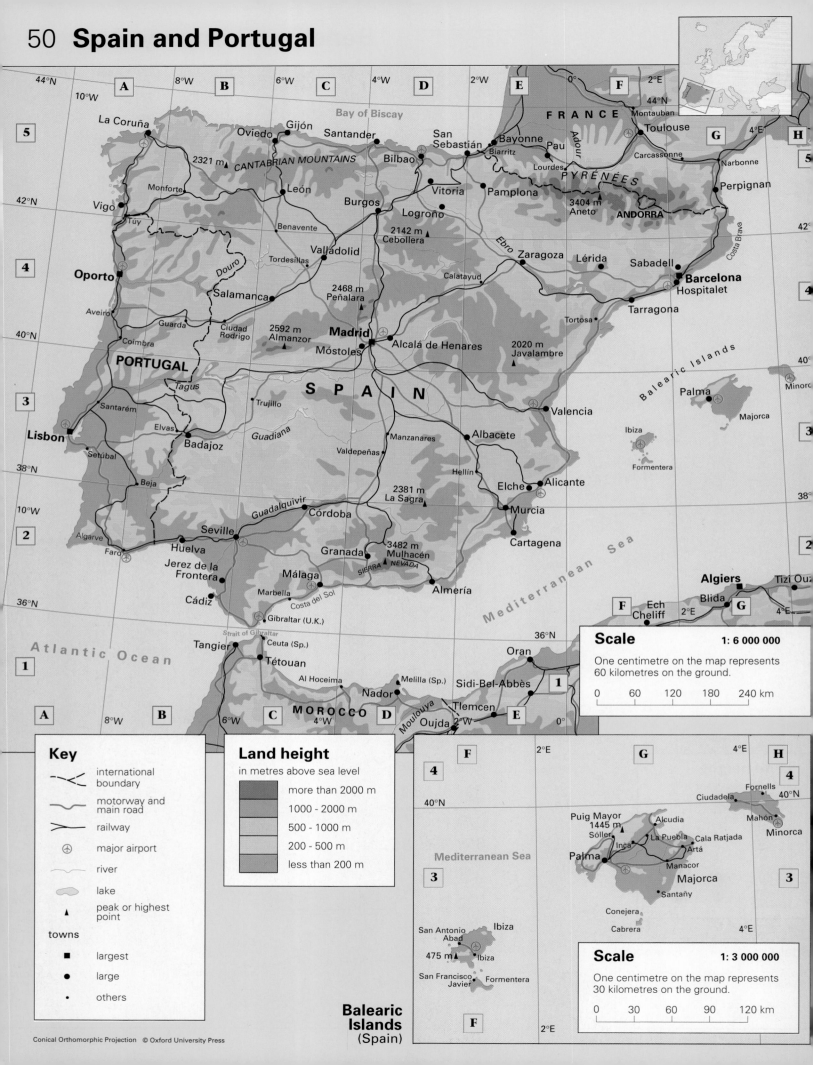

50 Spain and Portugal

Key

- —‹— international boundary
- motorway and main road
- railway
- ⊕ major airport
- river
- lake
- ▲ peak or highest point

towns
- ■ largest
- ● large
- · others

Land height
in metres above sea level

- more than 2000 m
- 1000 - 2000 m
- 500 - 1000 m
- 200 - 500 m
- less than 200 m

Scale   1: 6 000 000

One centimetre on the map represents 60 kilometres on the ground.

0   60   120   180   240 km

Scale   1: 3 000 000

One centimetre on the map represents 30 kilometres on the ground.

0   30   60   90   120 km

Balearic Islands (Spain)

Conical Orthomorphic Projection © Oxford University Press

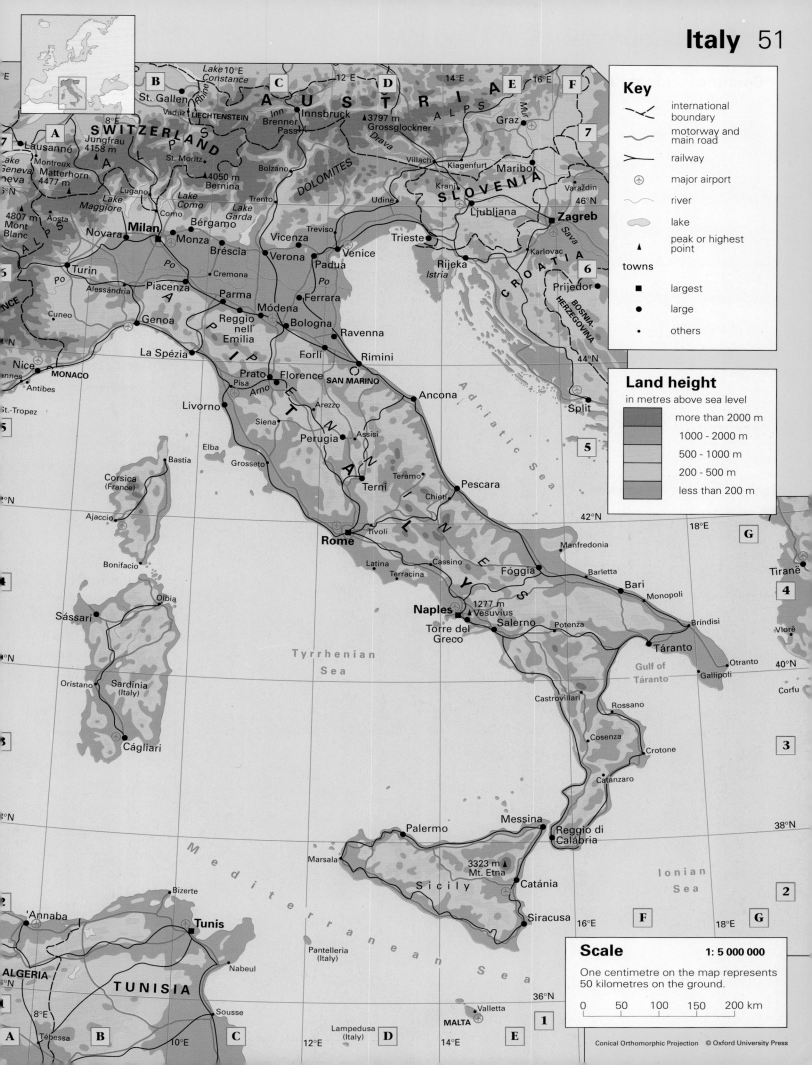

Key

international boundary	
motorway and main road	
railway	
major airport	
river	
lake	
peak or highest point	

towns

largest	
large	
others	

Land height
in metres above sea level

- more than 2000 m
- 1000 - 2000 m
- 500 - 1000 m
- 200 - 500 m
- less than 200 m

Scale   1: 5 000 000
One centimetre on the map represents 50 kilometres on the ground.

0   50   100   150   200 km

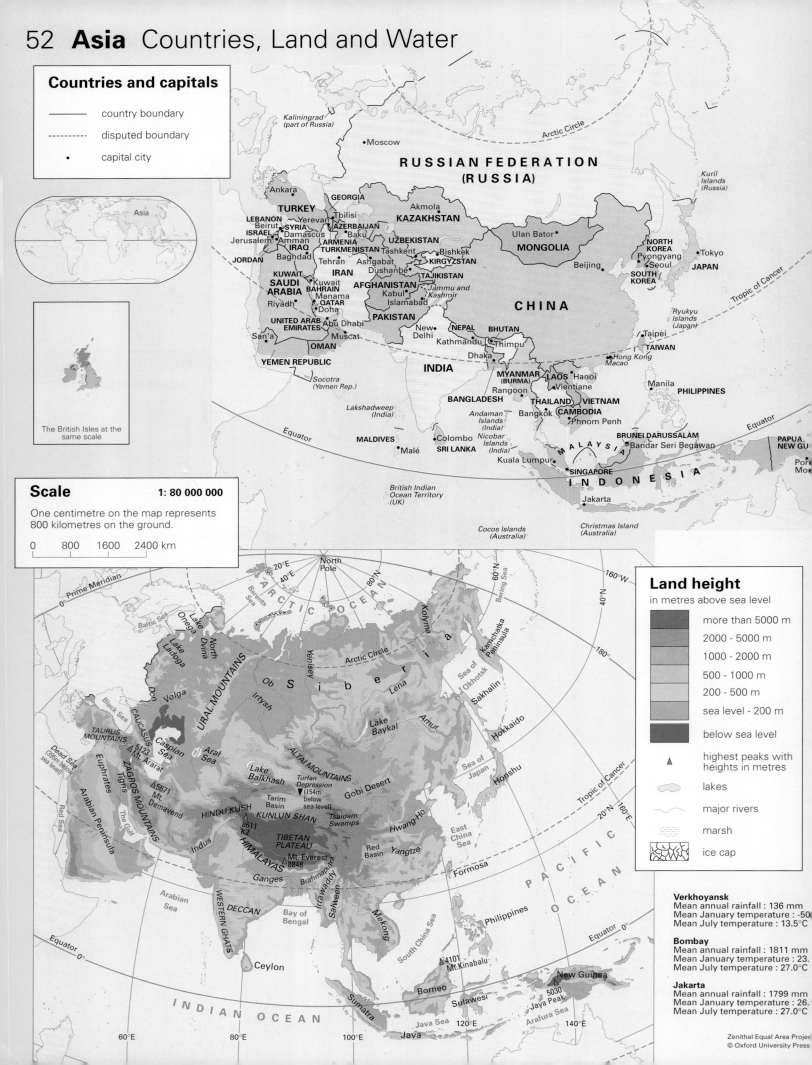

Countries and capitals

—— country boundary

- - - - disputed boundary

• capital city

Asia

The British Isles at the same scale

Scale
1 : 80 000 000

One centimetre on the map represents 800 kilometres on the ground.

0   800   1600   2400 km

Kaliningrad (part of Russia)

• Moscow

RUSSIAN FEDERATION (RUSSIA)

Arctic Circle

Kuril Islands (Russia)

• Ankara
GEORGIA
TURKEY
Yerevan •Tbilisi
LEBANON
Beirut
SYRIA •Damascus
ISRAEL •Amman
Jerusalem **IRAQ**
JORDAN Baghdad
Tehrān

Akmola
KAZAKHSTAN

Ulan Bator •
MONGOLIA

NORTH KOREA
Pyongyang • •Tokyo
Beijing • **SOUTH KOREA** Seoul **JAPAN**

AZERBAIJAN
ARMENIA Baku
TURKMENISTAN Tashkent
UZBEKISTAN
Ashgabat **KIRGYZSTAN** Bishkek
Dushanbe **TAJIKISTAN**

KUWAIT
Kuwait
SAUDI ARABIA
IRAN
BAHRAIN
Manama
QATAR
Riyadh • •Doha
UNITED ARAB EMIRATES
Abu Dhabi
San'a
OMAN Muscat

AFGHANISTAN
Kabul *Jammu and Kashmir*
Islamabad

CHINA

Ryukyu Islands (Japan)

Tropic of Cancer

•Taipei
TAIWAN

PAKISTAN
New Delhi • **NEPAL** **BHUTAN**
Kathmandu •Thimpu
Dhaka

•Hong Kong
Macao

YEMEN REPUBLIC

INDIA
MYANMAR (BURMA) **LAOS** Hanoi •
Rangoon Vientiane •
BANGLADESH **THAILAND** **VIETNAM**
Bangkok **CAMBODIA**
Phnom Penh

•Manila
PHILIPPINES

Socotra (Yemen Rep.)

Lakshadweep (India)

Andaman Islands (India)

Equator

BRUNEI DARUSSALAM
•Bandar Seri Begawan

PAPUA NEW GU

MALDIVES
•Malé

•Colombo
SRI LANKA

Nicobar Islands (India)

MALAYSIA

Equator

Por Mor

British Indian Ocean Territory (UK)

Kuala Lumpur •
SINGAPORE
INDONESIA

•Jakarta

Cocos Islands (Australia)

Christmas Island (Australia)

Land height
in metres above sea level

more than 5000 m
2000 - 5000 m
1000 - 2000 m
500 - 1000 m
200 - 500 m
sea level - 200 m
below sea level

▲ highest peaks with heights in metres

lakes

major rivers

marsh

ice cap

20°E
40°E
North Pole
0° Prime Meridian
80°N
ARCTIC OCEAN
160°W
60°N
40°N
180°

Baltic Sea
Barents Sea
Lake Onega
North Dvina
Lake Ladoga
URAL MOUNTAINS
Yenisey
Ob
S i b e r i a
Lena
Kolyma
Arctic Circle
Bering Sea
Kamchatka Peninsula

Black Sea
CAUCASUS
Don
Volga
Irtysh
Sea of Okhotsk
Sakhalin

TAURUS MOUNTAINS
Caspian Sea
△5123 Mt. Ararat
Aral Sea
Lake Balkhash
ALTAI MOUNTAINS
Lake Baykal
Amur
Hokkaido

Dead Sea (395m below sea level)
ZAGROS MOUNTAINS
Euphrates
Tigris
△5671 Mt Demavend
Turfan Depression (154m below sea level)
Gobi Desert
Sea of Japan
Honshu

Red Sea
Arabian Peninsula
The Gulf
HINDU KUSH
KUNLUN SHAN
Tarim Basin
Tsaidam Swamps
Hwang-Ho
East China Sea

Indus
8611 K2
TIBETAN PLATEAU
Red Basin
Yangtze

HIMALAYAS
△Mt. Everest 8848
Brahmaputra
Formosa

Ganges
DECCAN
Irrawaddy
Salween
Mekong
WESTERN GHATS
Arabian Sea
Bay of Bengal

Equator
60°E
80°E
100°E

Ceylon

Tropic of Cancer
20°N
160°E

PACIFIC OCEAN

Philippines

△4101 Mt.Kinabalu

Sumatra
Borneo
Sulawesi
Java Sea
120°E
Java
Arafura Sea
140°E

New Guinea
5030 Jaya Peak

INDIAN OCEAN

Equator 0°

Verkhoyansk
Mean annual rainfall : 136 mm
Mean January temperature : -50
Mean July temperature : 13.5°C

Bombay
Mean annual rainfall : 1811 mm
Mean January temperature : 23.
Mean July temperature : 27.0°C

Jakarta
Mean annual rainfall : 1799 mm
Mean January temperature : 26.
Mean July temperature : 27.0°C

Zenithal Equal Area Proje
© Oxford University Press

Verkhoyansk (100 m)

degrees Celsius

15
10
5
0
−5
−10
−15
−20
−25
−30
−35
−40
−45
−50
−55

millimetres

100
50

J F M A M J J A S O N D

Bombay (11 m)

degrees Celsius

35
30
25
20
15
10
5
0

650
600
550
500
450
400
350
300
250
200
150
100
50

millimetres

J F M A M J J A S O N D

Jakarta (8 m)

degrees Celsius

30
25
20
15
10
5
0

350
300
250
200
150
100
50

millimetres

J F M A M J J A S O N D

Climatic regions

Hot tropical rainy

rain all year

monsoon

dry in winter

Very dry

with no reliable rain

with a little rain

Influenced by the sea: warm summers, mild winters

with dry summers (Mediterranean type)

with dry winters

with no dry season

Cool

with dry winters

rain all year

Cold polar

no warm season and fairly dry

Mountain

height of the land strongly affects the climate

Ocean currents

→ warm

→ cold

Scale 1: 80 000 000

One centimetre on the map represents 800 kilometres on the ground.

0   800   1600   2400 km

Ecosystems

Vegetation types are those which would occur naturally without interference by people

coniferous forest

deciduous and mixed forest

tropical rain forest

evergreen trees and shrubs

thorn forest

temperate grasslands

semi-desert

desert

tundra

mountains

— country boundary

More information about these ecosystems can be found on page 8.

Zenithal Equal Area Projection
© Oxford University Press

Farming, forestry, and fishing

main farming types

little or no farming : because the area is too dry or otherwise harsh.

nomadic herding : animals provide the needs of the wandering families.

shifting cultivation : small areas farmed until soils exhausted, then family moves.

mixed subsistence : crops and animals for family food.

rice subsistence : where heavy rainfall will allow a main crop of rice.

subsistance crops : mostly intensive with the aid of irrigation. Family food only.

grazing and stock rearing : on a large scale, for profit.

mixed farming : animals and crops for profit.

grain farming : mostly wheat, on a large scale, for profit.

plantation : well organized, specializing in one crop for profit, e.g. tea or rubber.

mediterranean farming : cereals, animals, vegetables, fruit, wine, surplus for profit.

specialized horticulture : mostly on oases supported by underground water

dairy farming : milk, butter, and cheese for profit.

forestry

cutting and replacement of timber for profit

cash crops

groundnuts		fruit	
palm products		dates	
coffee		sugar	
tea		cotton	
tobacco		rubber	

animal products

wool		fish	
meat			

Energy, Minerals, and Industry

energy

coalfield

oil field (with associated gas, and sometimes off shore)

gas field

hydro-electric power stations

largest (over 3000 megawatts)

smaller (500 - 3000 megawatts)

industry

main centres of industry

country boundary

minerals
(main mining areas)

iron ore		nickel	
silver		bauxite	
gold		diamonds	
tin		copper	
phosphates			

Scale

1 : 80 000 000

One centimetre on the map represents 800 kilometres on the ground.

0   800   1600   2400 km

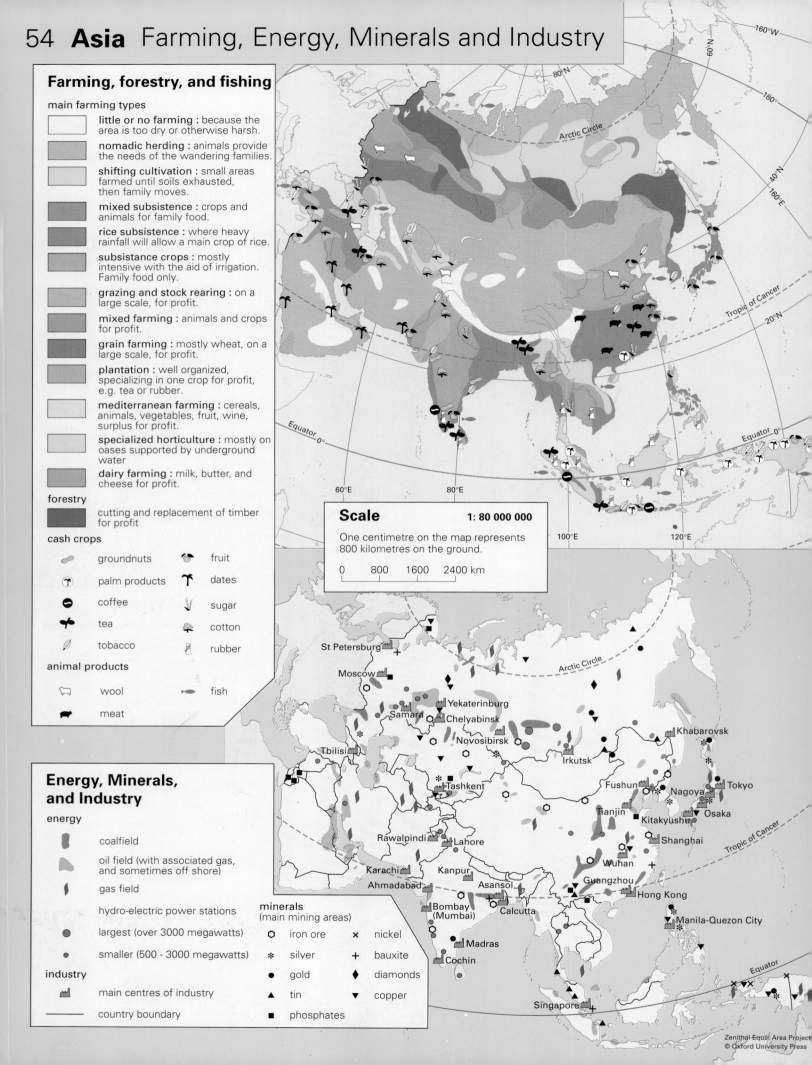

St Petersburg
Moscow
Yekaterinburg
Samara
Chelyabinsk
Novosibirsk
Khabarovsk
Tbilisi
Irkutsk
Tashkent
Fushun
Tokyo
Nagoya
Tianjin
Kitakyushu
Osaka
Rawalpindi
Lahore
Shanghai
Karachi
Kanpur
Wuhan
Ahmadabad
Asansol
Guangzhou
Bombay (Mumbai)
Calcutta
Hong Kong
Madras
Manila-Quezon City
Cochin
Singapore

Zenithal Equal Area Project
© Oxford University Press

Population density

number of people
per square kilometre

— country boundary

high		more than 100
moderate		10 - 100
sparse		1 -10
very low		less than 1

○ major cities and
built up areas
of at least
3 million people

● cities with
1 - 3 million
people

Population structure of China

Males   Age   Females

80
70
60
50
40
30
20
10
0

6 5 4 3 2 1 0   0 1 2 3 4 5 6

percent of total population in 1990
Total population : 1130.5 million

Population structure of India

Males   Age   Females

70
60
50
40
30
20
10
0

7 6 5 4 3 2 1 0   0 1 2 3 4 5 6 7

percent of total population in 1993
Total population : 883.9 million

© Oxford University Press

Scale

1: 80 000 000

One centimetre on the map represents
800 kilometres on the ground.

0   800   1600   2400 km

Environmental issues

tropical deforestation

existing areas
of rainforest

former areas
of rainforest

desertification

existing areas
of desert

high risk areas

moderate risk
areas

sea pollution

areas severely polluted
for all or part of the year

areas persistently
affected by pollution

▼ deep sea dump sites

✳ major oil spills
(over 100 000 tonnes)

✳ major oil spills
(less than
100 000 tonnes)

acid rain

areas where
acid rain is becoming
a problem

air pollution

◆ cities where sulphur
dioxide emmissions
are recorded,
and exceed
recommended levels

global warming

addition of greenhouse gases
in tonnes of carbon per person
(look at the world map on page 17)

Zenithal Equal Area Projection

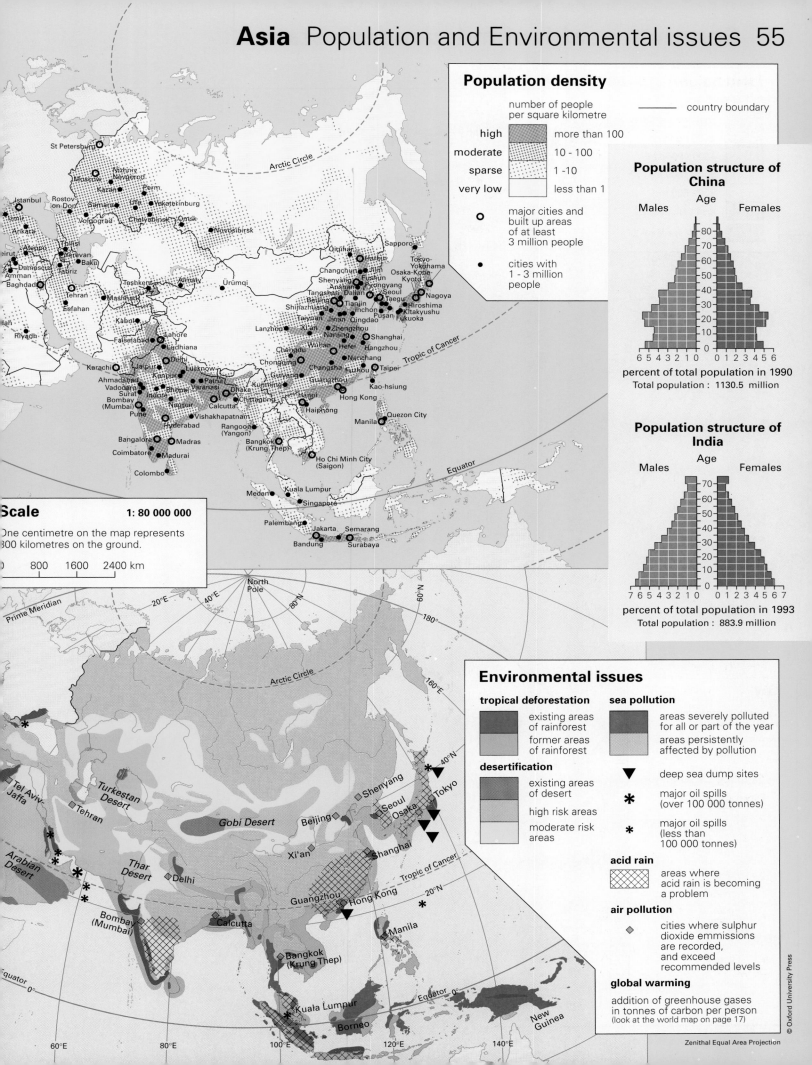

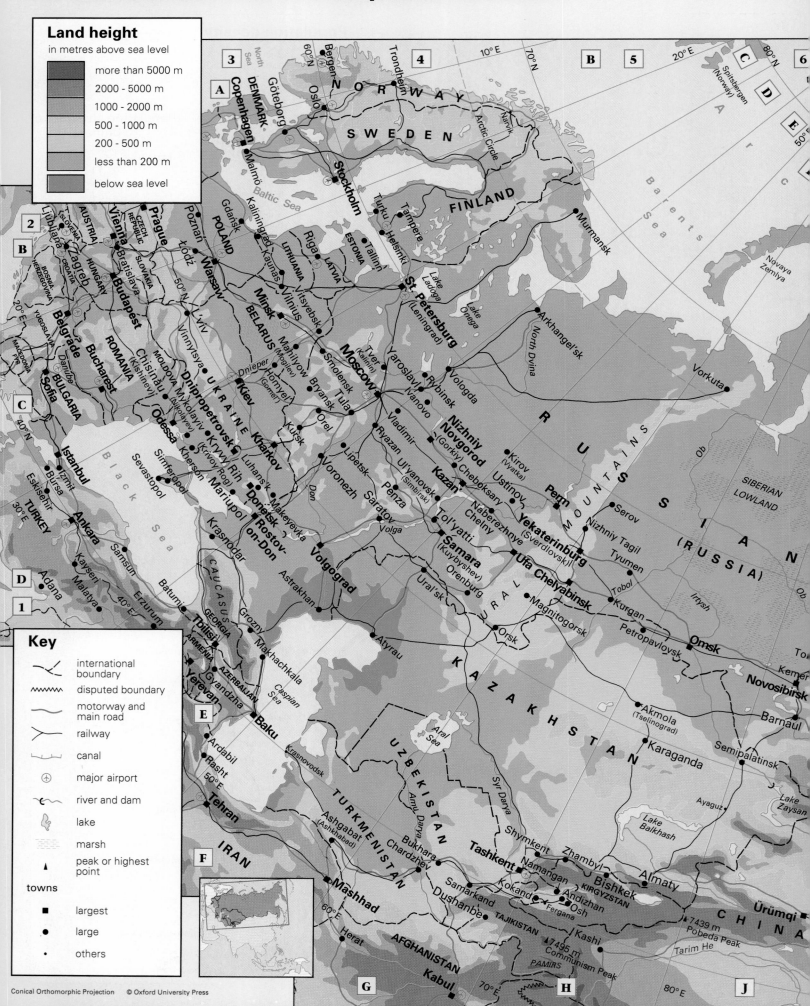

Land height
in metres above sea level

- more than 5000 m
- 2000 - 5000 m
- 1000 - 2000 m
- 500 - 1000 m
- 200 - 500 m
- less than 200 m
- below sea level

Key

- ⌇ international boundary
- ⌁ disputed boundary
- ⌇ motorway and main road
- ⌇ railway
- ⌇ canal
- ⊕ major airport
- ⌁ river and dam
- ⌁ lake
- ⌁ marsh
- ▲ peak or highest point

towns

- ■ largest
- ● large
- · others

Scale 1: 20 000 000

One centimetre on the map represents
200 kilometres on the ground.

0 200 400 600 800 km

Key

⌁⌁⌁	international boundary	
wwww	disputed boundary	
⌁⌁	motorway and main road	
⋋⋌	railway	
✈	major airport	

⌁	river and dam	
◯	lake	
⋯	marsh	

towns

■ largest
● large
· others

Land height
in metres above sea level

more than 5000 m
2000 - 5000 m
1000 - 2000 m
500 - 1000 m
200 - 500 m
less than 200 m
below sea level

Scale
1: 20 000 000

One centimetre on the map represents 200 kilometres on the ground.

0   200   400   600   800 km

Conical Orthomorphic Projection © Oxford University Press

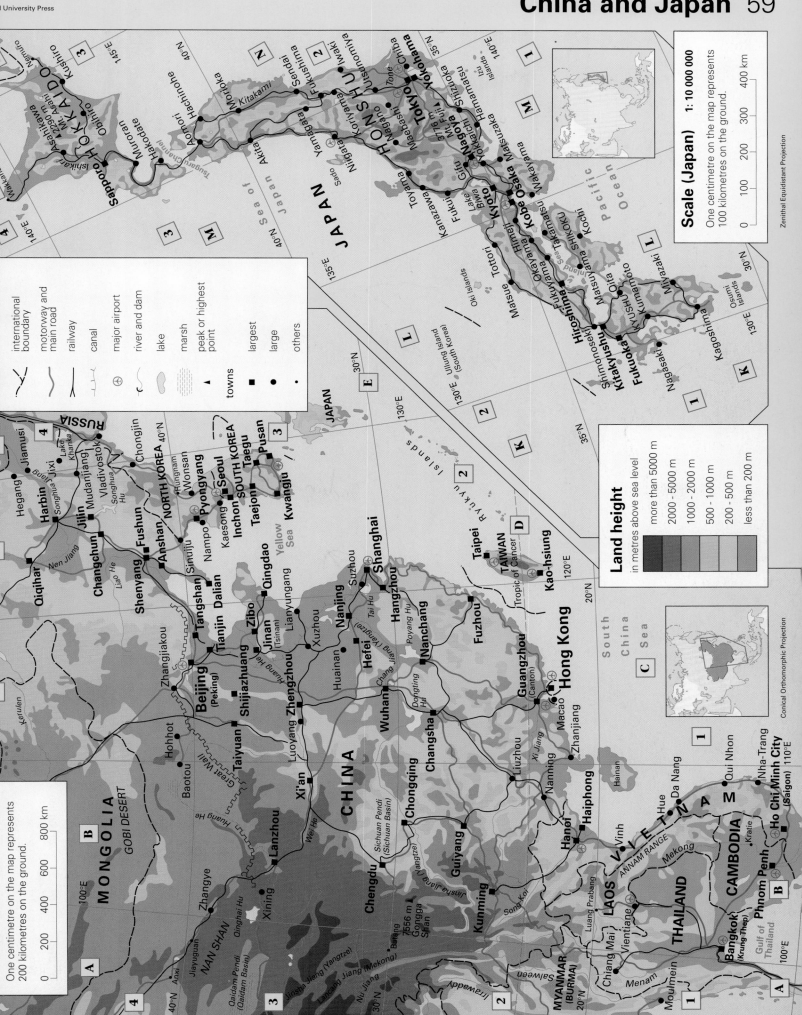

rd University Press

Scale (Japan)   1: 10 000 000

One centimetre on the map represents
100 kilometres on the ground.

0   100   200   300   400 km

Zenithal Equidistant Projection

Land height

in metres above sea level

more than 5000 m
2000 - 5000 m
1000 - 2000 m
500 - 1000 m
200 - 500 m
less than 200 m

Conical Orthomorphic Projection

international boundary
motorway and main road
railway
canal
major airport
river and dam
lake
marsh
peak or highest point

largest
large
others

towns

One centimetre on the map represents
200 kilometres on the ground.

0   200   400   600   800 km

JAPAN

HOKKAIDO
HONSHU
SHIKOKU
KYUSHU

Sapporo
Wakkanai
Asahikawa
Mt. Asahi 2290 m
Kushiro
Obihiro
Muroran
Hakodate
Tsugaru Channel
Aomori
Hachinohe
Morioka
Kitakami
Akita
Sendai
Yamagata
Fukushima
Niigata
Nagano
Toyama
Kanazawa
Fukui
Maebashi
Utsunomiya
Mt. Fuji 3776 m
TOKYO
Yokohama
Chiba
Gifu
Nagoya
Shizuoka
Hamamatsu
Yokkaichi
KYOTO
Osaka
Kobe
Wakayama
Okayama
Himeji
Takamatsu
Kochi
Matsuyama
Oita
Hiroshima
Shimonoseki
Kitakyushu
Fukuoka
Kumamoto
Miyazaki
Nagasaki
Kagoshima
Osumi Islands
Izu Islands
Lake Biwa
Iwaki
Koriyama
Sado
Oki Islands
Tone
Shinano

Sea of Japan
Pacific Ocean
Ryukyu Islands
South China Sea

RUSSIA
MONGOLIA
GOBI DESERT
CHINA
NORTH KOREA
SOUTH KOREA
Yellow Sea
TAIWAN
Tropic of Cancer

Jiamusi
Hegang
Jixi
Harbin
Mudanjiang
Qiqihar
Jilin
Changchun
Vladivostok
Chongjin
Hunchun
Hamhung
Wonsan
Pyongyang
Nampo
Sinuiju
Kaesong
Seoul
Inchon
Taejon
Taegu
Pusan
Kwangju
Shenyang
Fushun
Anshan
Tangshan
Dalian
Tianjin
Qingdao
Zibo
Jinan (Tsinan)
Lianyungang
Suzhou
Shanghai
Hangzhou
Nanjing
Xuzhou
Zhengzhou
Luoyang
Hefei
Nanchang
Fuzhou
Taipei
Kao-hsiung
Guangzhou (Canton)
Macao
Hong Kong
Zhanjiang
Nanning
Liuzhou
Wuhan
Changsha
Chongqing
Guiyang
Kunming
Chengdu
Lanzhou
Xining
Zhangye
Zhangjiakou
Hohhot
Baotou
Taiyuan
Shijiazhuang
Xi'an
Beijing (Peking)
Jiayuguan
Anxi

Lake Khanka
Songhua Jiang
Nen Jiang
Liao He
Huang He
Wei He
Great Wall
Yangtze
Chang Jiang (Yangtze)
Huai He
Jinsha Jiang (Yangtze)
Lancang Jiang (Mekong)
Nu Jiang
Salween
Dongting Hu
Poyang Hu
Tai Hu
Xi Jiang
Hainan
Qinghai Hu
Qaidam Pendi (Qaidam Basin)
NAN SHAN
Sichuan Pendi (Sichuan Basin)
Gongga Shan 7556 m
Kerulen

MYANMAR (BURMA)
LAOS
THAILAND
VIETNAM
CAMBODIA

Moulmein
Chiang Mai
Bangkok (Krung Thep)
Gulf of Thailand
Menam
Vientiane
Luang Prabang
Hanoi
Haiphong
Vinh
Hue
Da Nang
Qui Nhon
Nha-Trang
Ho Chi Minh City (Saigon)
Phnom Penh
Kratie
Mekong
Song Koi
ANNAM RANGE
Irrawaddy
Salween

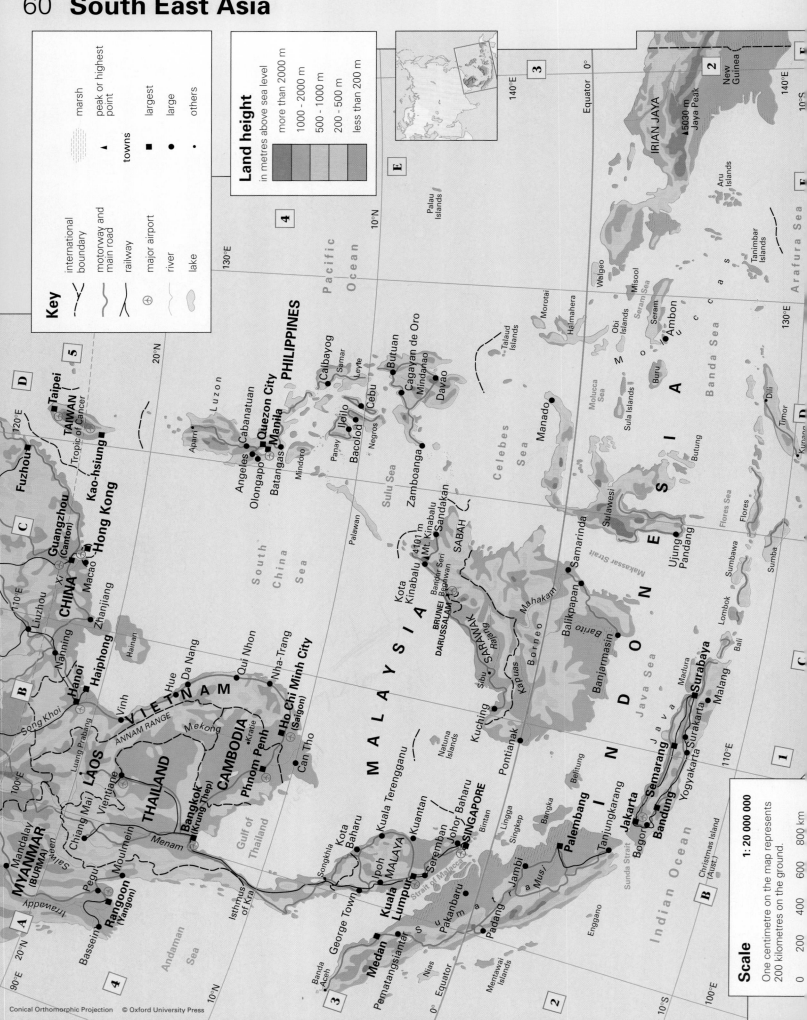

Key

towns
- ▲ peak or highest point
- ▦ marsh
- ■ largest
- ● large
- ・ others

- international boundary
- motorway and main road
- railway
- ⊕ major airport
- river
- lake

Land height
in metres above sea level

- more than 2000 m
- 1000 - 2000 m
- 500 - 1000 m
- 200 - 500 m
- less than 200 m

Scale   1: 20 000 000

One centimetre on the map represents 200 kilometres on the ground.

0   200   400   600   800 km

Conical Orthomorphic Projection   © Oxford University Press

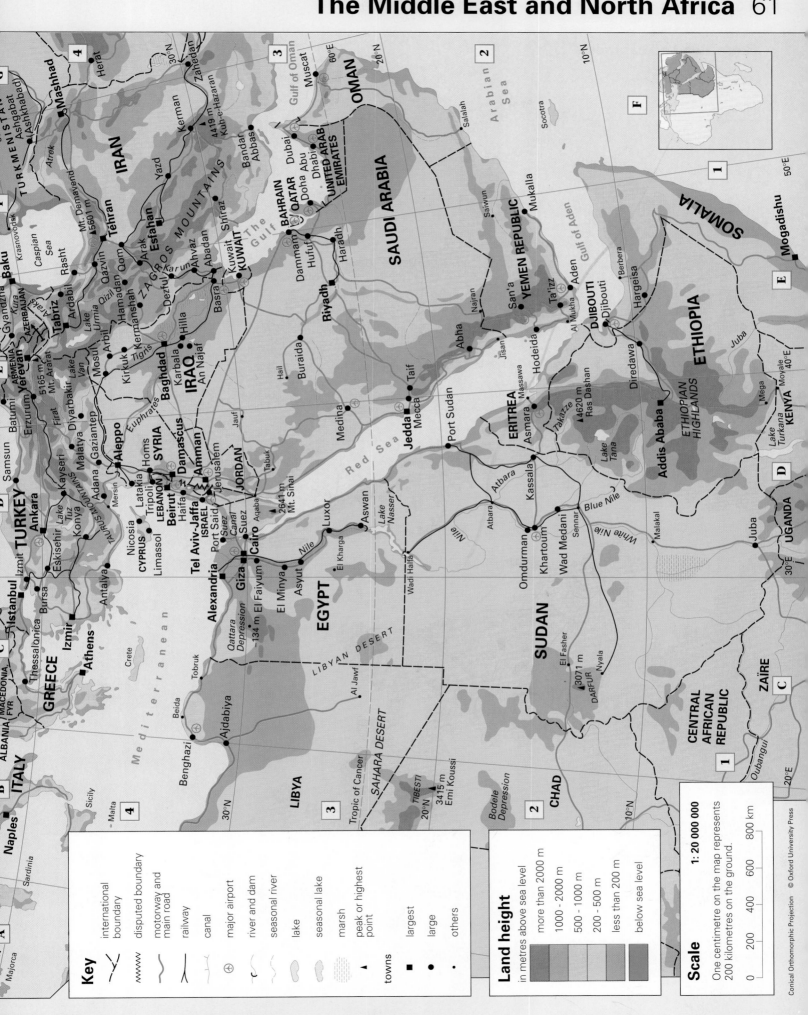

Key

⌇⌇	international boundary
⌇⌇	disputed boundary
∿∿	motorway and main road
⟋	railway
⟋	canal
⊕	major airport
⟋	river and dam
⟋	seasonal river
⬭	lake
⬭	seasonal lake
▨	marsh
▲	peak or highest point

towns

■	largest
●	large
•	others

Land height

in metres above sea level

	more than 2000 m
	1000 - 2000 m
	500 - 1000 m
	200 - 500 m
	less than 200 m
	below sea level

Scale   1: 20 000 000

One centimetre on the map represents 200 kilometres on the ground.

0	200	400	600	800 km

Conical Orthomorphic Projection   © Oxford University Press

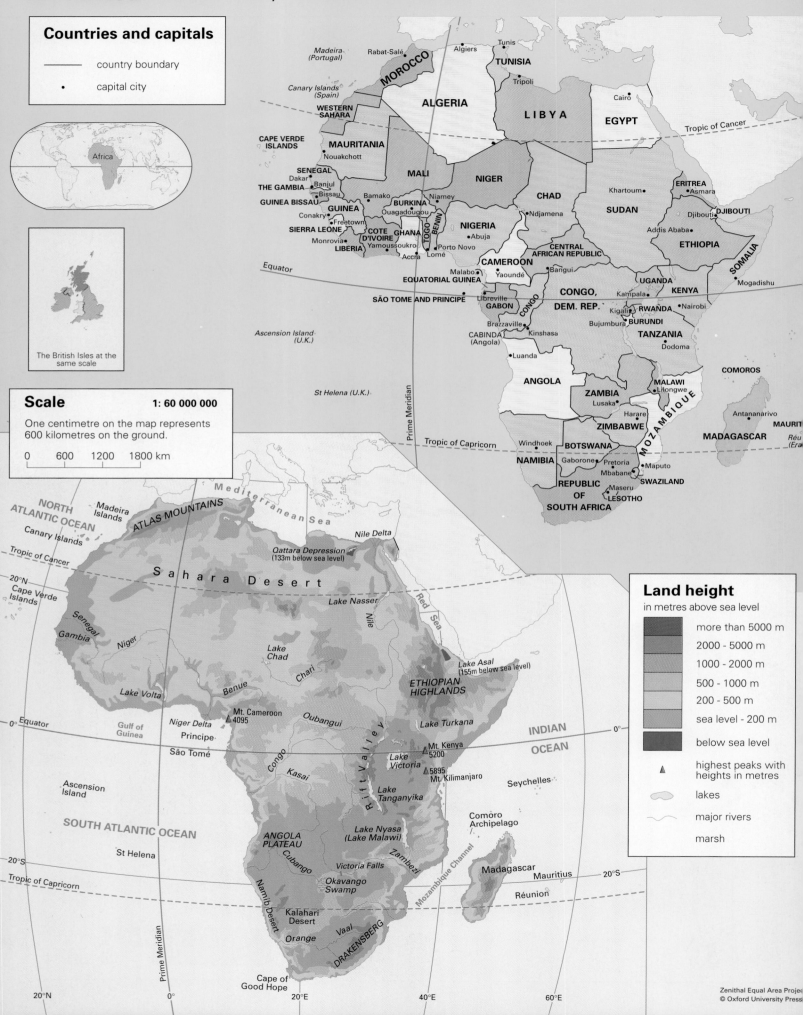

Countries and capitals

— country boundary

• capital city

Africa

The British Isles at the same scale

Scale

1 : 60 000 000

One centimetre on the map represents 600 kilometres on the ground.

0   600   1200   1800 km

Countries and capitals (map labels)

Madeira (Portugal)
Rabat-Salé
MOROCCO
Algiers
Tunis
TUNISIA
Tripoli
Canary Islands (Spain)
WESTERN SAHARA
ALGERIA
LIBYA
Cairo
EGYPT
Tropic of Cancer
CAPE VERDE ISLANDS
MAURITANIA
Nouakchott
MALI
NIGER
CHAD
Khartoum
ERITREA
Asmara
DJIBOUTI
SENEGAL
Dakar
Banjul
THE GAMBIA
Bissau
GUINEA BISSAU
Bamako
Niamey
BURKINA
Ouagadougou
SUDAN
Djibouti
Addis Ababa
GUINEA
Conakry
Freetown
SIERRA LEONE
COTE D'IVOIRE
GHANA
TOGO
BENIN
NIGERIA
Abuja
Ndjamena
CENTRAL AFRICAN REPUBLIC
ETHIOPIA
SOMALIA
Monrovia
Yamoussoukro
LIBERIA
Accra
Lomé
Porto Novo
CAMEROON
Yaoundé
Bangui
Mogadishu
Equator
Malabo
EQUATORIAL GUINEA
UGANDA
Kampala
KENYA
Nairobi
SÃO TOMÉ AND PRINCIPE
Libreville
CONGO
GABON
CONGO, DEM. REP.
Kigali
RWANDA
Brazzaville
Bujumbura
BURUNDI
CABINDA (Angola)
Kinshasa
TANZANIA
Dodoma
Luanda
COMOROS
ANGOLA
MALAWI
Lilongwe
Antananarivo
ZAMBIA
Lusaka
MAURIT...
Harare
MOZAMBIQUE
MADAGASCAR
Ré... (Fra...)
Windhoek
ZIMBABWE
Tropic of Capricorn
NAMIBIA
BOTSWANA
Gaborone
Pretoria
Maputo
Mbabane
SWAZILAND
REPUBLIC OF SOUTH AFRICA
Maseru
LESOTHO

Prime Meridian
Ascension Island (U.K.)
St Helena (U.K.)

Physical map labels

NORTH ATLANTIC OCEAN
Madeira Islands
Mediterranean Sea
ATLAS MOUNTAINS
Nile Delta
Canary Islands
Tropic of Cancer
Qattara Depression (133m below sea level)
20°N
Sahara Desert
Cape Verde Islands
Lake Nasser
Red Sea
Nile
Senegal
Gambia
Niger
Lake Chad
Chari
Lake Asal (155m below sea level)
ETHIOPIAN HIGHLANDS
Benue
Lake Volta
Mt. Cameroon △ 4095
0° Equator
Gulf of Guinea
Niger Delta
Principe
Oubangui
Lake Turkana
INDIAN OCEAN
São Tomé
Mt. Kenya △ 5200
0°
Congo
Kasai
Rift Valley
Lake Victoria
△ 5895 Mt. Kilimanjaro
Ascension Island
Lake Tanganyika
Seychelles
SOUTH ATLANTIC OCEAN
ANGOLA PLATEAU
Lake Nyasa (Lake Malawi)
Comoro Archipelago
St Helena
Cubango
Victoria Falls
Zambezi
Madagascar
Mauritius
20°S
20°S
Tropic of Capricorn
Namib Desert
Okavango Swamp
Kalahari Desert
Mozambique Channel
Réunion
Vaal
DRAKENSBERG
Orange
20°N
0°
20°E
40°E
60°E
Cape of Good Hope
Prime Meridian

Zenithal Equal Area Projec...
© Oxford University Press

Land height

Land height

in metres above sea level

- more than 5000 m
- 2000 - 5000 m
- 1000 - 2000 m
- 500 - 1000 m
- 200 - 500 m
- sea level - 200 m
- below sea level
- ▲ highest peaks with heights in metres
- lakes
- major rivers
- marsh

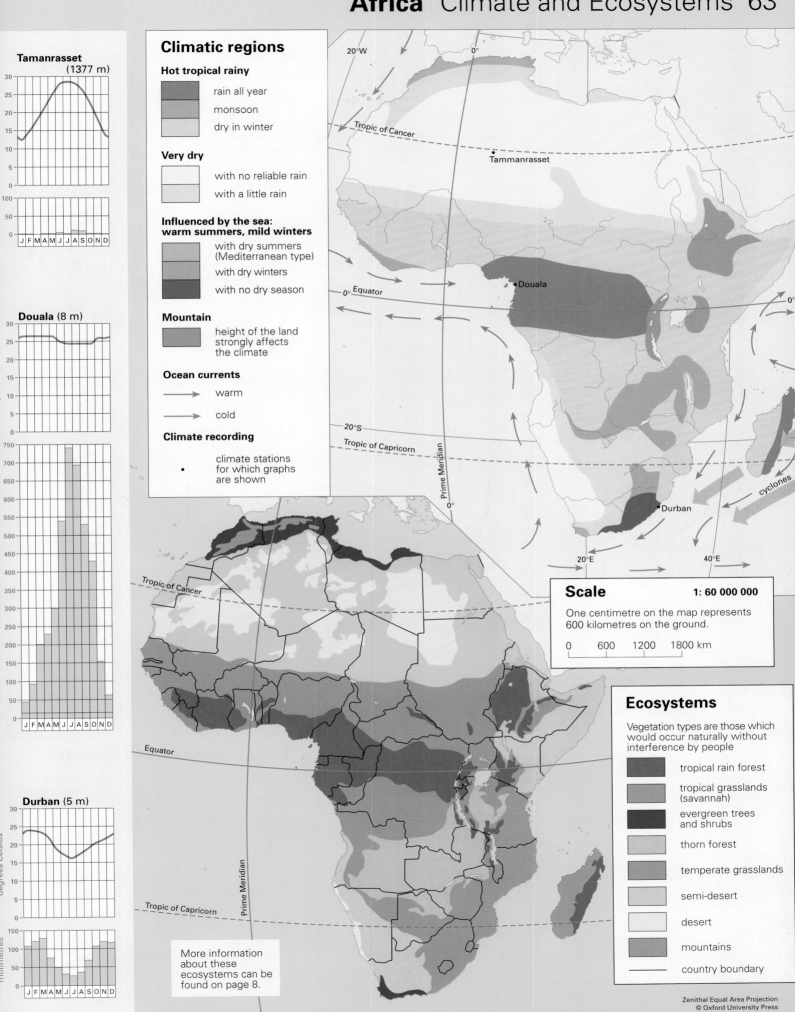

Tamanrasset
(1377 m)

Douala (8 m)

Durban (5 m)

degrees Celsius

millimetres

J F M A M J J A S O N D

Climatic regions

Hot tropical rainy

rain all year

monsoon

dry in winter

Very dry

with no reliable rain

with a little rain

**Influenced by the sea:
warm summers, mild winters**

with dry summers
(Mediterranean type)

with dry winters

with no dry season

Mountain

height of the land
strongly affects
the climate

Ocean currents

→ warm

→ cold

Climate recording

• climate stations
for which graphs
are shown

20°W 0°

Tropic of Cancer

• Tammanrasset

Equator 0°

• Douala

20°S

Tropic of Capricorn

Prime Meridian

0°

• Durban

cyclones

20°E 40°E

Scale   1: 60 000 000

One centimetre on the map represents
600 kilometres on the ground.

0   600   1200   1800 km

Tropic of Cancer

Equator

Prime Meridian

Tropic of Capricorn

Ecosystems

Vegetation types are those which
would occur naturally without
interference by people

tropical rain forest

tropical grasslands
(savannah)

evergreen trees
and shrubs

thorn forest

temperate grasslands

semi-desert

desert

mountains

—— country boundary

More information
about these
ecosystems can be
found on page 8.

Zenithal Equal Area Projection
© Oxford University Press

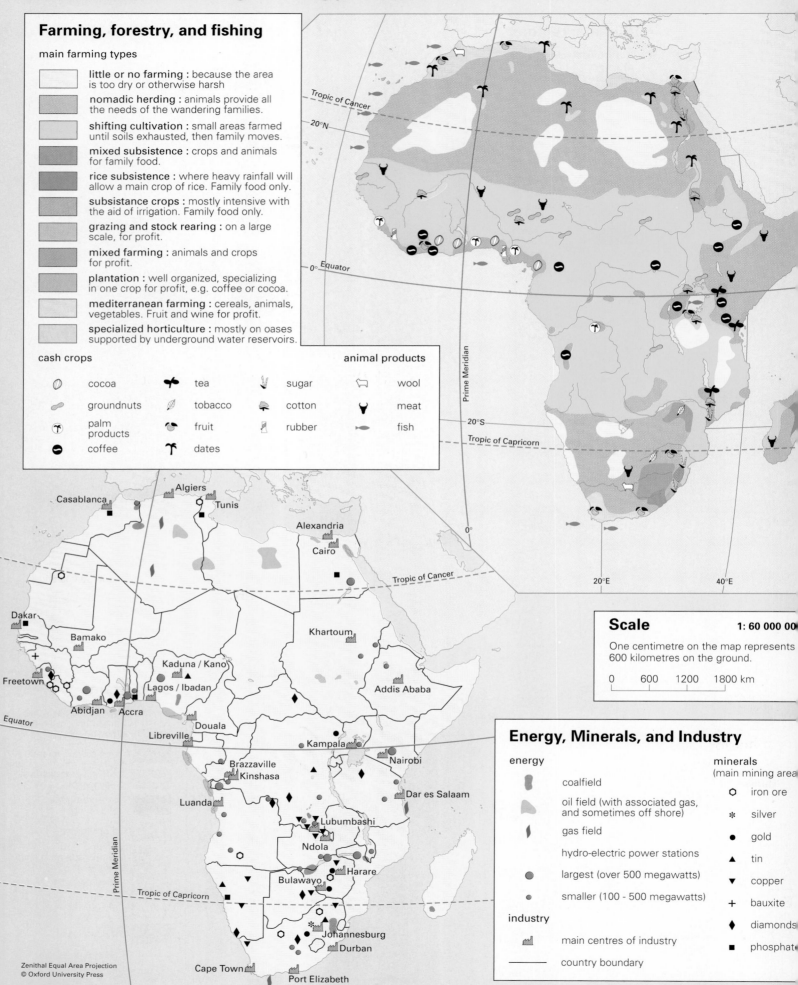

Farming, forestry, and fishing

main farming types

	little or no farming : because the area is too dry or otherwise harsh
	nomadic herding : animals provide all the needs of the wandering families.
	shifting cultivation : small areas farmed until soils exhausted, then family moves.
	mixed subsistence : crops and animals for family food.
	rice subsistence : where heavy rainfall will allow a main crop of rice. Family food only.
	subsistance crops : mostly intensive with the aid of irrigation. Family food only.
	grazing and stock rearing : on a large scale, for profit.
	mixed farming : animals and crops for profit.
	plantation : well organized, specializing in one crop for profit, e.g. coffee or cocoa.
	mediterranean farming : cereals, animals, vegetables. Fruit and wine for profit.
	specialized horticulture : mostly on oases supported by underground water reservoirs.

cash crops

- cocoa
- groundnuts
- palm products
- coffee
- tea
- tobacco
- fruit
- dates
- sugar
- cotton
- rubber

animal products

- wool
- meat
- fish

Scale

1: 60 000 00

One centimetre on the map represents 600 kilometres on the ground.

| 0 | 600 | 1200 | 1800 km |

Zenithal Equal Area Projection
© Oxford University Press

Energy, Minerals, and Industry

energy

- coalfield
- oil field (with associated gas, and sometimes off shore)
- gas field
- hydro-electric power stations
  - largest (over 500 megawatts)
  - smaller (100 - 500 megawatts)

industry

- main centres of industry
- country boundary

minerals
(main mining area

- ○ iron ore
- ✳ silver
- ● gold
- ▲ tin
- ▼ copper
- ✛ bauxite
- ◆ diamonds
- ■ phosphate

Population structure of Kenya

Males | Age | Females

80
70
60
50
40
30
20
10

7 6 5 4 3 2 1 0   0 1 2 3 4 5 6 7 8 9

ercent of total population in 1989
Total population : 21.4 million

Population structure of Egypt

Males | Age | Females

70
60
50
40
30
20
10
0

7 6 5 4 3 2 1 0   0 1 2 3 4 5 6 7 8

ercent of total population in 1992
Total population : 55.2 million

Population density

number of people
per square kilometre

high	more than 100
moderate	10 - 100
sparse	1 - 10
very low	less than 1

○ major cities and built up areas of at least 3 million people

● cities with 1 - 3 million people

— country boundary

Scale

1 : 60 000 000

One centimetre on the map represents 600 kilometres on the ground.

0   600   1200   1800 km

Cities and labels on the main map

Rabat-Salé
Casablanca
Algiers
Tunis
Alexandria
Giza
Cairo
Tropic of Cancer
Dakar
Addis Ababa
Ibadan
Abidjan
Lagos
Mogadishu
Equator
Kinshasa
Nairobi
Luanda
Dar es Salaam
Harare
Antananarivo
Tropic of Capricorn
Pretoria
Johannesburg
Maputo
Durban
Cape Town

Environmental issues map labels

Sahara Desert
Tropic of Cancer
20°N
Sahel
Somali Desert
Equator
Prime Meridian
Congo Basin
Madagascar
20°S
Namib Desert
Tropic of Capricorn
Kalahari Desert
20°W
0°
20°E
40°E

Environmental issues

tropical deforestation
- existing areas of rainforest
- former areas of rainforest

desertification
- existing areas of desert
- high risk areas
- moderate risk areas

sea pollution
- areas severely polluted for all or part of the year
- areas persistently affected by pollution

▼ deep sea dump sites

✳ major oil spills (over 100 000 tonnes)

∗ major oil spills (less than 100 000 tonnes)

acid rain
- areas where acid rain is becoming a problem

tsetse fly
- areas affected by the tsetse fly

global warming

addition of greenhouse gases in tonnes of carbon per person
(look at the world map on page 17)

Zenithal Equal Area Projection
© Oxford University Press

Scale   1: 20 000 000

One centimetre on the map represents 200 kilometres on the ground.

0   200   400   600   800 km

SPAIN

Gibraltar
Tangier
Tétouan
Oran
Algiers
'Annaba
Tunis
Sousse
Constantine
Sfax

Kenitra
Rabat-Salé
Fès
Casablanca
Meknes
Oujda

Safi

Tripoli
Misurata

Beida
Tobruk
Benghazi
Ajdabiya

Marrakesh
4165 m
Mt. Toubkal
Béchar

ATLAS MOUNTAINS
TUNISIA

Mediterranean
Sea

Agadir

Touggourt

Hassi Messaoud

Canary Islands

MOROCCO

ALGERIA

LIBYA

Tenerife

Las Palmas

El Aaiun

Sebha

LIBYAN DESERT

WESTERN
SAHARA

Tropic of Cancer

S A H A R A   D E S E R T

Al Jawf

Nouadhibou

AHAGGAR
3002 m
Tamanrasset
Mt. Tahat

MAURITANIA

TIBESTI
3415 m
Emi
Koussi

Bodele
Depression

Nouakchott

MALI

NIGER

CHAD

SUDAN
El Fa
DARFUR
307
Ny

Timbuktu

Agadès

Lake
Chad

St. Louis
Senegal
Dakar

SENEGAL

Kayes

Niger

Niamey

Zinder

Nguru

Maiduguri

Ndjamena

Banjul
THE GAMBIA

Bamako

BURKINA
Ouagadougou

Sokoto

Kano

Chari

Bissau

Kankan

Bobo-Dioulasso

Zaria
Kaduna

GUINEA-
BISSAU

GUINEA

Niger

BENIN

JOS
PLATEAU

Sarh

Conakry

Black Volta

GHANA

Kainji
Reservoir

Abuja

NIGERIA

Freetown
SIERRA
LEONE

Bo

1752 m
Mt. Nimba

Bouaké

Kumasi

Lake
Volta

TOGO

Ogbomosho

Ibadan

Onitsha

Benue

ADAMAWA HIGHLANDS
Ngaoundéré

CENTRAL
AFRICAN REPUBLIC

Monrovia

LIBERIA

CÔTE
D'IVOIRE

Yamoussoukro

Lomé

Lagos
Porto Novo
Cotonou

CAMEROON

Bangui

Abidjan

Accra

Sekondi-
Takoradi

Port
Harcourt

Mt. Cameroun
4070 m
Douala
Malabo

Yaoundé

Oubangui

South Atlantic
Ocean

Gulf of Guinea

SÃO TOMÉ
AND PRINCIPE

Principe

EQ. GUINEA

Bata

Zaïre

Equator

São Tomé

Libreville

GABON

Mbandaka

ZAÏRE

Port-Gentil

CONGO

Congo (Zaïre)

Lake
Mai-Ndombe

Kasai

Ilebo

Land height

in metres above sea level

more than 2000 m

1000 - 2000 m

500 - 1000 m

200 - 500 m

less than 200 m

below sea level

Brazzaville
Kinshasa

Pointe Noire
CABINDA
(Angola)

Kikwit

Kananga

Matadi

Luanda

Malanje

ANGOLA

Cuanza

B   20°E   C   El Fasher   30°E   D   40°E   ERITREA   E   Gulf of Aden

6   CHAD   ▲3071 m   Wad Medani   ▲4620 m Ras Dashan   DJIBOUTI   6
Sennar   Djibouti
DARFUR   Nyala   White Nile   Blue Nile   Lake Tana   Berbera
Chari   SUDAN   ETHIOPIA   Hargeisa
Sarh   Addis Ababa   Diredawa
Ngaoundéré   ETHIOPIAN
NIGERIA   ADAMAWA HIGHLANDS   CENTRAL   HIGHLANDS
CAMEROON   AFRICAN REPUBLIC   Malakal   SOMALIA   5
Sanaga   Bangui   Oubangui   Juba   Mega   10°N
Yaoundé   Uele   Lake   Moyale
Turkana
GUINEA   Lake Mobutu   Lake   KENYA   Mogadishu
Kyoga
GABON   Kisangani   Mt.   UGANDA   Kampala   5199 m
Ruwenzori   Entebbe   Kisumu   Mt. Kenya   Equator 0°
Mbandaka   5118 m   Lake Edward   Lake
CONGO   Boyoma Falls   CONGO, DEM. REP.   Kigali   Victoria   Nairobi
Lake   Lualaba   Lake Kivu   RWANDA   5895 m
Mai-Ndombe   Bukavu   Mwanza   Mt. Kilimanjaro
Brazzaville   Congo   Kasai   Ilebo   Bujumbura   Mombasa   Indian   4
CABINDA   Kinshasa   BURUNDI   Tabora   Tanga
(Angola)   Kikwit   Kigoma   TANZANIA   Ocean
Matadi   Kananga   Mbuji-Mayi   Kalemie   Dodoma   Zanzibar
WESTERN RIFT VALLEY   Dar es Salaam
Lake
Tanganyika
Luanda   Lake   Aldabra   10°S
Mweru   Lake   Islands
Malanje   Rukwa
Lake   EASTERN RIFT VALLEY
Bangweulu   Ruvuma   COMOROS   Moroni
Likasi   Lubumbashi   Lake Nyasa
ANGOLA   Kasai   Kitwe   (Lake Malawi)   Mozambique   Mahajanga   3
Lobito   Huambo   Ndola   MALAWI   Nampula   Mozambique Channel
Benguela   Cuanza   Kabwe   Lilongwe
Lubango   Cunene   Zambezi   ZAMBIA   Lake   Blantyre   Toamasina
Cubango   Lusaka   Cabora Bassa
Etosha   Zambezi   Lake   Harare   Beira   Antananarivo   20°S
Pan   Kariba   MOZAMBIQUE
NAMIBIA   Okavango   Victoria   ZIMBABWE   MADAGASCAR
Swamp   Falls
Walvis Bay   BOTSWANA   Bulawayo   Europa
Windhoek   Toliara   Tropic of Capricorn   2
NAMIB DESERT   KALAHARI
DESERT   Limpopo
Gaborone   Maputo
Lüderitz   Pretoria   Mbabane
Johannesburg   SWAZILAND   40°E   50°E
HIGH VELD   DRAKENSBERG   30°S
Orange   Kimberley   Vaal   ▲3482 m   Pietermaritzburg   E
Bloemfontein   Maseru   Durban
Atlantic Ocean   REPUBLIC OF   LESOTHO
SOUTH AFRICA
GREAT KARROO   1
East London
Cape Town   Port Elizabeth
10°E   B   Cape of   20°E   C   30°E   D
Good Hope

Scale   1: 20 000 000

One centimetre on the map represents
200 kilometres on the ground.

0   200   400   600   800 km

For explanations of the symbols and colours used on
this map look at the oppsite page.

Zenithal Equal Area Projection   © Oxford University Press

68 Oceania Countries, Land and water

Countries and capitals

— country boundary
• capital city

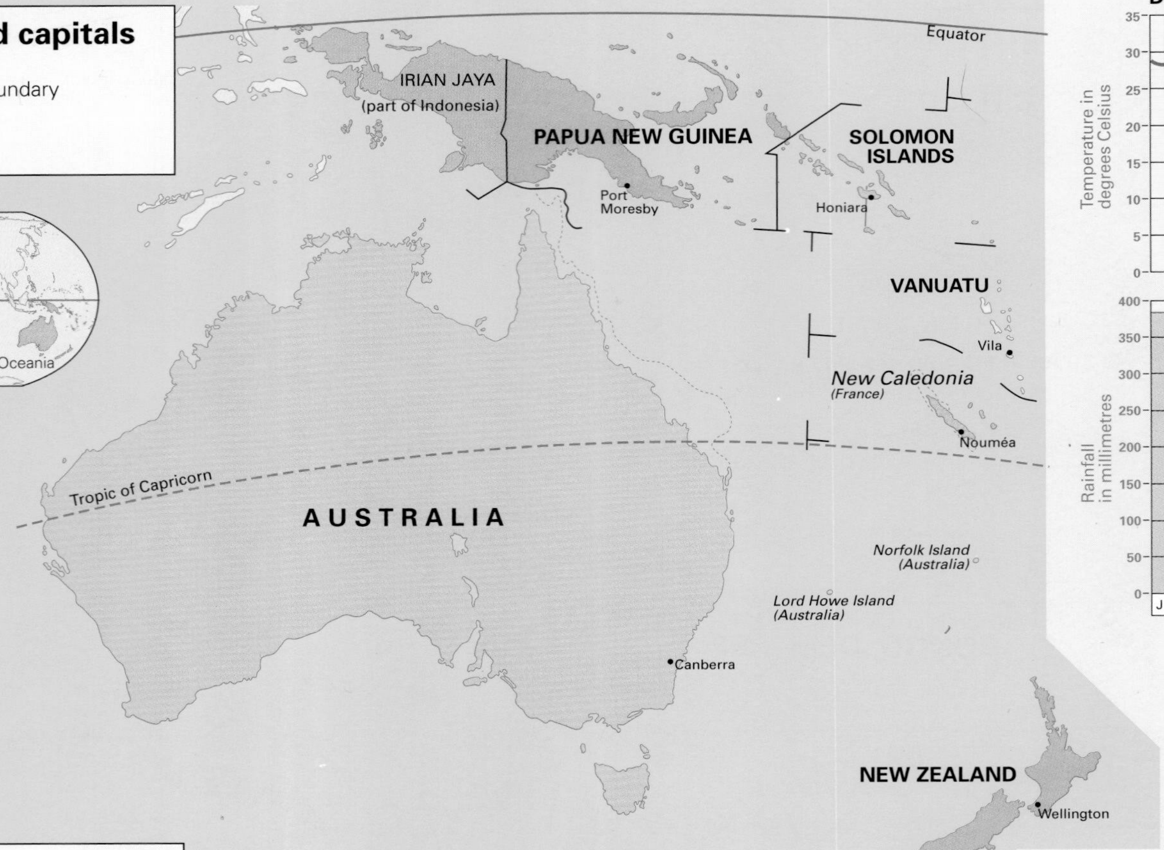

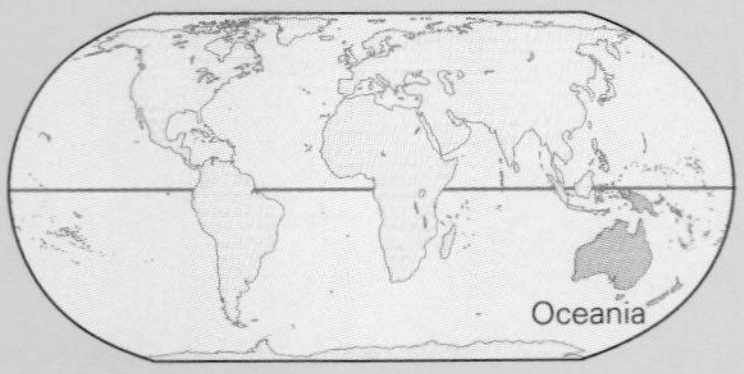

Oceania

The British Isles at the same scale

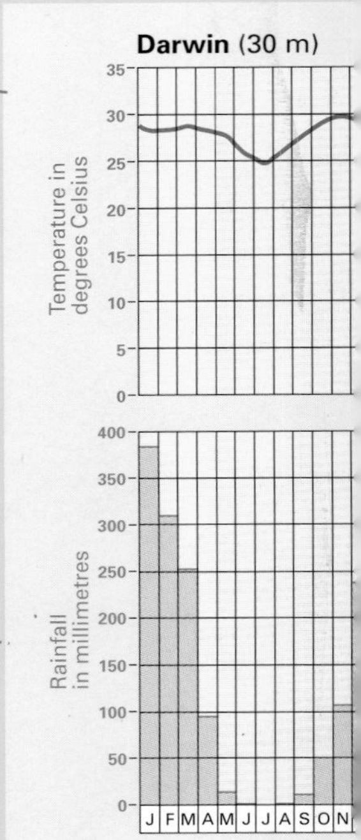

Scale
1 : 44 000 000

One centimetre on the map represents 440 kilometres on the ground.

0   440   880   1320 km

Land height
in metres above sea level

more than 2000 m
1000 - 2000 m
500 - 1000 m
200 - 500 m
sea level - 200 m
below sea level

▲ highest peaks with heights in metres

lakes

major rivers

major seasonal rivers

coral reef

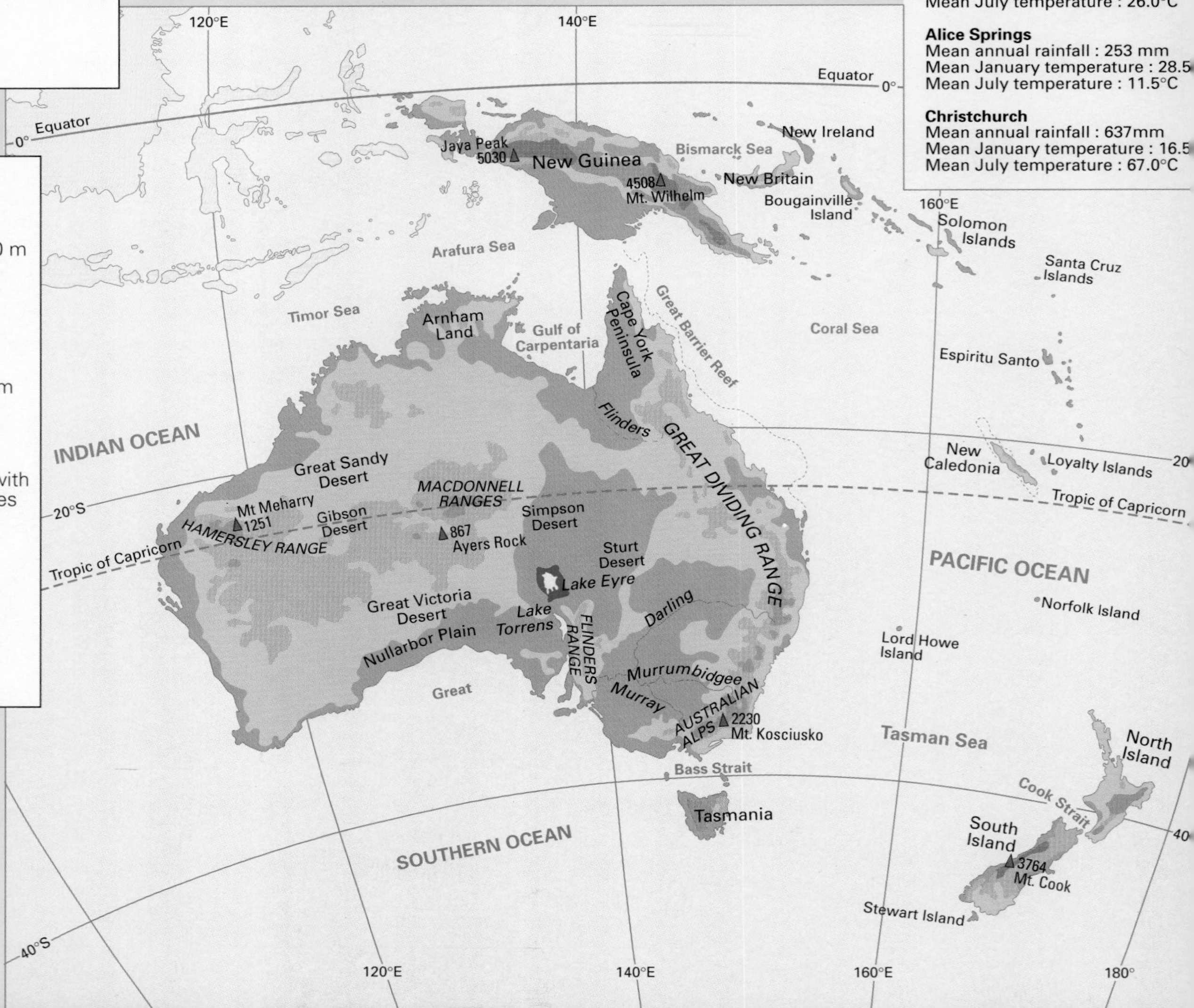

Modified Zenithal Equidistant Projection
© Oxford University Press

Top map labels
Equator

IRIAN JAYA
(part of Indonesia)

PAPUA NEW GUINEA

SOLOMON ISLANDS

Port Moresby

Honiara

VANUATU

Vila •

New Caledonia
(France)

Nouméa •

Tropic of Capricorn

AUSTRALIA

Norfolk Island
(Australia)

Lord Howe Island
(Australia)

• Canberra

NEW ZEALAND

Wellington •

Darwin (30 m)

Temperature in degrees Celsius

Rainfall in millimetres

J F M A M J J A S O N

Darwin
Mean annual rainfall : 1492 mm
Mean January temperature : 28.5
Mean July temperature : 26.0°C

Alice Springs
Mean annual rainfall : 253 mm
Mean January temperature : 28.5
Mean July temperature : 11.5°C

Christchurch
Mean annual rainfall : 637mm
Mean January temperature : 16.5
Mean July temperature : 67.0°C

Lower map labels

120°E   140°E

Equator   0°

0° Equator

Jaya Peak 5030 ▲   New Guinea   Bismarck Sea   New Ireland

4508 ▲   New Britain
Mt. Wilhelm   Bougainville Island

160°E   Solomon Islands

Arafura Sea

Santa Cruz Islands

Timor Sea   Arnham Land   Gulf of Carpentaria   Cape York Peninsula   Coral Sea   Espiritu Santo

Great Barrier Reef

Flinders   GREAT DIVIDING RANGE

New Caledonia   Loyalty Islands   20°

Tropic of Capricorn

INDIAN OCEAN

Great Sandy Desert   MACDONNELL RANGES   Simpson Desert

PACIFIC OCEAN

20°S   Mt Meharry ▲ 1251   Gibson Desert   ▲ 867   Sturt Desert
HAMERSLEY RANGE   Ayers Rock

Tropic of Capricorn

Great Victoria Desert   Lake Eyre   Norfolk Island

Lake Torrens   Darling   Lord Howe Island

Nullarbor Plain   FLINDERS RANGE   Murrumbidgee

Great   Murray   AUSTRALIAN ALPS ▲ 2230
Mt. Kosciusko   Tasman Sea   North Island

Bass Strait   Cook Strait

SOUTHERN OCEAN   Tasmania   South Island

▲ 3764 Mt. Cook

Stewart Island

40°S   120°E   140°E   160°E   180°   40°

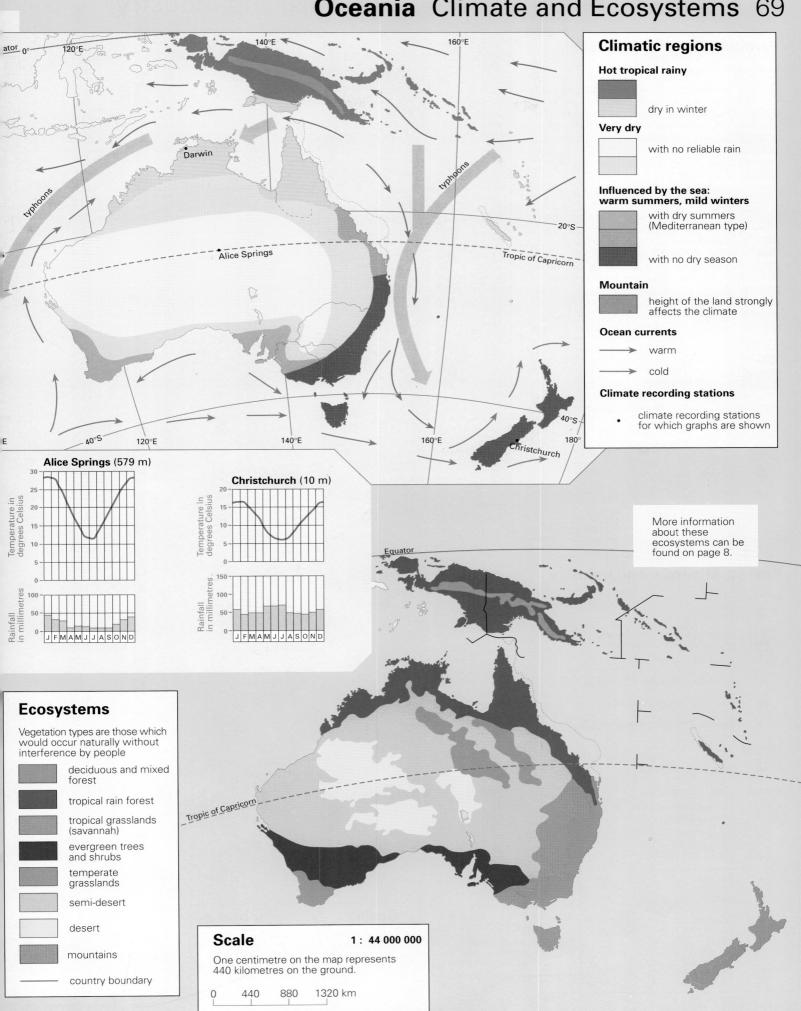

Climatic regions

Hot tropical rainy

dry in winter

Very dry

with no reliable rain

**Influenced by the sea:
warm summers, mild winters**

with dry summers
(Mediterranean type)

with no dry season

Mountain

height of the land strongly
affects the climate

Ocean currents

→ warm

→ cold

Climate recording stations

• climate recording stations
for which graphs are shown

Alice Springs (579 m)

Temperature in degrees Celsius

Rainfall in millimetres

J F M A M J J A S O N D

Christchurch (10 m)

Temperature in degrees Celsius

Rainfall in millimetres

J F M A M J J A S O N D

More information
about these
ecosystems can be
found on page 8.

Ecosystems

Vegetation types are those which
would occur naturally without
interference by people

deciduous and mixed forest

tropical rain forest

tropical grasslands (savannah)

evergreen trees and shrubs

temperate grasslands

semi-desert

desert

mountains

— country boundary

Scale

1 : 44 000 000

One centimetre on the map represents
440 kilometres on the ground.

0   440   880   1320 km

Darwin

Alice Springs

Tropic of Capricorn

Christchurch

Equator

Tropic of Capricorn

typhoons

typhoons

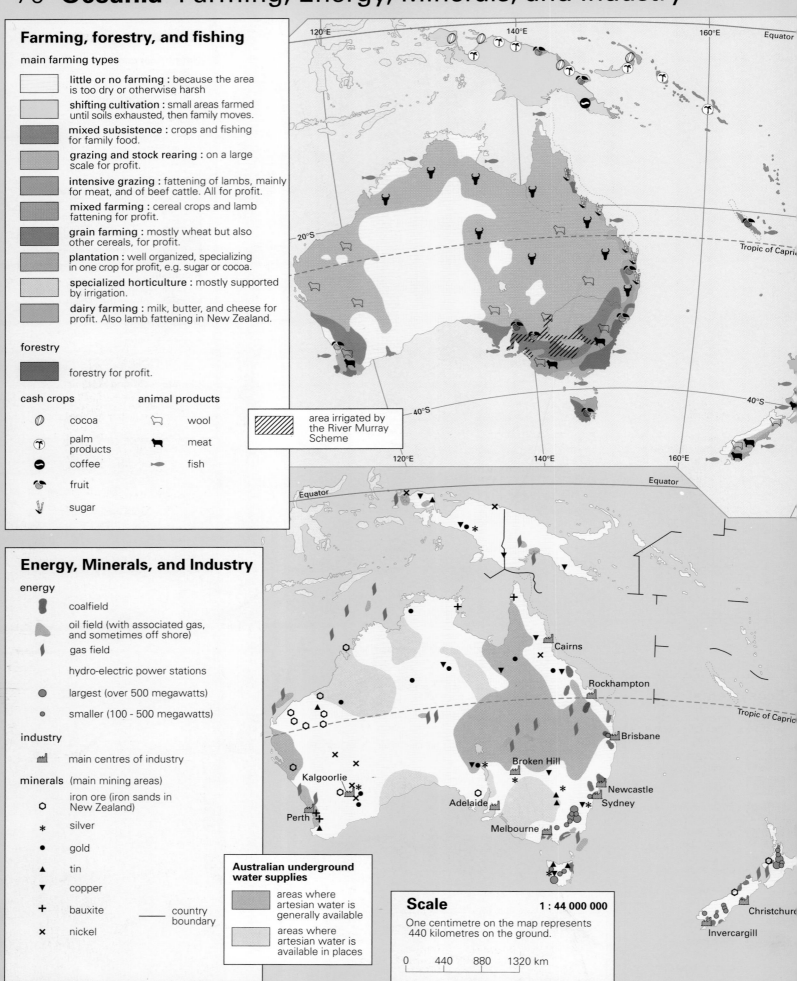

Farming, forestry, and fishing

main farming types

- **little or no farming** : because the area is too dry or otherwise harsh
- **shifting cultivation** : small areas farmed until soils exhausted, then family moves.
- **mixed subsistence** : crops and fishing for family food.
- **grazing and stock rearing** : on a large scale for profit.
- **intensive grazing** : fattening of lambs, mainly for meat, and of beef cattle. All for profit.
- **mixed farming** : cereal crops and lamb fattening for profit.
- **grain farming** : mostly wheat but also other cereals, for profit.
- **plantation** : well organized, specializing in one crop for profit, e.g. sugar or cocoa.
- **specialized horticulture** : mostly supported by irrigation.
- **dairy farming** : milk, butter, and cheese for profit. Also lamb fattening in New Zealand.

forestry

- forestry for profit.

cash crops

- ⊘ cocoa
- ⑂ palm products
- ● coffee
- ◓ fruit
- ⸎ sugar

animal products

- 🐑 wool
- 🐖 meat
- 🐟 fish

area irrigated by the River Murray Scheme

Energy, Minerals, and Industry

energy

- coalfield
- oil field (with associated gas, and sometimes off shore)
- gas field
- hydro-electric power stations
  - ● largest (over 500 megawatts)
  - • smaller (100 - 500 megawatts)

industry

- 🏭 main centres of industry

minerals (main mining areas)

- ○ iron ore (iron sands in New Zealand)
- ∗ silver
- • gold
- ▲ tin
- ▼ copper
- + bauxite
- × nickel

— country boundary

Australian underground water supplies

- areas where artesian water is generally available
- areas where artesian water is available in places

Scale   1 : 44 000 000

One centimetre on the map represents 440 kilometres on the ground.

0   440   880   1320 km

Kalgoorlie
Perth
Adelaide
Melbourne
Broken Hill
Sydney
Newcastle
Brisbane
Rockhampton
Cairns
Christchurch
Invercargill

Modified Zenithal Equidistant Pro
© Oxford University

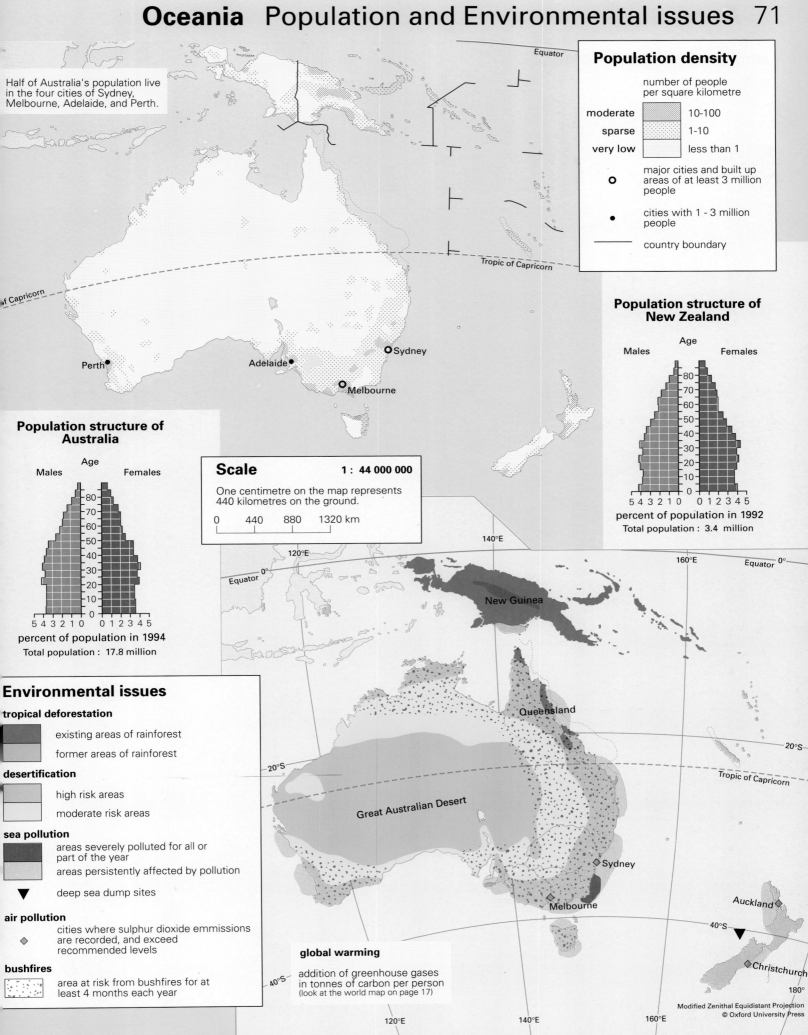

Half of Australia's population live in the four cities of Sydney, Melbourne, Adelaide, and Perth.

Population density

number of people per square kilometre

moderate	10-100
sparse	1-10
very low	less than 1

○ major cities and built up areas of at least 3 million people

● cities with 1 - 3 million people

— country boundary

Population structure of New Zealand

Age — Males — Females

5 4 3 2 1 0   0 1 2 3 4 5

percent of population in 1992
Total population : 3.4 million

Population structure of Australia

Age — Males — Females

5 4 3 2 1 0   0 1 2 3 4 5

percent of population in 1994
Total population : 17.8 million

Scale

1 : 44 000 000

One centimetre on the map represents 440 kilometres on the ground.

0   440   880   1320 km

Environmental issues

tropical deforestation

existing areas of rainforest

former areas of rainforest

desertification

high risk areas

moderate risk areas

sea pollution

areas severely polluted for all or part of the year

areas persistently affected by pollution

▼ deep sea dump sites

air pollution

◆ cities where sulphur dioxide emmissions are recorded, and exceed recommended levels

bushfires

area at risk from bushfires for at least 4 months each year

global warming

addition of greenhouse gases in tonnes of carbon per person
(look at the world map on page 17)

New Guinea

Queensland

Great Australian Desert

Sydney

Melbourne

Auckland

Christchurch

Equator

Tropic of Capricorn

Modified Zenithal Equidistant Projection
© Oxford University Press

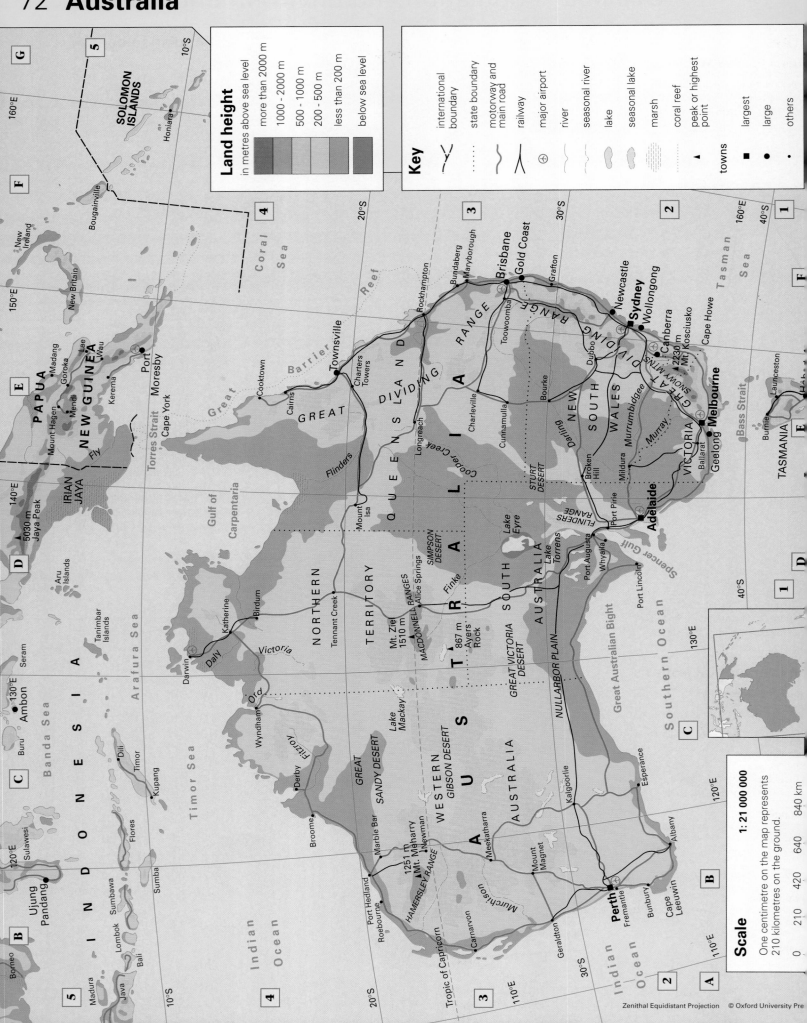

Land height

in metres above sea level

- more than 2000 m
- 1000 - 2000 m
- 500 - 1000 m
- 200 - 500 m
- less than 200 m
- below sea level

Key

- international boundary
- state boundary
- motorway and main road
- railway
- major airport
- river
- seasonal river
- lake
- seasonal lake
- marsh
- coral reef
- peak or highest point

towns

- largest
- large
- others

Scale 1: 21 000 000

One centimetre on the map represents 210 kilometres on the ground.

0 210 420 630 840 km

Zenithal Equidistant Projection   © Oxford University Press

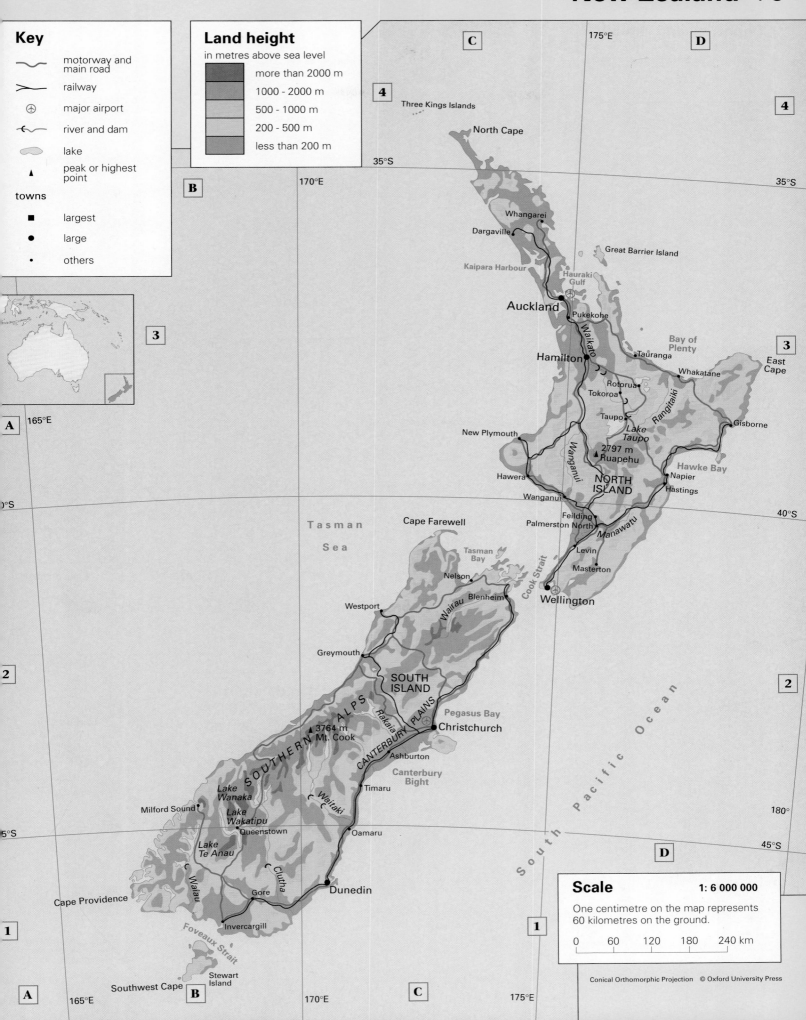

Key

〜	motorway and main road
⤙	railway
⊕	major airport
⊷	river and dam
▨	lake
▲	peak or highest point

towns

■	largest
●	large
·	others

Land height
in metres above sea level

- more than 2000 m
- 1000 – 2000 m
- 500 – 1000 m
- 200 – 500 m
- less than 200 m

Scale 1: 6 000 000
One centimetre on the map represents 60 kilometres on the ground.

0 60 120 180 240 km

Conical Orthomorphic Projection © Oxford University Press

Three Kings Islands
North Cape
Whangarei
Dargaville
Great Barrier Island
Kaipara Harbour
Hauraki Gulf
Auckland
Pukekohe
Hamilton
Waikato
Bay of Plenty
Tauranga
Whakatane
East Cape
Rotorua
Tokoroa
Rangitaiki
Taupo
Lake Taupo
Gisborne
New Plymouth
2797 m Ruapehu
Wanganui
NORTH ISLAND
Hawke Bay
Hawera
Napier
Wanganui
Hastings
Feilding
Palmerston North
Manawatu
Levin
Masterton
Cape Farewell
Tasman Sea
Tasman Bay
Nelson
Cook Strait
Wellington
Westport
Wairau
Blenheim
Greymouth
SOUTH ISLAND
Pegasus Bay
SOUTHERN ALPS
Rakaia
CANTERBURY PLAINS
Christchurch
3764 m Mt. Cook
Ashburton
Canterbury Bight
Lake Wanaka
Waitaki
Timaru
Milford Sound
Lake Wakatipu
Queenstown
Oamaru
Lake Te Anau
Clutha
Waiau
Gore
Dunedin
Cape Providence
Invercargill
Foveaux Strait
Southwest Cape
Stewart Island
South Pacific Ocean

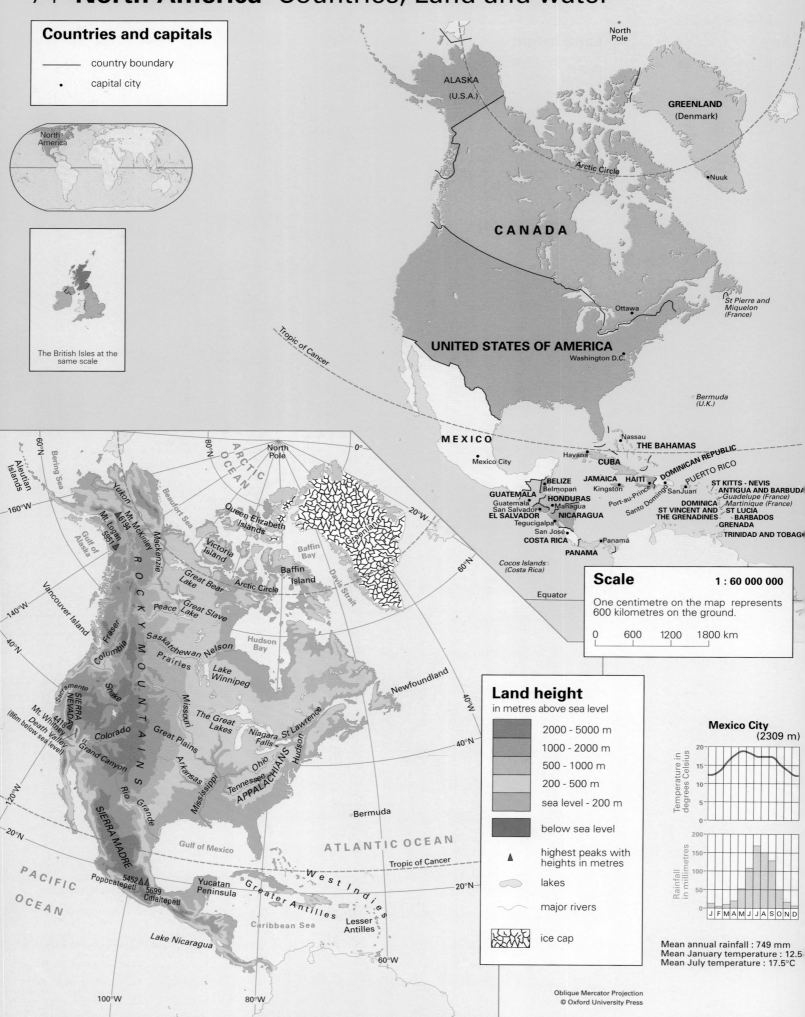

Countries and capitals

— country boundary

• capital city

North America

The British Isles at the same scale

ALASKA (U.S.A.)

North Pole

GREENLAND (Denmark)

Arctic Circle

• Nuuk

CANADA

St Pierre and Miquelon (France)

Tropic of Cancer

• Ottawa

UNITED STATES OF AMERICA

Washington D.C. •

Bermuda (U.K.)

MEXICO

• Nassau   THE BAHAMAS

Mexico City •   Havana •   CUBA   DOMINICAN REPUBLIC   PUERTO RICO

BELIZE   JAMAICA   HAITI   ST KITTS - NEVIS

Belmopan   Kingston   Port-au-Prince   San Juan   ANTIGUA AND BARBUDA

GUATEMALA   Guadelupe (France)

Guatemala   HONDURAS   Santo Domingo   DOMINICA   Martinique (France)

San Salvador   Managua   ST VINCENT AND   ST LUCIA

EL SALVADOR   NICARAGUA   THE GRENADINES   BARBADOS

Tegucigalpa   GRENADA

San José   TRINIDAD AND TOBAGO

COSTA RICA   • Panamá

Cocos Islands   PANAMA

(Costa Rica)

Equator

Scale   1 : 60 000 000

One centimetre on the map represents 600 kilometres on the ground.

0   600   1200   1800 km

Aleutian Islands

Bering Sea

60°N

ARCTIC OCEAN

80°N

North Pole

0°

Beaufort Sea

Queen Elizabeth Islands

20°W

160°W

Yukon   Mt McKinley 6194 ▲

Mt Logan 5951 ▲

Gulf of Alaska

Mackenzie

Victoria Island

Greenland

Baffin Bay

Davis Strait

60°N

Vancouver Island

140°W

R O C K Y

Great Bear Lake

Peace Lake

Arctic Circle

Baffin Island

Columbia

Fraser

Saskatchewan   Nelson

Great Slave Lake

Hudson Bay

40°W

40°N

120°W

Sacramento   SIERRA NEVADA   Snake

Prairies

Lake Winnipeg

Newfoundland

M O U N T A I N S

4418 ▲   Missouri

The Great Lakes

Mt Whitney

Death Valley   Grand Canyon   Colorado

Great Plains

Niagara Falls   St Lawrence

40°N

(86m below sea level)

Arkansas

Mississippi

Ohio   Hudson

Tennessee   APPALACHIANS

SIERRA MADRE

Rio Grande

Bermuda

20°N

PACIFIC OCEAN

Popocatepetl   5452 ▲▲

5699   Yucatan Peninsula

Citlaltepetl

Gulf of Mexico

Greater Antilles

ATLANTIC OCEAN

Tropic of Cancer

W e s t   I n d i e s

20°N

Caribbean Sea

Lesser Antilles

Lake Nicaragua

100°W   80°W   60°W

Land height

in metres above sea level

2000 - 5000 m

1000 - 2000 m

500 - 1000 m

200 - 500 m

sea level - 200 m

below sea level

▲ highest peaks with heights in metres

lakes

major rivers

ice cap

Mexico City

(2309 m)

Mean annual rainfall : 749 mm

Mean January temperature : 12.5

Mean July temperature : 17.5°C

Oblique Mercator Projection

© Oxford University Press

Vancouver (14 m)

Temperature in degrees Celsius

Rainfall in millimetres

J F M A M J J A S O N D

Cheyenne (1871 m)

Temperature in degrees Celsius

Rainfall in millimetres

J F M A M J J A S O N D

Climatic regions

Hot tropical rainy

rain all year

monsoon

dry in winter

Very dry

with no reliable rain

with a little rain

Influenced by the sea: warm summers, mild winters

with dry summers (Mediterranean type)

with no dry season

Cool

with dry winters

Cold polar

no warm season and fairly dry

Mountain

height of the land strongly affects the climate

Ocean currents

→ warm

→ cold

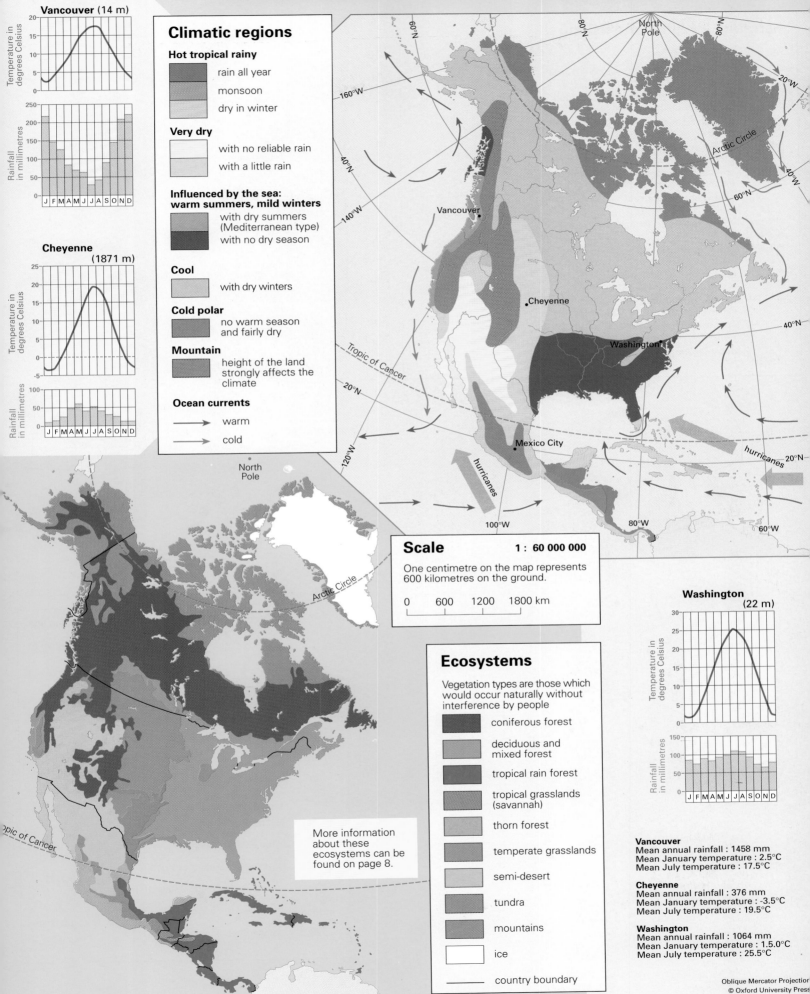

Scale

1 : 60 000 000

One centimetre on the map represents 600 kilometres on the ground.

0   600   1200   1800 km

Ecosystems

Vegetation types are those which would occur naturally without interference by people

coniferous forest

deciduous and mixed forest

tropical rain forest

tropical grasslands (savannah)

thorn forest

temperate grasslands

semi-desert

tundra

mountains

ice

country boundary

More information about these ecosystems can be found on page 8.

Washington (22 m)

Temperature in degrees Celsius

Rainfall in millimetres

J F M A M J J A S O N D

Vancouver
Mean annual rainfall : 1458 mm
Mean January temperature : 2.5°C
Mean July temperature : 17.5°C

Cheyenne
Mean annual rainfall : 376 mm
Mean January temperature : -3.5°C
Mean July temperature : 19.5°C

Washington
Mean annual rainfall : 1064 mm
Mean January temperature : 1.5.0°C
Mean July temperature : 25.5°C

Oblique Mercator Projection
© Oxford University Press

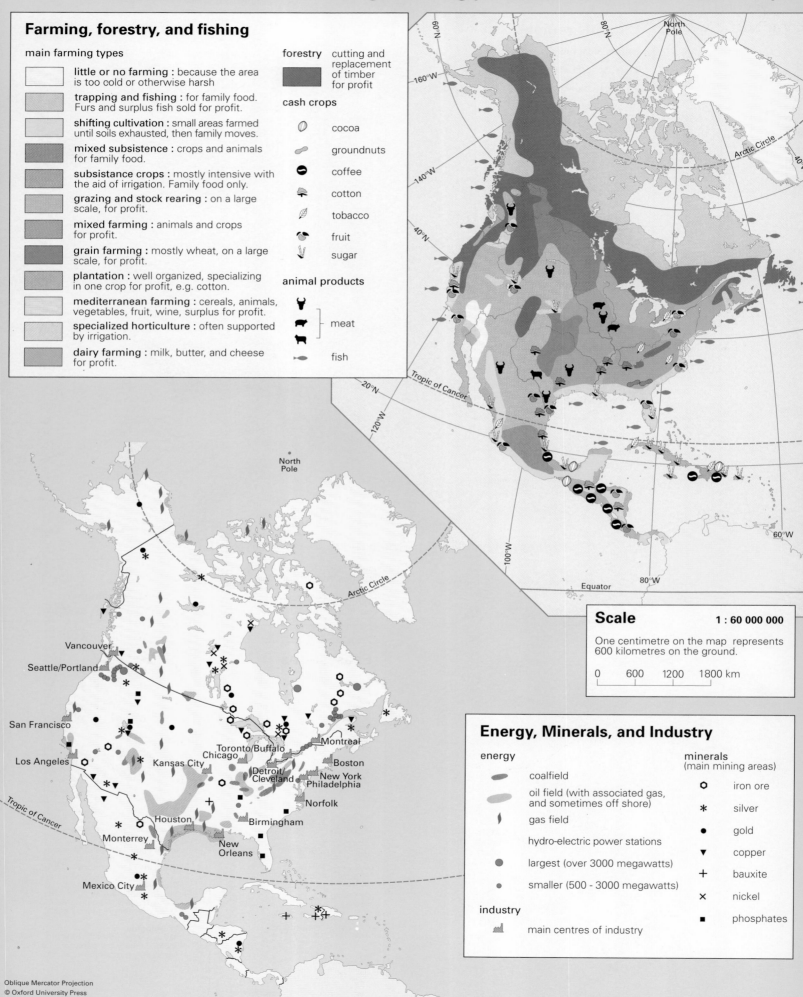

Farming, forestry, and fishing

main farming types

little or no farming : because the area is too cold or otherwise harsh

trapping and fishing : for family food. Furs and surplus fish sold for profit.

shifting cultivation : small areas farmed until soils exhausted, then family moves.

mixed subsistence : crops and animals for family food.

subsistance crops : mostly intensive with the aid of irrigation. Family food only.

grazing and stock rearing : on a large scale, for profit.

mixed farming : animals and crops for profit.

grain farming : mostly wheat, on a large scale, for profit.

plantation : well organized, specializing in one crop for profit, e.g. cotton.

mediterranean farming : cereals, animals, vegetables, fruit, wine, surplus for profit.

specialized horticulture : often supported by irrigation.

dairy farming : milk, butter, and cheese for profit.

forestry — cutting and replacement of timber for profit

cash crops

- cocoa
- groundnuts
- coffee
- cotton
- tobacco
- fruit
- sugar

animal products

- meat
- fish

Scale

1 : 60 000 000

One centimetre on the map represents 600 kilometres on the ground.

0   600   1200   1800 km

Energy, Minerals, and Industry

energy

- coalfield
- oil field (with associated gas, and sometimes off shore)
- gas field

hydro-electric power stations

- largest (over 3000 megawatts)
- smaller (500 - 3000 megawatts)

minerals
(main mining areas)

- iron ore
- silver
- gold
- copper
- bauxite
- nickel
- phosphates

industry

- main centres of industry

Vancouver
Seattle/Portland
San Francisco
Los Angeles
Kansas City
Toronto/Buffalo
Chicago
Detroit/Cleveland
Montreal
Boston
New York
Philadelphia
Norfolk
Birmingham
Houston
New Orleans
Monterrey
Mexico City

North Pole
Arctic Circle
Tropic of Cancer

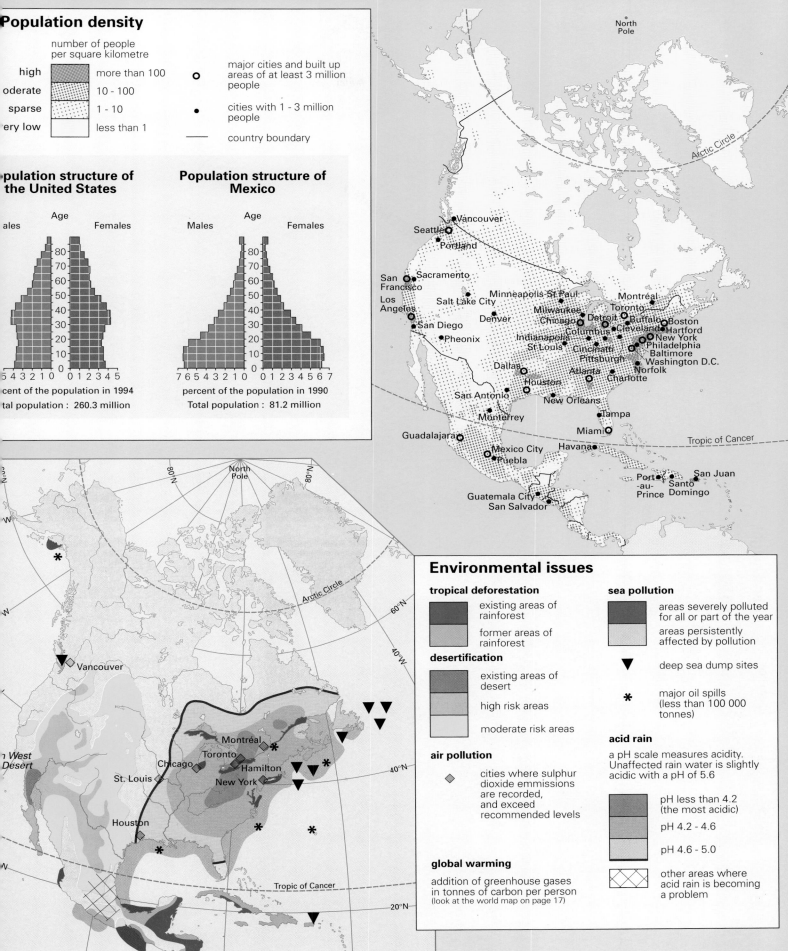

Population density

number of people
per square kilometre

high	more than 100
moderate	10 - 100
sparse	1 - 10
very low	less than 1

○ major cities and built up areas of at least 3 million people

• cities with 1 - 3 million people

— country boundary

Population structure of the United States

Age

Males   Females

80
70
60
50
40
30
20
10
0

5 4 3 2 1 0   0 1 2 3 4 5

percent of the population in 1994

Total population : 260.3 million

Population structure of Mexico

Age

Males   Females

80
70
60
50
40
30
20
10
0

7 6 5 4 3 2 1 0   0 1 2 3 4 5 6 7

percent of the population in 1990

Total population : 81.2 million

Environmental issues

tropical deforestation

existing areas of rainforest

former areas of rainforest

desertification

existing areas of desert

high risk areas

moderate risk areas

air pollution

◆ cities where sulphur dioxide emmissions are recorded, and exceed recommended levels

global warming

addition of greenhouse gases in tonnes of carbon per person (look at the world map on page 17)

sea pollution

areas severely polluted for all or part of the year

areas persistently affected by pollution

▼ deep sea dump sites

✻ major oil spills (less than 100 000 tonnes)

acid rain

a pH scale measures acidity. Unaffected rain water is slightly acidic with a pH of 5.6

pH less than 4.2 (the most acidic)

pH 4.2 - 4.6

pH 4.6 - 5.0

other areas where acid rain is becoming a problem

Oblique Mercator Projection
© Oxford University Press

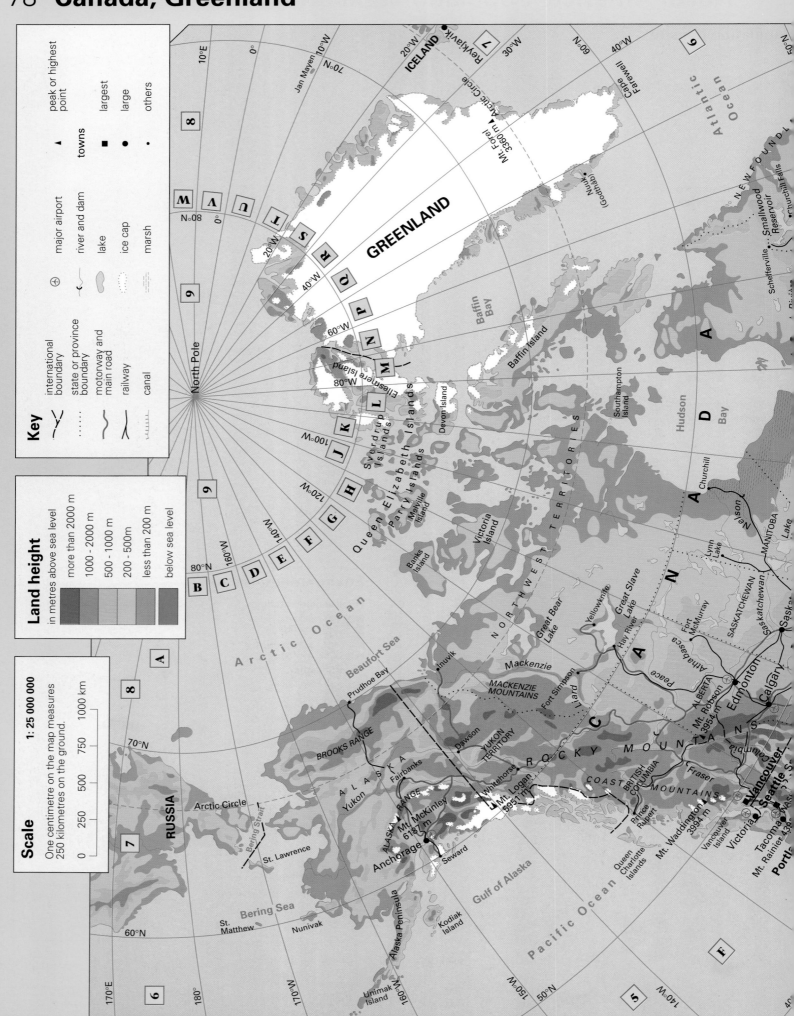

Key

international boundary	
state or province boundary	
motorway and main road	
railway	
canal	

major airport	
river and dam	
lake	
ice cap	
marsh	

peak or highest point	▲

towns
- ■ largest
- ● large
- · others

Land height
in metres above sea level

- more than 2000 m
- 1000 - 2000 m
- 500 - 1000 m
- 200 - 500m
- less than 200 m
- below sea level

Scale

1 : 25 000 000

One centimetre on the map measures 250 kilometres on the ground.

0 250 500 750 1000 km

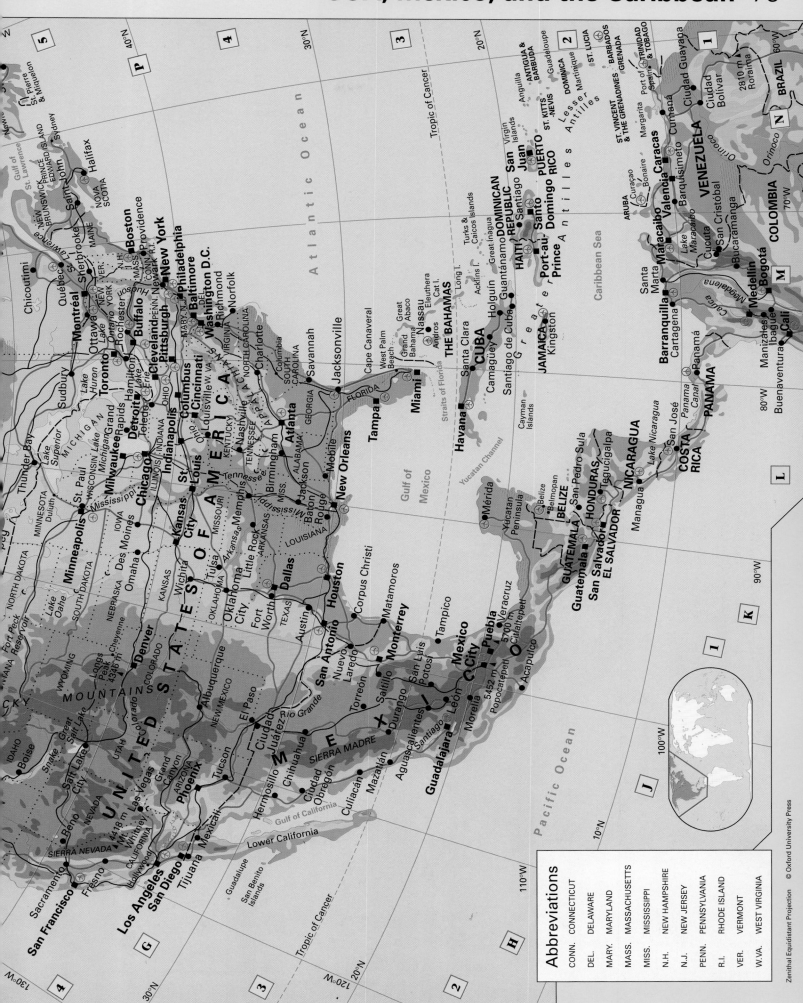

Zenithal Equidistant Projection

Abbreviations

CONN.	CONNECTICUT
DEL.	DELAWARE
MARY.	MARYLAND
MASS.	MASSACHUSETTS
MISS.	MISSISSIPPI
N.H.	NEW HAMPSHIRE
N.J.	NEW JERSEY
PENN.	PENNSYLVANIA
R.I.	RHODE ISLAND
VER.	VERMONT
W.VA.	WEST VIRGINIA

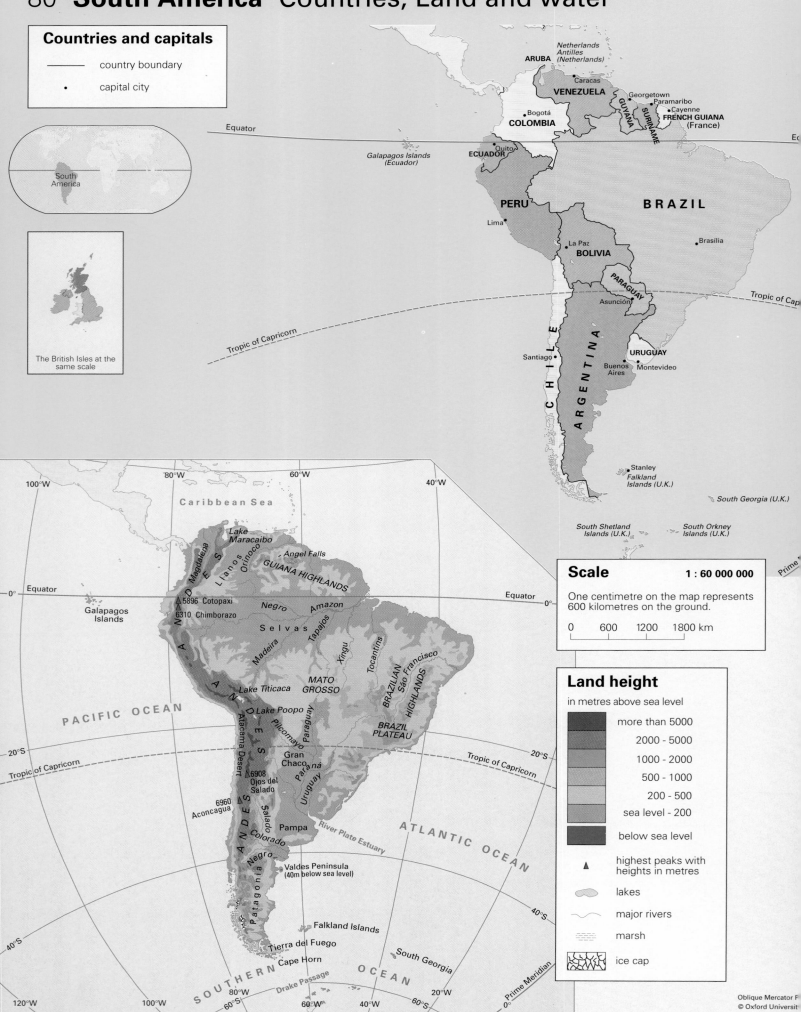

Countries and capitals

— country boundary

• capital city

South America

The British Isles at the same scale

Equator

Galapagos Islands (Ecuador)

ARUBA

Netherlands Antilles (Netherlands)

• Caracas

VENEZUELA

Georgetown
• Paramaribo
Cayenne

GUYANA
SURINAME
FRENCH GUIANA
(France)

• Bogotá
COLOMBIA

•Quito
ECUADOR

PERU

• Lima

B R A Z I L

• Brasília

La Paz
•
BOLIVIA

PARAGUAY

Asunción
•

Tropic of Capricorn

Santiago
•

C H I L E

A R G E N T I N A

Buenos Aires
•

URUGUAY

• Montevideo

•Stanley
Falkland Islands (U.K.)

South Georgia (U.K.)

South Shetland Islands (U.K.)

South Orkney Islands (U.K.)

Prime

Equator

Ec

Tropic of Cap

Caribbean Sea

100°W 80°W 60°W 40°W

Lake Maracaibo

Angel Falls

GUIANA HIGHLANDS

Magdalena
Llanos
Orinoco

Equator 0° 0°

Galapagos Islands

△5896 Cotopaxi
6310 Chimborazo

Negro
Amazon

S e l v a s

Madeira
Tapajos
Xingu
Tocantins

MATO GROSSO

Lake Titicaca

Lake Poopo

BRAZILIAN HIGHLANDS
São Francisco

BRAZIL PLATEAU

Pilcomayo
Paraguay

PACIFIC OCEAN

Atacama Desert

△6908
Ojos del Salado

Gran Chaco
Paraná
Uruguay

20°S 20°S

Tropic of Capricorn

6960
Aconcagua

Salado
Colorado

Pampa

Negro

River Plate Estuary

ATLANTIC OCEAN

Valdes Peninsula
(40m below sea level)

A N D E S

Patagonia

Falkland Islands

Tierra del Fuego

South Georgia

Cape Horn

S O U T H E R N **O C E A N**

Drake Passage

120°W 100°W 80°S 80°W 60°W 40°W 20°W Prime Meridian 0° 20°E

Scale   1 : 60 000 000

One centimetre on the map represents 600 kilometres on the ground.

0   600   1200   1800 km

Land height

in metres above sea level

more than 5000

2000 - 5000

1000 - 2000

500 - 1000

200 - 500

sea level - 200

below sea level

▲ highest peaks with heights in metres

lakes

major rivers

marsh

ice cap

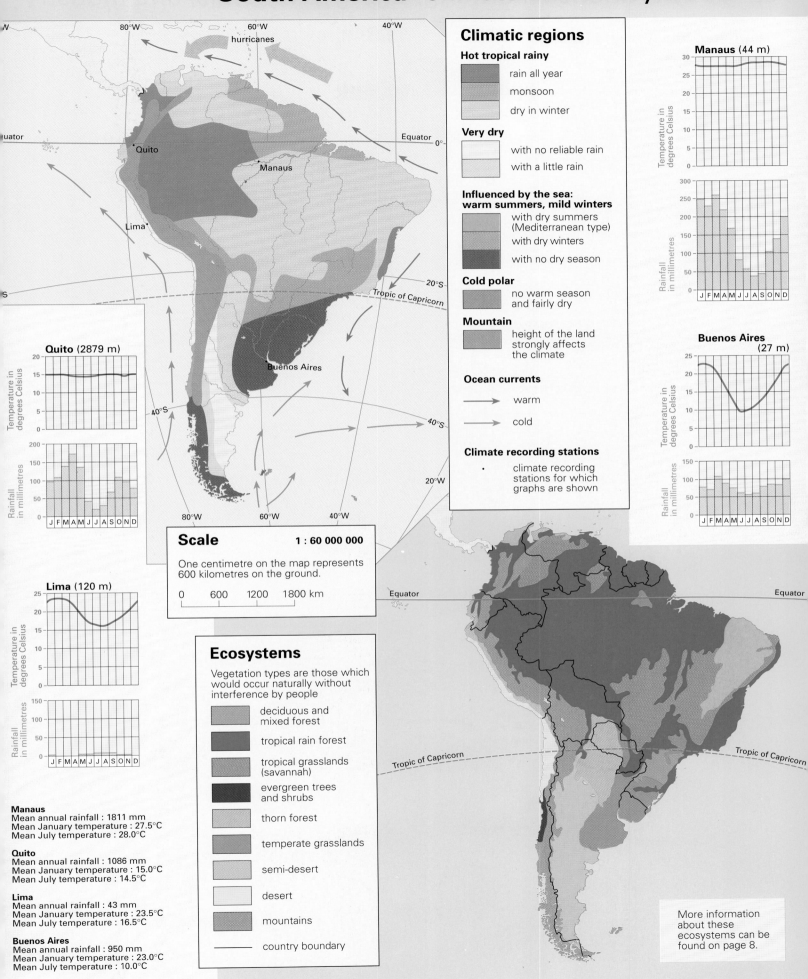

Climatic regions

Hot tropical rainy
- rain all year
- monsoon
- dry in winter

Very dry
- with no reliable rain
- with a little rain

Influenced by the sea: warm summers, mild winters
- with dry summers (Mediterranean type)
- with dry winters
- with no dry season

Cold polar
- no warm season and fairly dry

Mountain
- height of the land strongly affects the climate

Ocean currents
- → warm
- → cold

Climate recording stations
- • climate recording stations for which graphs are shown

Manaus (44 m)

Quito (2879 m)

Lima (120 m)

Buenos Aires (27 m)

Scale   1 : 60 000 000

One centimetre on the map represents 600 kilometres on the ground.

0   600   1200   1800 km

Ecosystems

Vegetation types are those which would occur naturally without interference by people

- deciduous and mixed forest
- tropical rain forest
- tropical grasslands (savannah)
- evergreen trees and shrubs
- thorn forest
- temperate grasslands
- semi-desert
- desert
- mountains
- — country boundary

Manaus
Mean annual rainfall : 1811 mm
Mean January temperature : 27.5°C
Mean July temperature : 28.0°C

Quito
Mean annual rainfall : 1086 mm
Mean January temperature : 15.0°C
Mean July temperature : 14.5°C

Lima
Mean annual rainfall : 43 mm
Mean January temperature : 23.5°C
Mean July temperature : 16.5°C

Buenos Aires
Mean annual rainfall : 950 mm
Mean January temperature : 23.0°C
Mean July temperature : 10.0°C

More information about these ecosystems can be found on page 8.

Oblique Mercator Projection

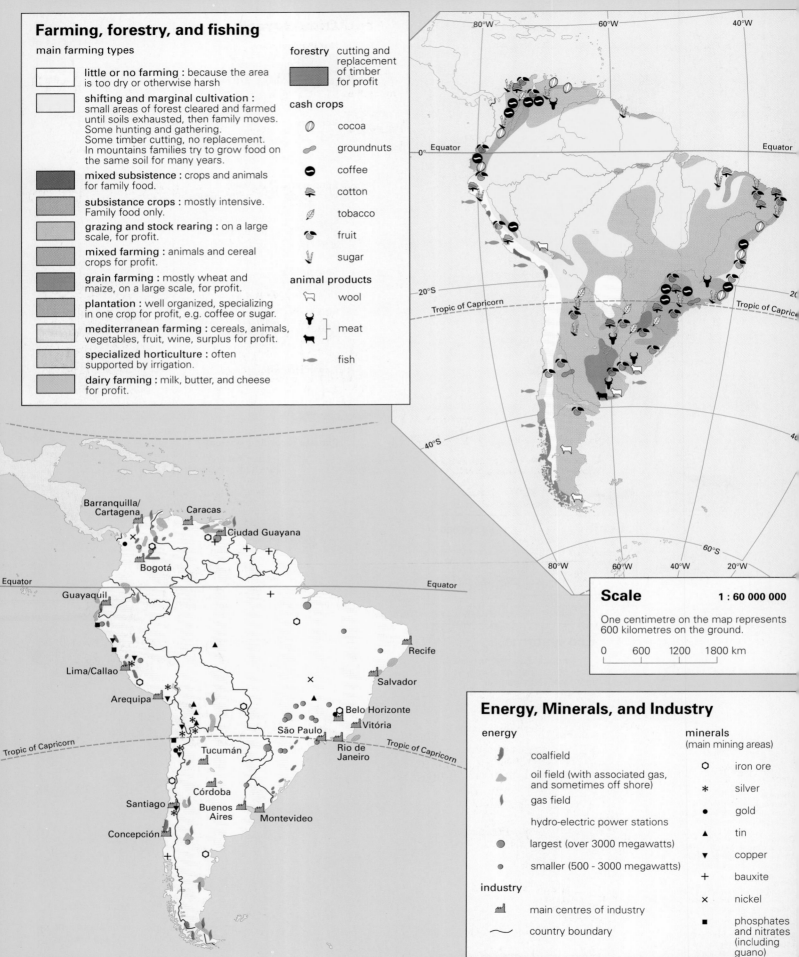

Farming, forestry, and fishing

main farming types

little or no farming : because the area is too dry or otherwise harsh	
shifting and marginal cultivation : small areas of forest cleared and farmed until soils exhausted, then family moves. Some hunting and gathering. Some timber cutting, no replacement. In mountains families try to grow food on the same soil for many years.	
mixed subsistence : crops and animals for family food.	
subsistance crops : mostly intensive. Family food only.	
grazing and stock rearing : on a large scale, for profit.	
mixed farming : animals and cereal crops for profit.	
grain farming : mostly wheat and maize, on a large scale, for profit.	
plantation : well organized, specializing in one crop for profit, e.g. coffee or sugar.	
mediterranean farming : cereals, animals, vegetables, fruit, wine, surplus for profit.	
specialized horticulture : often supported by irrigation.	
dairy farming : milk, butter, and cheese for profit.	

forestry cutting and replacement of timber for profit

cash crops

- cocoa
- groundnuts
- coffee
- cotton
- tobacco
- fruit
- sugar

animal products

- wool
- meat
- fish

Scale

1 : 60 000 000

One centimetre on the map represents 600 kilometres on the ground.

| 0 | 600 | 1200 | 1800 km |

Energy, Minerals, and Industry

energy

- coalfield
- oil field (with associated gas, and sometimes off shore)
- gas field

hydro-electric power stations

- largest (over 3000 megawatts)
- smaller (500 - 3000 megawatts)

industry

- main centres of industry
- country boundary

minerals
(main mining areas)

- ○ iron ore
- ✳ silver
- ● gold
- ▲ tin
- ▼ copper
- + bauxite
- × nickel
- ■ phosphates and nitrates (including guano)

Barranquilla/ Cartagena
Caracas
Ciudad Guayana
Bogotá
Guayaquil
Lima/Callao
Arequipa
Tucumán
Córdoba
Santiago
Buenos Aires
Concepción
Montevideo
Recife
Salvador
Belo Horizonte
Vitória
São Paulo
Rio de Janeiro

Equator
Tropic of Capricorn
Prime Meridian

Oblique Mercator Projection
© Oxford University Press

Population density

number of people per square kilometre

high		more than 100
moderate		10 - 100
sparse		1 - 10
very low		less than 1

◯ major cities and built up areas of at least 3 million people

• cities with 1 - 3 million people

— country boundary

Population structure of Brazil

Age

Males ... Females

80
70
60
50
40
30
20
10
0

6 5 4 3 2 1 0   0 1 2 3 4 5 6

percent of the population in 1992
Total population : 149.2 million

Population structure of Argentina

Age

Males ... Females

80
70
60
50
40
30
20
10
0

6 5 4 3 2 1 0   0 1 2 3 4 5 6

percent of the population in 1993
Total population : 33.7 million

Scale   1 : 60 000 000

One centimetre on the map represents 600 kilometres on the ground.

0   600   1200   1800 km

Environmental issues

tropical deforestation

existing areas of rainforest

former areas of rainforest

desertification

existing areas of desert

high risk areas

moderate risk areas

global warming   addition of greenhouse gases in tonnes of carbon per person (look at the world map on page 17)

sea pollution

areas severely polluted for all or part of the year

areas persistently affected by pollution

✳ major oil spills (over 100 000 tonnes)

✳ major oil spills (less than 100 000 tonnes)

acid rain   a pH scale measures acidity. Unaffected rain water is slightly acidic with a pH of 5.6

areas where acid rain is becoming a problem

air pollution

◆ cities where sulphur dioxide emmissions are recorded, and exceed recommended levels

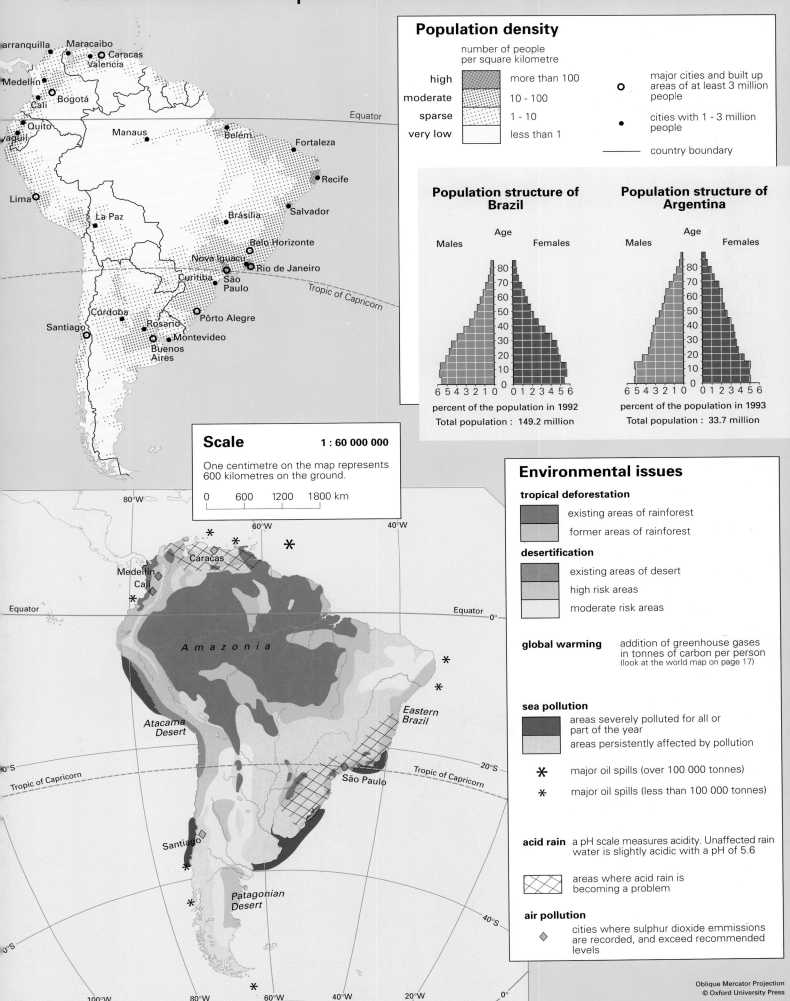

Oblique Mercator Projection
© Oxford University Press

Key

	international boundary
	motorway and main road
	railway
	canal
⊕	major airport
	river and dam
	lake

	ice cap
	marsh
▲	peak or highest point

towns
■	largest
●	large
·	others

Land height
in metres above sea level

- more than 5000 m
- 2000 - 5000 m
- 1000 - 2000 m
- 500 - 1000 m
- 200 - 500 m
- less than 200 m

Scale

1: 21 000 000

One centimetre on the map represents
210 kilometres on the ground.

| 0 | 210 | 420 | 630 | 840 km |

© Oxford University Press

Transverse Mercator Projection

South Atlantic

Ocean

South Georgia
(U.K.)

Southern Ocean

Pacific

Ocean

Stanley

Falkland
Islands (U.K.)

South Orkney
Islands

South Shetland
Islands (U.K.)

Antarctic
Peninsula

ANTARCTICA

Antarctic Circle

Joinville

Florianópolis

Caxias do Sul

Porto Alegre

Rio Grande

Pelotas

URUGUAY

Montevideo

River Plate
Estuary

Corrientes

Resistencia

Santiago
del Estero

Paraná

Uruguay

Salado

Córdoba

Santa Fe

Paraná

Rosario

Buenos Aires

La Plata

Mar del Plata

San Juan

Mendoza

ARGENTINA

Colorado

Negro

Bahía Blanca

Chillán

PATAGONIA

Esquel

Comodoro
Rivadavia

Aconcagua
7035 m

Viña del Mar

Valparaíso

Santiago

Talca

Talcahuano

Concepción

Temuco

Valdivia

Osorno

Puerto Montt

Chiloé
Island

Juan
Fernández
Islands

CHILE

ANDES

Tierra
del Fuego

Punta Arenas

Cape Horn

30°S

40°S

50°S

60°S

30°S

40°S

50°S

60°S

80°W

70°W

60°W

50°W

40°W

30°W

90°W

100°W

A B C D E F

1 2 3 4 5

The Arctic Ocean

- ice cap (up to 3350 metres thick in Greenland)
- sea covered by ice all year
- sea covered by ice for part of the year
- ▲ highest points, with height given in metres
- ⊕ position of magnetic north in 1994
- country boundary
- ■ capital city

The Arctic is mostly ocean. Antarctica is a group of islands covered by a sheet of ice which overruns the coast as floating ice called 'shelf ice'.

The ice sheet in Antarctica is 7 times the size of the Arctic ice sheet (in Greenland), and contains 8 times as much ice.

In the Arctic, the area north of 60°N contains land areas belonging to 8 different countries.
In Antarctica, an international treaty suspends all land claims and preserves the area south of 60°S for scientific research and international cooperation.

Parts of the Arctic are inhabited. Antarctica is unihabited except for the scientists who occupy the research stations.

The first person to reach the North Pole was Peary, in 1909. In 1911 Amundsen reached the South Pole, closely followed by Scott in 1912.

Scale   1: 40 000 000

One centimetre on the map represents 400 kilometres on the ground.

0   400   800   1200   2000 km

The British Isles at the same scale

Antarctica

- land not covered by ice
- ice cap (up to 4000 metres thick)
- sea covered by ice all year
- sea covered by ice for part of the year
- ▲ highest points, with height given in metres
- ⊕ position of magnetic south in 1990
- ⚑ scientific stations, permanently occupied

Zenithal Equidistant Projection
© Oxford University Press

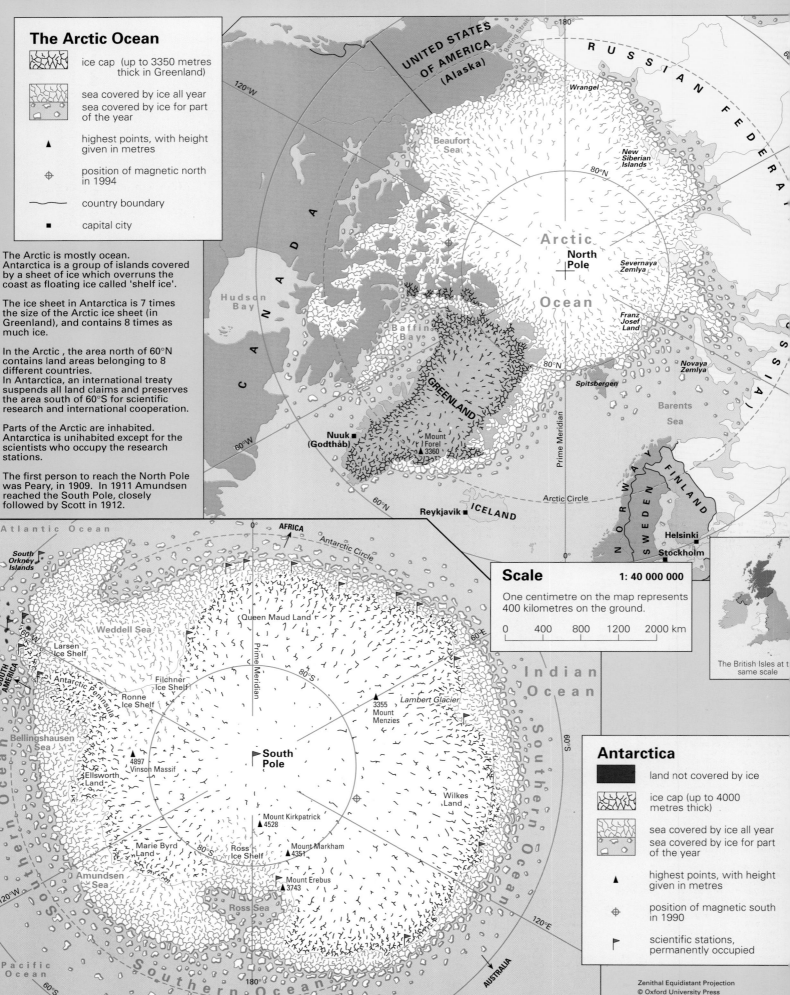

How to use the index

To find a place on an atlas map use either the grid code or latitude and longitude.

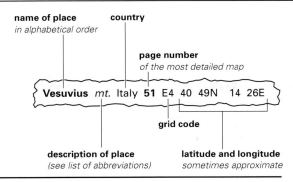

name of place
in alphabetical order

country

page number
of the most detailed map

Vesuvius *mt.* Italy **51** E4 40 49N 14 26E

grid code

description of place
(see list of abbreviations)

latitude and longitude
sometimes approximate

Grid code

Vesuvius is in grid square E4

Vesuvius *mt.* Italy **51** E4 40 49N 14 26E

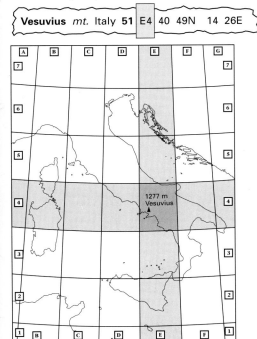

Latitude and longitude

Vesuvius is at latitude 40 49N longitude 14 26E

Vesuvius *mt.* Italy **51** E4 40 49N 14 26E

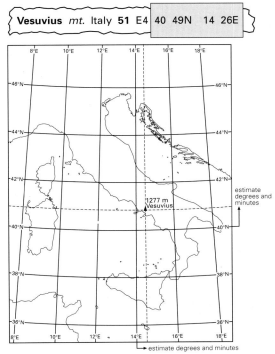

Abbreviations used in the index

admin.	administrative area
b.	bay or harbour
bor.	borough
c.	cape, point or headland
co.	county
est.	estuary
geog.reg.	geographical region
i.	island
is.	islands
l.	lake, lakes, lagoon
mt.	mountain
mts.	mountains
p.	peninsula
pk.	peak
plat.	plateau
pt.	point
r.	river
res.	reservoir
sd.	sound, strait or channel
sum.	summit
tn.	town
u.a.	unitary authority
vol.	volcano

A

Aachen Germany **49** D4 50 46N 6 06E
Aare *r.* Switzerland **49** D2 47 15N 7 30E
Abadan Iran **61** E4 30 20N 48 15E
Abbeville France **48** D5 50 06N 1 51E
Aberaeron Wales **36** C2 52 49N 44 43W
Aberchirder Scotland **31** G2 57 33N 2 38W
Aberconwy and Colwyn *u.a.* Wales **36** D3 53 10N 3 50W
Aberdare Wales **36** D1 51 43N 3 27W
Aberdeen Scotland **31** G2 57 10N 2 04W
Aberdeen City *u.a.* Scotland **31** G2 57 10N 2 00W
Aberdeenshire *u.a.* Scotland **31** G2 57 10N 2 50W
Aberfeldy Scotland **31** F1 56 37N 3 54W
Abergavenny Wales **36** D1 51 50N 3 00W
Abertillery Wales **36** D1 51 45N 3 09W
Aberystwyth Wales **36** C2 52 25N 4 05W
Abha Saudi Arabia **61** E2 18 14N 42 31E
Abidjan Côte d'Ivoire **66** B3 5 19N 4 01W
Abingdon England **38** C2 51 41N 1 17W
Aboyne Scotland **31** G2 57 05N 2 50W
Abu Dhabi United Arab Emirates **61** F3 24 28N 54 25E
Abuja Nigeria **66** C3 9 10N 7 11E
Acapulco Mexico **79** K2 16 51N 99 56W
Accra Ghana **66** B3 5 33N 0 15W
Acklins Island The Bahamas **79** M3 22 30N 74 30W
Aconcagua *mt.* Argentina **85** B4 32 40S 70 02W
Adamawa Highlands Africa **66** D3 7 00N 13 00E
Adana Turkey **43** P3 37 00N 35 19E
Addis Ababa Ethiopia **61** D1 9 03N 38 42E
Adelaide Australia **72** D2 34 55S 138 36E
Aden Yemen Republic **61** E2 12 50N 45 03E
Aden, Gulf of Indian Ocean **61** E2 12 30N 47 30E
Adour *r.* France **48** C1 43 45N 0 30W
Adriatic Sea Mediterranean Sea **51** E5 43 00N 15 00E
Aegean Sea Mediterranean Sea **42** L3 39 00N 24 00E
AFGHANISTAN 58 B4
Agadès Niger **66** C4 17 00N 7 56E
Agadir Morocco **66** B6 30 30N 9 40W
Agra India **58** C3 27 09N 78 00E
Aguascalientes Mexico **79** J3 21 51N 102 18W
Ahaggar *mts.* Algeria **66** C5 23 50N 6 00E

Ahmadabad India **58** C3 23 03N 72 40E
Ahvaz Iran **61** E4 31 17N 48 43E
Ailsa Craig *i.* Scotland **32** D3 55 16N 5 07W
Aïn Sefra Algeria **42** F2 32 45N 0 35W
Airdrie Scotland **33** F3 55 52N 3 59W
Aire *r.* England **34** C2 54 00N 2 05W
Aix-en-Provence France **48** F1 43 31N 5 27E
Ajaccio Corsica **51** B4 41 55N 8 43E
Ajdabiya Libya **66** E6 30 46N 20 14E
Akita Japan **59** N2 39 44N 140 05E
Akmola (*Tselinograd*) Kazakhstan **56** H3 51 10N 71 28E
Akureyri Iceland **42** C9 65 41N 18 04W
Alabama *state* U.S.A. **79** J4 32 00N 87 00W
Alaska *state* U.S.A. **78** D7 63 00N 150 00W
Alaska, Gulf of U.S.A. **78** E6 58 00N 147 00W
Alaska Peninsula U.S.A. **78** D6 56 30N 159 00W
Alaska Range *mts.* U.S.A. **78** D7/E7 62 30N 152 30W
Albacete Spain **50** E3 39 00N 1 52W
ALBANIA 42 L4
Albany Australia **72** B2 35 00S 117 53E
Alberta *province* Canada **78** H6 55 00N 115 00W
Ålborg Denmark **42** H7 57 05N 9 50E
Albuquerque U.S.A. **79** J4 35 05N 106 38W
Alcalá de Henares Spain **50** D4 40 28N 3 22W
Alcudia Balearic Islands **50** G3 39 51N 3 06E
Aldabra Islands Indian Ocean **67** E4 9 00S 46 00E
Aldeburgh England **39** F3 52 09N 1 35E
Alderney *i.* Channel Islands British Isles **41** E2 49 43N 2 12W
Aldershot England **38** D2 51 15N 0 47W
Aleppo Syria **61** D4 36 14N 37 10E
Alessándria Italy **51** B6 44 55N 8 37E
Alexandria Egypt **61** C4 31 13N 29 55E
Alexandria Scotland **33** E3 55 59N 4 36W
Algarve *geog. reg.* Portugal **50** A2 37 30N 8 00W
ALGERIA 66 C5
Algiers Algeria **66** C6 36 50N 3 00E
Al Hoceima Morocco **50** D1 35 14N 3 56W
Alicante Spain **50** E3 38 21N 0 29W
Alice Springs Australia **72** D3 23 41S 133 52E
Al Jawf Libya **66** E5 24 12N 23 18E
Allahabad India **58** D3 25 27N 81 50E

Allier *r.* France **48** E3 46 15N 3 15E
Alloa Scotland **33** F4 56 07N 3 49W
Almanzor *mt.* Spain **50** C4 40 15N 5 18W
Almaty Kazakhstan **56** H2 43 19N 76 55E
Almería Spain **50** D2 36 50N 2 26W
Al Mukha Yemen Republic **61** E2 13 20N 43 16E
Aln *r.* England **33** H3 55 30N 1 50W
Alnwick England **33** H3 55 25N 1 42W
Alps *mts.* Europe **49** D2/G2 46 00N 7 30E
Altai Mountains Mongolia **57** K2 47 00N 92 30E
Alton England **38** D2 51 09N 0 59W
Alyth Scotland **31** F1 56 37N 3 13W
Amazon *r.* Brazil **84** D7 2 30S 65 30W
Amble England **33** H3 55 20N 1 34W
Ambleside England **34** C3 54 26N 2 58W
Ambon Indonesia **60** D2 3 41S 128 10E
Amesbury England **38** C2 51 10N 1 47W
Amiens France **48** E4 49 54N 2 18E
Amlwch Wales **36** C3 53 25N 4 20W
Amman Jordan **61** D4 31 04N 46 17E
Ammanford Wales **36** D1 51 48N 3 58W
Amritsar India **58** C4 31 35N 74 56E
Amsterdam Netherlands **49** C5 52 22N 4 54E
Amu Darya *r.* Asia **56** G2 41 00N 61 00E
Amundsen Sea Southern Ocean **86** 72 00S 130 00W
Amur *r.* Asia **57** N3 54 00N 122 00E
Anchorage U.S.A. **78** E7 61 10N 150 00W
Ancona Italy **51** D5 43 37N 13 31E
Andaman Islands India **58** E2 12 00N 94 00E
Andaman Sea Indian Ocean **58** E2 13 00N 95 00E
Andes *mts.* South America **84/85** B8/C5 10 00S 77 00W
Andizhan Uzbekistan **56** H2 40 40N 72 12E
ANDORRA 50 F5
Andover England **38** C2 51 13N 1 28W
Andros *i.* The Bahamas **79** M3 24 00N 78 00W
Aneto *mt.* Spain **50** F5 42 37N 0 40E
Angara *r.* Russia **57** K3 59 00N 97 00E
Angeles The Philippines **60** D4 15 09N 120 33E
Angers France **48** C3 47 29N 0 32W
Anglesey *u.a.* Wales **36** C3 53 18N 4 25W
ANGOLA 67 B3
Angoulême France **48** D2 45 40N 0 10E
Anguilla *i.* Leeward Islands **79** N2 18 14N 63 05W

Angus *u.a.* Scotland **31** F1/G1 56 45N 3 00W
Ankara Turkey **43** N3 39 55N 32 50E
'Annaba Algeria **66** C6 36 55N 7 47E
An Najaf Iraq **61** E4 31 59N 44 19E
Annam Range *mts.* Laos/Vietnam **60** B4 19 00N 104 00E
Annan Scotland **33** F2 54 59N 3 16W
Annan *r.* Scotland **33** F3 55 05N 3 20W
Annapurna *mt.* Nepal **58** D3 28 34N 83 50E
Annecy France **48** G2 45 54N 6 07E
Anshan China **59** D4 41 05N 122 58E
Anstruther Scotland **33** G4 56 14N 2 42W
Antalya Turkey **43** N3 36 53N 30 42E
Antananarivo Madagascar **67** E3 18 52S 47 30E
Antarctic Peninsula Antarctica **86** 68 00S 65 00W
Antibes France **48** G1 43 35N 7 07E
Antigua *i.* Antigua & Barbuda **84** C9 17 09N 61 49W
ANTIGUA AND BARBUDA 79 N2
Antofagasta Chile **84** B5 23 40S 70 23W
Antrim Northern Ireland **32** C2 54 43N 6 13W
Antrim *district* Northern Ireland **32** C2 54 45N 6 25W
Antrim Mountains Northern Ireland **32** C3/D2 55 00N 6 10W
Antwerp Belgium **49** C4 51 13N 4 25E
Anxi China **59** A5 40 32N 95 57E
Aomori Japan **59** N3 40 50N 140 43E
Aosta Italy **51** A6 45 43N 7 19E
Aparri The Philippines **60** D4 18 22N 121 40E
Apeldoorn Netherlands **49** C5 52 13N 5 57E
Appalachians *mts.* U.S.A. **79** L4 37 00N 82 00W
Appennines *mts.* Italy **51** C6/F4 44 30N 10 00E
Appleby-in-Westmorland England **34** C3 53 36N 2 29W
Aqaba Jordan **61** D3 29 32N 35 00E
Arabian Sea Indian Ocean **7** 17 00N 60 00E
Aracaju Brazil **84** F6 10 54S 37 07W
Arad Romania **42** L5 46 10N 21 19E
Arafura Sea Australia **72** D5 9 00S 133 00E
Araguaia *r.* Brazil **84** D6 12 30S 51 00W
Arak Iran **61** E4 34 05N 49 42E
Araks *r.* Asia **61** E4 39 30N 48 00E
Aral Sea Asia **56** G2 45 00N 60 00E
Aran Fawddy *mt.* Wales **36** D2 52 47N 3 41W

Ararat, Mount Turkey **43** Q3 39 44N 44 15E
Arbil Iraq **61** E4 36 12N 44 01E
Arbroath Scotland **31** G1 56 34N 2 35W
Arctic Ocean 86
Ardabil Iran **61** E4 38 15N 48 18E
Ardbeg Scotland **32** D3 55 42N 6 05W
Ardminish Scotland **32** D3 55 42N 5 44W
Ardres France **39** F1 50 51N 1 59E
Ards *district* Northern Ireland **32** D2 54 30N 5 30W
Ards Peninsula Northern Ireland **32** D2 54 25N 5 30W
Arequipa Peru **84** B6 16 25S 71 32W
Arezzo Italy **51** C5 43 28N 11 53E
ARGENTINA 85 C4
Argyll and Bute *u.a.* Scotland **32/33** D4/E4 56 10N 5 00W
Århus Denmark **42** J7 56 15N 10 10E
Arica Chile **84** B6 18 30S 70 20W
Arisaig Scotland **30** D1 56 51N 5 51W
Arisaig, Sound of Scotland **30** D1 56 50N 5 50W
Arizona *state* U.S.A. **79** H4 34 00N 112 00W
Arkansas *r.* U.S.A. **79** K4 35 00N 93 00W
Arkansas *state* U.S.A. **79** K4 34 00N 93 00W
Arkhangel'sk Russia **56** E4 64 32N 40 40E
Arklow Wicklow Republic of Ireland **36** A2 52 48N 6 09W
Arles France **48** F1 43 41N 4 38E
Armagh Northern Ireland **32** C2 54 21N 6 39W
Armagh *district* Northern Ireland **32** C2 54 20N 6 40W
ARMENIA 43 Q4
Armentières France **39** G1 50 41N 2 53E
Arnhem Netherlands **49** C4 52 00N 5 53E
Arno *r.* Italy **51** C5 43 45N 11 00E
Arnold England **37** F2 53 00N 1 09W
Arran *i.* Scotland **32** D3 55 35N 5 15W
Arras France **48** E5 50 17N 2 46E
Artá Balearic Islands **50** G3 39 42N 3 20E
Arun *r.* England **38** D2 51 05N 0 30W
Arundel England **38** D1 50 51N 0 34W
Asahikawa Japan **59** N3 43 46N 142 23E
Asahi, Mount Japan **59** N3 43 42N 142 54E
Asansol India **58** D3 23 40N 86 59E
Ascension Island Atlantic Ocean **5** 7 57S 14 22W
Ashbourne England **37** F2 53 01N 1 43W
Ashburton New Zealand **73** C2 43 54S 171 45E
Ashford England **39** E2 51 09N 0 53E
Ashgabat *(Ashkhabad)* Turkmenistan **56** F1 37 58N 58 24E
Ashington England **33** H3 55 11N 1 34W
Ashkhabad *see* Ashgabat
Asmara Eritrea **61** D2 15 20N 38 58E
Assisi Italy **51** D5 43 04N 12 37E
Astrakhan Russia **56** E2 46 22N 48 04E
Asunción Paraguay **85** D5 25 15S 57 40W
Aswan Egypt **61** D3 24 05N 32 56E
Asyut Egypt **61** D3 27 14N 31 07E
Atacama Desert Chile **84/85** B5 22 30S 70 00W
Atbara Sudan **61** D2 17 42N 34 00E
Atbara *r.* Sudan **61** D2 17 00N 35 00E
Athabasca *r.* Canada **78** H6 57 30N 112 00W
Athens Greece **42** L3 38 00N 23 44E
Atlanta U.S.A. **79** L4 33 45N 84 23W
Atlantic Ocean 79 N4
Atlas Mountains Morocco **66** B6 32 00N 2 00W
Atrek *r.* Iran/Turkmenistan **61** F4 38 00N 57 00E
Atyrau Kazakhstan **56** F2 47 08N 51 59E
Auchterarder Scotland **31** F1 56 18N 3 43W
Auchtermuchty Scotland **33** E4 56 17N 3 15W
Auckland New Zealand **73** C3 36 51S 174 46E
Auderville France **41** F2 49 43N 1 56W
Augsburg Germany **49** F3 48 21N 10 54E
Austin U.S.A. **79** K4 30 18N 97 47W
AUSTRALIA 72
AUSTRIA 42 J5
Auxerre France **48** E3 47 48N 3 35E
Aveiro Portugal **50** A4 40 38N 8 40W
Aviemore Scotland **31** F2 57 12N 3 50W
Avignon France **48** F1 43 56N 4 48E
Avon *r.* Warwickshire/Hereford and Worcester England **37** F2 52 15N 1 55W
Avon *r.* Wiltshire/Bath and North East Somerset/North Somerset England **38** B2 51 20N 2 05W
Avon *r.* Wiltshire/Hampshire/Dorset England **38** C1 50 55N 1 50W
Axe *r.* England **41** E3 50 50N 2 50W
Axminster England **41** E3 50 47N 3 00W
Ayaguz Kazakhstan **56** J2 47 59N 80 27E
Ayers Rock *mt.* Australia **72** D3 25 20S 131 01E
Aylesbury England **38** D2 51 50N 0 50W
Ayr Scotland **33** E3 55 28N 4 38W
Ayr *r.* Scotland **33** E3 55 30N 4 20W
Ayre, Point of *c.* Isle of Man British Isles **33** E2 54 25N 4 22W
AZERBAIJAN 56 E2
Azores *is.* Atlantic Ocean **4** 38 30N 28 00W
Azov, Sea of Asia **43** P5 46 00N 36 00E

B

Babruysk Belarus **42** M6 53 08N 29 10E
Bacolod The Philippines **60** D4 10 38N 122 58E
Badajoz Spain **50** B3 38 53N 6 58W
Baden-Baden Germany **49** E3 48 45N 8 15E
Baffin Bay Canada **78** N8 72 00N 64 00W
Baffin Island Canada **78** M7 70 00N 75 00W
Baghdad Iraq **61** E4 33 20N 44 26E
BAHAMAS, THE 79 M3
Bahia Blanca Argentina **85** C4 38 45S 62 15W
BAHRAIN 61 F3
Baie de la Seine *b.* France **41** G2 49 40N 0 30W
Bakewell England **37** F3 53 13N 1 40W
Baku Azerbaijan **56** F2 40 22N 49 53E
Bala Wales **36** D2 52 54N 3 35W
Balakovo Russia **43** R6 52 04N 47 46E
Bala Lake Wales **36** D2 52 53N 3 38W
Balearic Islands Spain **50** F3/H4 40 00N 2 00E
Bali *i.* Indonesia **60** C2 8 30S 115 00E

Balikesir Turkey **42** M3 39 37N 27 51E
Balikpapan Indonesia **60** C2 1 15S 116 50E
Balkhash, Lake Kazakhstan **56** H2 46 00N 75 00E
Ballantrae Scotland **32** D3 55 06N 5 00W
Ballarat Australia **72** E2 37 33S 143 52E
Ballater Scotland **31** F2 57 03N 3 03W
Ballybofey Donegal Republic of Ireland **32** B2 54 48N 7 47W
Ballycastle Northern Ireland **32** C3 55 12N 6 15W
Ballymena Northern Ireland **32** C2 54 52N 6 17W
Ballymena *district* Northern Ireland **32** C2 54 55N 6 20W
Ballymoney Northern Ireland **32** C3 55 04N 6 31W
Ballymoney *district* Northern Ireland **32** C3 55 00N 6 30W
Ballyshannon Donegal Republic of Ireland **32** A2 54 30N 8 11W
Baltic Sea Europe **42** K7 55 15N 17 00E
Baltimore U.S.A. **79** M4 39 18N 76 38W
Bamako Mali **66** B4 12 40N 7 59W
Bamberg Germany **49** F3 49 54N 10 54E
Bamburgh England **33** H3 55 36N 1 42W
Banbridge Northern Ireland **32** C2 54 21N 6 16W
Banbridge *district* Northern Ireland **32** C2 54 20N 6 20W
Banbury England **38** C3 52 04N 1 20W
Banchory Scotland **31** G2 57 30N 2 30W
Banda Aceh Indonesia **60** A3 5 30N 95 20E
Bandar Abbas Iran **61** F3 27 12N 56 15E
Bandar Seri Begawan Brunei Darussalam **60** C3 4 53N 114 57E
Banda Sea Indonesia **60** D2 5 50S 124 00E
Bandung Indonesia **60** B2 6 57S 107 34E
Banff Scotland **31** G2 57 40N 2 33W
Bangalore India **58** C2 12 58N 77 35E
Bangka *i.* Indonesia **60** B2 2 30S 107 00E
Bangkok *(Krung Thep)* Thailand **60** B4 13 44N 100 30E
BANGLADESH 58 D3/E3
Bangor Northern Ireland **32** D2 54 40N 5 40W
Bangor Wales **36** C3 53 13N 4 08W
Bangui Central African Republic **67** B5 4 23N 18 37E
Bangweulu, Lake Zambia **67** C3 11 15S 29 45E
Banja Luka Bosnia-Herzegovina **42** K4 44 47N 17 11E
Banjarmasin Indonesia **60** C2 3 22S 114 33E
Banjul The Gambia **66** A4 13 28N 16 39W
Banks Island Canada **78** G8 73 15N 121 30W
Bann *r.* Northern Ireland **32** C2 54 55N 6 30W
Baotou China **59** B4 40 38N 109 59E
BARBADOS 79 P2
Barbuda *i.* Antigua & Barbuda **84** C9 17 41N 61 48W
Barcelona Spain **50** G4 41 25N 2 10E
Bareilly India **58** C3 28 20N 79 24E
Barents Sea Arctic Ocean **86** 75 00N 40 00E
Barfleur France **41** F2 49 40N 1 16W
Bari Italy **51** F4 41 07N 16 52E
Barito *r.* Indonesia **60** C2 0 00S 115 00E
Barking England **39** E2 51 33N 0 06E
Barletta Italy **51** F4 41 20N 16 17E
Barmouth Wales **36** C2 52 43N 4 03W
Barnard Castle England **34** D3 54 33N 1 55W
Barnaul Russia **56** J3 53 21N 83 45E
Barnet England **38** D2 51 39N 0 12W
Barnoldswick England **34** C2 53 56N 2 16W
Barnsley England **35** D2 53 34N 1 28W
Barnstaple England **40** C4 51 05N 4 04W
Barquisimeto Venezuela **84** C9 10 03N 69 18W
Barra *i.* Scotland **30** B1/2 57 00N 7 25W
Barranquilla Colombia **84** B9 11 10N 74 50W
Barreiras Brazil **84** E6 12 09S 44 58W
Barrow-in-Furness England **34** B3 54 07N 3 14W
Barry Wales **36** D1 51 24N 3 18W
Barton-upon-Humber England **35** E2 53 41N 0 27W
Basildon England **39** E2 51 34N 0 25W
Basingstoke England **38** C2 51 16N 1 05W
Basle Switzerland **49** E3 47 33N 7 36E
Basra Iraq **61** E4 30 30N 47 50E
Bassein Myanmar **58** E2 16 46N 94 45E
Bass Strait Australia **72** E2 39 51S 145 53E
Bastia France **51** B5 42 14N 9 26E
Bata Equatorial Guinea **66** C5 1 51N 9 49E
Batang China **59** A3 30 02N 99 01E
Batangas The Philippines **60** D4 13 46N 121 01E
Bath England **38** B2 51 23N 2 22W
Bath and North East Somerset *u.a.* England **38** B2 51 25N 2 30W
Bathgate Scotland **33** F3 55 55N 3 39W
Baton Rouge U.S.A. **79** K4 30 30N 91 10W
Batumi Georgia **56** E2 41 37N 41 36E
Bavaria *admin.* Germany **49** F3/G3 49 00N 12 00E
Bayeux France **48** C4 49 16N 0 42W
Baykal, Lake Russia **57** L3 54 00N 109 00E
Bayonne France **48** C1 43 30N 1 28W
Bayreuth Germany **49** F3 49 27N 11 35E
Beachy Head *c.* England **39** E1 50 44N 0 16E
Bearsden Scotland **33** E3 55 56N 4 20W
Beaufort Sea Arctic Ocean **78** E7 72 00N 140 00W
Beauly *r.* Scotland **31** E2 57 30N 4 30W
Beauvais France **48** E4 49 26N 2 05E
Beccles England **39** F3 52 28N 1 34E
Bechar Algeria **66** B6 31 35N 2 17W
Bedford England **38** D3 52 08N 0 29W
Bedfordshire *co.* England **38** D3 52 08N 0 29W
Bedworth England **37** F2 52 29N 1 28W
Beersheba Israel **43** N2 31 15N 34 47E
Beida Libya **66** E6 32 00N 21 30E
Beijing *(Peking)* China **59** C3 39 55N 116 26E
Beinn Dearg *mt.* Scotland **31** E2 57 47N 4 56W
Beira Mozambique **67** D3 19 49S 34 52E
Beirut Lebanon **61** D4 33 52N 35 30E
Beja Portugal **50** B3 38 01N 7 52W
Bejaïa Algeria **42** H3 36 49N 5 03E
BELARUS 56 C3
Belém Brazil **84** E7 1 27S 48 29W
Belfast Northern Ireland **32** D2 54 35N 5 55W
Belfast *district* Northern Ireland **32** C2/D2 54 30N 5 58W
Belfast Lough *est.* Northern Ireland **32** D2 54 40N 5 45W
Belfort France **48** G3 47 38N 6 52E
Belgaum India **58** C2 15 54N 74 36E

BELGIUM 49 C4
Belgrade Serbia Yugoslavia **42** L4 44 50N 20 30E
Belitung *i.* Indonesia **60** B2 2 30S 107 30E
BELIZE 79 L2
Belize Belize **79** L2 17 29N 88 10W
Belle Isle *i.* France **48** B3 47 20N 3 10W
Bellingshausen Sea Southern Ocean **86** 71 00S 85 00W
Belmopan Belize **79** L2 17 13N 88 48W
Belo Horizonte Brazil **84** E6 19 54S 43 54W
Beltsy Moldova **42** M5 47 44N 28 41E
Ben Alder *mt.* Scotland **31** E1 56 49N 4 28W
Benavente Spain **50** C5 42 00N 5 40W
Benbecula *i.* Scotland **30** B2 57 25N 7 20W
Ben Cruachan *mt.* Scotland **30** D1 56 26N 5 09W
Bengal, Bay of Indian Ocean **58** D2 17 00N 88 00E
Benghazi Libya **66** E6 32 07N 20 04E
Benguela Angola **67** B3 12 34S 13 24E
Ben Hope *mt.* Scotland **31** E3 58 24N 4 37W
BENIN 66 C4
Ben Klibreck *mt.* Scotland **31** E3 58 14N 4 22W
Ben Lawers *mt.* Scotland **31** E1 56 33N 4 15W
Ben Lomond *mt.* Scotland **31** E1 56 12N 4 38W
Ben More *mt.* Argyll and Bute Scotland **30** C1 56 25N 6 02W
Ben More *mt.* Stirling Scotland **31** E1 56 25N 6 02W
Ben More Assynt *mt.* Scotland **31** E3 58 07N 4 52W
Ben Nevis *mt.* Scotland **31** D1 56 48N 5 00W
Benue *r.* Nigeria/Cameroon **66** C3/D3 9 00N 10 00E
Ben Wyvis *mt.* Scotland **31** E2 57 40N 4 35W
Berbera Somalia **66** E6 10 28N 45 02E
Berezniki Russia **43** T7 59 26N 56 49E
Bérgamo Italy **51** B6 45 42N 9 40E
Bergen Norway **42** H8 60 23N 5 20E
Bergerac France **48** D2 44 50N 0 29E
Bering Sea Pacific Ocean **57** S3 58 00N 170 00W
Bering Strait Russia/U.S.A. **78** C7 69 00N 169 00W
Berkshire *co.* England **38** C2/D2 51 28N 1 00W
Berlin Germany **49** G5 52 32N 13 25E
Bermuda *i.* Atlantic Ocean **79** N4 32 50N 64 20W
Bern Switzerland **49** D2 46 57N 7 26E
Berneray *i.* Scotland **30** B2 57 45N 7 10W
Bernina *mt.* Europe **49** E2 46 23N 9 54E
Berwick-upon-Tweed England **33** G3 55 46N 2 00W
Besançon France **48** F3 47 14N 6 02E
Bethesda Wales **36** C3 53 11N 4 03W
Béthune France **48** E5 50 32N 2 38E
Beverley England **35** E2 53 51N 0 26W
Bewdley England **37** E2 52 22N 2 19W
Bexley England **39** E2 51 27N 0 09E
BHUTAN 58 D3/E3
Białystok Poland **42** L6 53 09N 23 10E
Biarritz France **48** C1 43 29N 1 33W
Bicester England **38** C2 51 54N 1 09W
Bideford England **40** C4 51 01N 4 13W
Bideford Bay England **40** C4 51 05N 4 25W
Bielefeld Germany **49** E5 52 02N 8 32E
Bigbury Bay England **40** D3 50 17N 4 00W
Biggar Scotland **33** F3 55 38N 3 32W
Biggleswade England **38** D3 52 05N 0 17W
Bikaner India **58** C3 28 01N 73 22E
Bilbao Spain **50** D5 43 15N 2 56W
Bintan *i.* Indonesia **60** B3 0 50N 104 30E
Birdum Australia **72** D4 15 39S 133 13E
Birkenhead England **34** B2 53 24N 3 02W
Birmingham England **37** F2 52 30N 1 50W
Birmingham U.S.A. **79** L4 33 30N 86 55W
Biscay, Bay of Atlantic Ocean **48** B2 45 30N 2 50W
Bishkek Kirgyzstan **56** H2 42 53N 74 46E
Bishop Auckland England **34** D3 54 40N 1 40W
Bishop's Stortford England **39** E2 51 53N 0 09E
Biskra Algeria **42** H2 34 50N 5 41E
Bissau Guinea-Bissau **66** A4 11 52N 15 39W
Bitola FYROM **42** L4 41 01N 21 21E
Biwa, Lake Japan **59** M2 35 20N 135 20E
Bizerte Tunisia **51** B3 37 18N 9 52E
Blackburn England **34** C2 53 45N 2 29W
Black Forest *mts.* Germany **49** E3 47 00N 8 00E
Black Mountains Wales **36** D1 51 55N 3 10W
Blackpool England **34** B2 53 50N 3 03W
Black Sea Europe **43** P4 43 00N 35 00E
Black Volta *r.* Africa **66** B3/4 10 00N 3 00W
Blackwater *r.* Northern Ireland **32** C2 54 30N 6 45W
Blackwater Reservoir Scotland **30** E1 56 41N 4 46W
Blaenau Ffestiniog Wales **36** D2 52 59N 3 56W
Blaenau Gwent *u.a.* Wales **36** D1 51 45N 3 10W
Blagoveshchensk Russia **57** N3 50 19N 127 30E
Blairgowrie Scotland **31** F1 56 36N 3 21W
Blandford Forum England **38** B1 50 52N 2 11W
Blantyre Malawi **67** D3 15 46S 35 00E
Blenheim New Zealand **73** C2 41 31S 173 57E
Blida Algeria **42** G3 36 30N 2 50E
Bloemfontein Republic of South Africa **67** C2 29 07S 26 14E
Blois France **48** D3 47 36N 1 20E
Blue Nile *r.* Ethiopia/Sudan **61** D2 12 00N 33 00E
Blyth England **33** H3 55 07N 1 30W
Blyth *r.* England **33** H3 55 10N 1 45W
Boa Vista Brazil **84** C8 3 23S 55 30W
Bobo Dioulasso Burkina **66** B4 11 11N 4 18W
Bochum Germany **49** D4 51 28N 7 11E
Bodele Depression Chad **66** D4 17 00N 17 50E
Bodmin England **40** C3 50 29N 4 43W
Bodmin Moor England **40** C3 50 35N 4 40W
Bodø Norway **42** J9 67 18N 14 26E
Bognor Regis England **38** D1 50 47N 0 41W
Bogor Indonesia **60** B2 6 34S 106 45E
Bogotá Colombia **84** B8 4 38N 74 05W
Boise U.S.A. **79** H5 43 38N 116 12W
BOLIVIA 84 C6
Bologna Italy **51** C6 44 30N 11 20E
Bolton England **34** C2 53 35N 2 26W
Bolzano Italy **51** C7 46 30N 11 22E
Bombay India **58** C2 18 56N 72 51E
Bonaire *i.* Lesser Antilles **79** N2 12 15N 68 27W
Bonar Bridge *tn.* Scotland **31** E2 57 53N 4 21W
Bo'ness Scotland **33** F4 56 01N 3 37W
Bonifacio Corsica **51** B4 41 23N 9 10E
Bonn Germany **49** D4 50 44N 7 06E
Bootle England **34** B2 53 28N 3 00W

Bordeaux France **48** C2 44 50N 0 34W
Borneo *i.* Indonesia/Malaysia **60** C3 1 00N 113 00E
Bornholm *i.* Denmark **42** J6 55 02N 15 00E
Boscastle England **40** C3 50 41N 4 42W
BOSNIA-HERZEGOVINA 42 K4
Boston England **35** E1 52 29N 0 01E
Boston U.S.A. **79** M5 42 20N 71 05W
Bothnia, Gulf of Finland/Sweden **42** L8 61 00N 19 10E
BOTSWANA 67 C2
Bouaké Côte d'Ivoire **66** B3 7 42N 5 00W
Bougainville *i.* Papua New Guinea **72** F6 6 15S 155 00E
Boulogne-sur-Mer France **48** E5 50 43N 1 37E
Bourges France **48** E3 47 05N 2 23E
Bourke Australia **72** E2 30 05S 145 58E
Bournemouth England **41** F3 50 43N 1 54W
Bou Saâda Algeria **42** G3 35 10N 4 09E
Bovey Tracey England **40** D3 50 36N 3 40W
Boyoma Falls Zaïre **67** C5 0 18N 25 30E
Bracknell England **38** D2 51 26N 0 46W
Bradford England **34** D2 53 48N 1 45W
Braemar Scotland **31** F2 57 00N 3 24W
Brahmaputra *r.* India/Bangladesh **58** E3 27 00N 94 00E
Brăila Romania **42** M5 45 17N 27 58E
Braintree England **39** E2 51 53N 0 32E
Brampton England **34** C3 54 57N 2 43W
Brandenburg Germany **49** G5 52 25N 12 34E
Branderburgh Scotland **31** F2 57 43N 3 18W
Brásilia Brazil **84** E6 15 45S 47 57W
Braşov Romania **42** M5 45 39N 25 35E
Bratislava Slovakia **42** K5 48 10N 17 10E
Bratsk Russia **57** L3 56 20N 101 50E
Braunton England **40** C4 51 07N 4 10W
Bray Wicklow Republic of Ireland **36** A3 53 12N 6 06W
BRAZIL 84 C7/E7
Brazilian Plateau Brazil **84** E6 17 00S 44 00W
Brazzaville Congo **66** D2 4 14S 15 14E
Brechin Scotland **31** G1 56 44N 2 40W
Brecon Wales **36** D1 51 57N 3 24W
Brecon Beacons *mts.* Wales **36** D1 51 53N 3 30W
Breda Netherlands **49** C4 51 35N 4 46E
Bremen Germany **49** E5 53 05N 8 48E
Bremerhaven Germany **49** E5 53 33N 8 35E
Brenner Pass Austria/Italy **49** F2 47 02N 11 32E
Brent England **38** D2 51 34N 0 17W
Brentwood England **39** E2 51 38N 0 18E
Bréscia Italy **51** C6 45 33N 10 13E
Bressay *i.* Scotland **29** D3 60 08N 1 05W
Brest Belarus **42** L6 52 08N 23 40E
Brest France **48** A4 48 23N 4 30W
Bridgend Wales **36** D1 51 31N 3 35W
Bridgend *u.a.* Wales **36** D1 51 32N 3 35W
Bridgnorth England **37** E2 52 33N 2 25W
Bridgwater England **41** D4 51 15N 3 00W
Bridgwater Bay England **41** D4 51 15N 3 20W
Bridlington England **35** D3 54 05N 0 12W
Bridport England **41** E3 50 44N 2 46W
Brigg England **35** E2 53 34N 0 30W
Brighouse England **34** D2 53 42N 1 47W
Brighton England **38** D1 50 50N 0 10W
Brindisi Italy **51** F4 40 37N 17 57E
Brisbane Australia **72** F3 27 28S 153 03E
Bristol England **38** B2 51 27N 2 35W
Bristol Channel United Kingdom **36** C1/D1 51 20N 3 50W
British Columbia *province* Canada **78** G6 55 00N 128 00W
Brittany *geog. reg.* France **48** B4 48 00N 3 00W
Brive France **48** D2 45 09N 1 32E
Brixham England **40** D3 50 23N 3 30W
Brno Czech Republic **42** K5 49 13N 16 40E
Broad Bay Scotland **30** C3 58 15N 6 10W
Broadford Scotland **30** D2 57 14N 5 54W
Broad Law *mt.* Scotland **33** F3 55 30N 3 22W
Broadway England **37** F2 52 02N 1 50W
Brodick Scotland **32** D3 55 35N 5 09W
Broken Hill *tn.* Australia **72** E2 31 57S 141 28E
Bromley England **39** E2 51 31N 0 01W
Bromsgrove England **37** E2 52 00N 2 03W
Bromyard England **37** E2 52 11N 2 30W
Brooks Range *mts.* U.S.A. **78** D7/E7 67 55N 155 00W
Broome Australia **72** C4 17 57S 122 13E
Brora Scotland **31** F3 58 01N 3 51W
Brough England **34** C3 54 32N 2 19W
Brough Head Scotland **29** B2 59 09N 3 19W
Brown Clee Hill England **37** E2 52 35N 2 36W
Brown Willy *sum.* England **40** C3 50 35N 4 36W
Bruges Belgium **49** B4 51 13N 3 14E
BRUNEI DARUSSALAM 60 C3
Brunswick Germany **49** F5 52 15N 10 30E
Brussels Belgium **49** C4 50 50N 4 21E
Bryansk Russia **56** D3 53 15N 34 09E
Bryher *i.* England **40** A2 49 57N 6 21W
Bucaramanga Colombia **84** B8 7 08N 73 10W
Buchan Ness *c.* Scotland **31** H2 57 28N 1 47W
Bucharest Romania **42** M4 44 25N 26 07E
Buckfastleigh England **40** D3 50 29N 3 46W
Buckhaven Scotland **33** F4 56 11N 3 03W
Buckie Scotland **31** G2 57 40N 2 58W
Buckingham England **38** D2 52 00N 1 00W
Buckinghamshire *co.* England **38** D2 51 50N 0 50W
Budapest Hungary **42** K5 47 30N 19 03E
Bude England **40** C3 50 50N 4 33W
Bude Bay England **40** C3 50 50N 4 40W
Buenaventura Colombia **84** B8 3 54N 77 02W
Buenos Aires Argentina **85** D4 34 40S 58 30W
Buffalo U.S.A. **79** M5 42 52N 78 55W
Builth Wells Wales **36** D2 52 09N 3 24W
Bujumbura Burundi **67** C4 3 22S 29 19E
Bukavu Zaïre **67** C4 2 30S 28 50E
Bukhara Uzbekistan **56** G1 39 47N 64 26E
Bulawayo Zimbabwe **67** C2 20 10S 28 43E
BULGARIA 42 M4
Bunbury Australia **72** B2 33 20S 115 39E
Buncrana Donegal Republic of Ireland **32** B3 55 08N 7 27W
Bundaberg Australia **72** F3 24 53S 152 21E
Bungay England **39** F3 52 28N 1 26E
Buraida Saudi Arabia **61** E3 26 20N 43 59E
Bure *r.* England **39** F3 52 47N 1 20E
Burgas Bulgaria **42** M4 42 30N 27 29E

Burghead *tn.* Scotland **31** F2 57 42N 3 30W
Burgos Spain **50** D5 42 21N 3 41W
Burgundy *geog. reg.* France **48** F3 47 00N 5 00E
BURKINA 66 B4
BURMA *see* MYANMAR
Burnie Australia **72** E1 41 03S 145 55E
Burnley England **34** C2 53 48N 2 14W
Burry Port Wales **36** C1 51 42N 4 15W
Bursa Turkey **42** M4 40 12N 29 04E
Burton upon Trent England **37** F2 52 48N 1 36W
Buru *i.* Indonesia **60** D2 3 30S 126 30E
BURUNDI 67 C4
Bury England **34** C2 53 36N 2 17W
Bury St. Edmunds England **39** E3 52 15N 0 43E
Bush *r.* Northern Ireland **32** C3 55 10N 6 30W
Bute *i.* Scotland **32** D3 55 50N 5 05W
Bute, Sound of Scotland **32** D3 55 45N 5 10W
Butt of Lewis *c.* Scotland **30** C3 58 30N 6 20W
Butuan The Philippines **60** D3 8 56N 125 31E
Butung *i.* Indonesia **60** D2 5 00S 122 45E
Buxton England **37** F3 53 16N 1 55W
Bydgoszcz Poland **42** K6 53 16N 18 00E

C

Cabanatuan The Philippines **60** D4 15 30N 120 58E
Cabinda *province* Angola **66** D2 5 00S 12 00E
Cabora Bassa, Lake Mozambique **67** D3 15 40S 31 40E
Cabrera *i.* Balearic Islands **50** G3 39 00N 2 59E
Cader Idris *mt.* Wales **36** C2 52 42N 3 54W
Cádiz Spain **50** B2 36 32N 6 18W
Caen France **48** C4 49 11N 0 22W
Caernarfon Wales **36** C3 53 08N 4 16W
Caernarfon Bay Wales **36** C3 53 05N 4 30W
Caernarfonshire and Merionethshire *u.a.* Wales **36** C2/D2 52 50N 3 54W
Caerphilly Wales **36** D1 51 35N 3 14W
Caerphilly *u.a.* Wales **36** D1 51 37N 3 5W
Cagayan de Oro The Philippines **60** D3 8 29N 124 40E
Cágliari Italy **51** B3 39 N 9 08E
Cairn Gorm *mt.* Scotland **31** F2 57 07N 3 40W
Cairngorms *mts.* Scotland **31** F2 57 10N 3 30W
Cairns Australia **72** E4 16 54S 145 45E
Cairo Egypt **61** D4 30 03N 31 15E
Calais France **48** D5 50 57N 1 52E
Cala Ratjada Balearic Islands **50** G3 39 43N 3 27E
Calatayud Spain **50** E4 41 21N 1 39W
Calbayog The Philippines **60** D4 12 04N 124 38E
Calcutta India **58** D3 22 30N 88 20E
Calgary Canada **78** H6 51 05N 114 05W
Cali Colombia **84** B8 3 24N 76 30W
Calicut India **58** C2 11 15N 75 45E
California *state* U.S.A. **79** H4 35 00N 119 00W
California, Gulf of Mexico **79** D3/D4 28 00N 111 00W
Callander Scotland **33** E4 56 15N 4 13W
Callao Peru **84** B6 12 05S 77 08W
Calligarry Scotland **30** C2 57 02N 5 58W
Calne England **38** B2 51 26N 2 00W
Cam *r.* England **39** E3 52 15N 0 15W
Camagüey Cuba **79** M3 21 25N 77 55W
Camberley England **38** D2 51 21N 0 45W
CAMBODIA 60 B4
Camborne England **40** B3 50 12N 5 19W
Cambrai France **48** E5 50 10N 3 14E
Cambrian Mountains Wales **36** D2 52 15N 3 45W
Cambridge England **39** E3 52 12N 0 07E
Cambridgeshire *co.* England **38/39** D3/E 52 30N 0 00
Camel *r.* England **40** C3 50 30N 4 45W
CAMEROON 66 D3
Cameroon, Mount Cameroon **66** C3 4 13N 9 10E
Campbeltown Scotland **32** D3 55 26N 5 36W
Campina Grande Brazil **84** F7 7 15S 35 50W
Campinas Brazil **84** E5 22 54S 47 06W
Campo Grande Brazil **84** D5 20 24S 54 35W
Campos Brazil **84** E5 21 46S 41 21W
Campsie Fells *hills* Scotland **33** E4 56 00N 4 15W
CANADA 78
Canary Islands Spain **66** A5 28 30N 15 10W
Canaveral, Cape U.S.A. **79** L3 28 28N 80 28W
Canberra Australia **72** E2 35 17S 149 09E
Canisp *mt.* Scotland **31** D3 58 07N 5 03W
Canna *i.* Scotland **30** C2 57 06N 6 35W
Cannes France **48** G1 43 33N 7 00E
Cannock England **37** E2 52 42N 2 01W
Cantabrian Mountains Spain **50** B5/C5 43 00N 5 30W
Canterbury England **39** F2 51 17N 1 05E
Canterbury Bight *b.* New Zealand **73** C2 44 00S 172 00E
Canterbury Plains New Zealand **73** C2 43 45S 171 56E
Can Tho Vietnam **60** B4 10 03N 105 46E
Canton *see* Guangzhou
Cap de la Hague *c.* France **41** F2 49 44N 1 56W
Cape Town Republic of South Africa **67** B1 33 56S 18 28E
CAPE VERDE 4
Cap Gris-Nez *c.* France **39** F1 50 52N 1 35E
Caracas Venezuela **84** C9 10 35N 66 56W
Carcassonne France **48** E1 43 13N 2 21E
Cardiff Wales **36** D1 51 30N 3 13W
Cardiff *u.a.* Wales **36** D1 51 32N 3 14W
Cardigan Wales **36** C2 52 06N 4 40W
Cardigan Bay Wales **36** C2 52 30N 4 30W
Cardiganshire *u.a.* Wales **36** C2/D2 52 20N 4 00W
Carentan France **41** F2 49 18N 1 14W
Caribbean Sea Central America **79** M2 15 00N 75 00W
Carlingford Lough *est.* Northern Ireland/
Republic of Ireland **32** C2 54 05N 6 10W
Carlisle England **34** C2 54 54N 2 55W
Carmarthen Wales **36** C1 51 51N 4 20W
Carmarthen Bay Wales **36** C1 51 40N 4 30W
Carmarthenshire *u.a.* Wales **36** C1/D1 51 55N 4 00W
Carmel Head Wales **36** C3 53 24N 4 35W
Carnarvon Australia **72** B3 24 53S 113 40E
Carn Eige *mt.* Scotland **31** D2 57 22N 5 07W
Carnforth England **34** C3 54 08N 2 46W
Carnoustie Scotland **31** G1 56 30N 2 44W
Carpathians *mts.* Europe **42** L5/M5 49 00N 22 00E
Carpentaria, Gulf of Australia **72** D4 14 39S 139 11E
Carrickfergus Northern Ireland **32** D2 54 43N 5 49W

Carrickfergus *district* Northern Ireland **32** D2 54 40N 5 50W
Cartagena Colombia **84** B9 10 24N 75 33W
Cartagena Spain **50** E2 37 36N 0 59W
Carteret France **41** F2 49 22N 1 48W
Casablanca Morocco **66** B6 33 39N 7 35W
Caspian Sea Asia **56** F2 41 00N 50 00E
Cassel France **39** G1 50 48N 2 28E
Cassino Italy **51** D4 41 29N 13 50E
Castlebay Scotland **30** B1 56 57N 7 28W
Castleblaney Monaghan Republic of Ireland **32** C2 54 07N 6 44W
Castle Douglas Scotland **33** F2 54 57N 3 56W
Castleford England **35** D2 43 44N 1 21W
Castlereagh *district* Northern Ireland **32** D2 54 35N 5 50W
Castletown Isle of Man British Isles **33** E2 54 04N 4 38W
Castrovillari Italy **51** F3 39 48N 16 12E
Catánia Italy **51** E2 37 31N 15 06E
Catanzaro Italy **51** F3 38 54N 16 36E
Cat Island The Bahamas **79** M3 24 30N 75 30W
Cauca *r.* Colombia **84** B7 8 00N 75 00W
Caucasus *mts.* Asia **56** E2 43 00N 43 00E
Cavan Cavan Republic of Ireland **32** B1 53 58N 7 21W
Caxias do Sul Brazil **85** D5 29 14S 51 10W
Cayenne French Guiana **84** D8 4 55N 52 18W
Cayman Islands Caribbean Sea **79** L2 19 20N 81 15W
Cebollera *mt.* Spain **50** D4 42 00N 2 40W
Cebu The Philippines **60** D4 10 17N 123 56E
Celebes Sea Indonesia **60** D3 3 00N 122 00E
Cemaes Head Wales **36** C2 53 10N 4 50W
CENTRAL AFRICAN REPUBLIC 67 B5/C5
Central Siberian Plateau Russia **57** L4 65 00N 110 00E
Ceuta *territory* Spain **50** C1 35 53N 5 19W
CHAD 66 D4
Chad, Lake West Africa **66** D4 13 50N 14 00E
Chagos Archipelago *is.* Indian Ocean **5** 6 00S 72 00E
Châlons-sur-Marne France **48** F4 48 58N 4 22E
Chalon-sur-Saône France **48** F3 46 47N 4 51E
Chambéry France **48** F2 45 34N 5 55E
Changchun China **59** D4 43 50N 125 20E
Chang Jiang *(Yangtze)* *r.* China **59** C3 30 00N 116 00E
Changsha China **59** C2 28 10N 113 00E
Channel Islands British Isles **41** E2 49 30N 2 30W
Channel Tunnel United Kingdom/France **39** F1/2 5 00N 1 30E
Chard England **41** E3 50 53N 2 58W
Chardzhev Turkmenistan **56** G1 39 09N 63 34E
Chardzhou Turkmenistan **56** G1 39 09N 63 34E
Chari *r.* Chad/Sudan **66** D4 11 00N 16 00E
Charleroi Belgium **49** C4 50 25N 4 27E
Charlestown of Aberlour Scotland **31** F2 57 28N 3 14W
Charleville Australia **72** E3 26 24S 146 14E
Charleville France **48** F4 49 46N 4 43E
Charlotte U.S.A. **79** L4 35 03N 80 50W
Charters Towers Australia **72** E3 20 04S 146 16E
Chartres France **48** D4 48 27N 1 30E
Châteauroux France **48** D3 46 49N 1 41E
Chatham England **39** E2 51 23N 0 32E
Cheadle England **34** C2 53 24N 2 13W
Cheb Czech Republic **49** G4 50 08N 12 28E
Cheboksary Russia **56** E3 56 08N 47 12E
Chelmsford England **39** E2 51 44N 0 28E
Cheltenham England **38** B2 51 54N 2 04W
Chelyabinsk Russia **56** G3 55 12N 61 25E
Chemnitz Germany **49** G4 50 50N 12 55E
Chengdu China **59** B3 30 37N 104 06E
Cher *r.* France **48** D3 47 15N 1 30E
Cherbourg France **48** C4 49 38N 1 37W
Cherepovets Russia **43** P7 59 09N 37 50E
Cherkassy Ukraine **42** N5 49 27N 32 04E
Chernihiv Ukraine **42** N6 51 30N 31 18E
Chernivtsi Ukraine **42** M5 48 19N 25 52E
Cherwell *r.* England **38** C2 51 55N 1 20W
Cheshire *co.* England **34** C2 53 30N 2 30W
Cheshunt England **38** D2 51 43N 0 02W
Chester England **34** C2 53 12N 2 54W
Chesterfield England **37** F3 53 15N 1 25W
Chester-le-Street England **34** D3 54 52N 1 34W
Cheviot Hills England/Scotland **33** G3 55 25N 2 20W
Cheviot, The *sum.* England **33** G3 55 29N 2 20W
Cheyenne U.S.A. **79** J5 41 08N 104 50W
Chiang Mai Thailand **60** A4 18 48N 98 59E
Chiba Japan **59** N2 35 38N 140 07E
Chicago U.S.A. **79** L5 41 50N 87 45W
Chichester England **38** D1 50 50N 0 48W
Chiclayo Peru **84** B7 6 47S 79 47W
Chicoutimi Canada **79** M5 48 26N 71 06W
Chieti Italy **51** E5 42 21N 14 10E
Chihuahua Mexico **79** J3 28 40N 106 06W
CHILE 84/85 B6/C2
Chillán Chile **85** B4 36 37S 72 10W
Chiloé Island Chile **85** B3 42 30S 74 00W
Chiltern Hills England **38** C2/D2 51 40N 1 00W
Chimbote Peru **84** B7 9 04S 78 34W
CHINA 59
Chippenham England **38** B2 51 28N 2 07W
Chipping Norton England **38** C2 51 56N 1 32W
Chipping Sodbury England **38** B2 51 33N 2 24W
Chisinău *(Kishnev)* Moldova **42** M5 47 00N 28 50E
Chita Russia **57** M3 52 03N 113 35E
Chittagong Bangladesh **58** E3 22 20N 91 48E
Cholet France **48** C3 47 04N 0 53W
Chongjin North Korea **59** D4 41 50N 129 55E
Chongqing China **59** B2 29 30N 106 35E
Chorley England **34** C2 53 40N 2 38W
Christchurch England **41** F3 50 44N 1 45W
Christchurch New Zealand **73** C2 43 32S 172 38E
Christmas Island Indian Ocean **60** B1 10 28S 105 35E
Churchill Canada **78** K6 58 45N 94 00W
Churchill Falls *tn.* Canada **78** N6 53 35N 64 00W
Cincinnati U.S.A. **79** L4 39 10N 83 30W
Cirencester England **38** C2 51 44N 1 59W
Citlaltépetl *mt.* Mexico **79** K2 19 00N 97 18W
City of Bristol *u.a.* England **38** B2 51 30N 2 30W
City of Edinburgh *u.a.* Scotland **33** F3 55 57N 3 15W
City of Glasgow *u.a.* Scotland **33** E3 55 50N 4 20W

City of Kingston upon Hull *u.a.* England **35** E2 53 45N 0 25W
Ciudad Bolívar Venezuela **84** C8 8 06N 63 36W
Ciudad Balearic Islands 50 G3 40 00N 3 50E
Ciudad Guayana Venezuela **84** C8 8 22N 62 37W
Ciudad Juárez Mexico **79** J4 31 42N 106 29W
Ciudad Obregón Mexico **79** J3 27 28N 109 59W
Ciudad Rodrigo Spain **50** B4 40 36N 6 33W
Clachan Scotland **32** D3 55 45N 5 34W
Clackmannanshire *u.a.* England **33** F4 56 10N 3 40W
Clacton on Sea England **39** F2 51 48N 1 09E
Claonaig Scotland **32** D3 55 46N 5 22W
Cleethorpes England **35** E2 53 34N 0 02W
Clermont-Ferrand France **48** E2 45 47N 3 05E
Clevedon England **38** B2 51 27N 2 51W
Cleveland Hills England **35** D3 54 25N 1 15W
Clisham *mt.* Scotland **30** C2 57 58N 6 50W
Clitheroe England **34** C2 53 53N 2 23W
Clones Monaghan Republic of Ireland **32** B2 54 11N 7 15W
Cluj-Napoca Romania **42** L5 46 47N 23 37E
Clutha *r.* New Zealand **73** B1 46 00S 169 30E
Clwyd *r.* Wales **36** D3 53 15N 3 25W
Clyde *r.* Scotland **33** F3 55 45N 3 55W
Clydebank Scotland **33** E3 55 54N 4 24W
Coalisland Northern Ireland **32** C2 54 32N 6 42W
Coalville England **37** F2 52 44N 1 20W
Coast Mountains Canada **78** G6 58 50N 132 40W
Coatbridge Scotland **33** E3 55 52N 4 01W
Coburg Germany **49** F4 50 15N 10 58E
Cochabamba Bolivia **84** C6 17 26S 66 10W
Cochin India **58** C1 9 56N 76 15E
Cockermouth England **34** B3 54 40N 3 21W
Cognac France **48** C2 45 42N 0 19W
Coimbatore India **58** C2 11 00N 76 57E
Coimbra Portugal **50** A4 40 12N 8 25W
Colchester England **39** E2 51 54N 0 54E
Coldstream *tn.* Scotland **33** G3 55 39N 2 15W
Coleraine Northern Ireland **32** C3 55 08N 6 40W
Coleraine *district* Northern Ireland **32** C3 55 00N 6 40W
Coll *i.* Scotland **30** C1 56 40N 6 35W
Colmar France **48** G4 48 05N 7 21E
Colne England **34** C2 53 52N 2 09W
Colne *r.* England **39** E2 51 53N 0 45E
Cologne Germany **49** D4 50 56N 6 57E
COLOMBIA 84 B8
Colombo Sri Lanka **58** C1 6 55N 79 52E
Colonsay *i.* Scotland **30** C2 56 05N 6 15W
Colorado *r.* Argentina **85** C4 37 30S 69 00W
Colorado *r.* U.S.A./Mexico **79** D4 30 00N 109 00W
Colorado *state* U.S.A. **79** J4 39 00N 106 00W
Columbia U.S.A. **79** L4 34 00N 81 00W
Columbia *r.* Canada/U.S.A. **78** H6 50 30N 119 00W
Columbus U.S.A. **79** L4 39 59N 83 03W
Colwyn Bay *tn.* Wales **36** D3 53 18N 3 43W
Communism Peak Tajikistan **56** H1 38 59N 72 01E
Como Italy **51** B6 45 48N 9 05E
Comodoro Rivadavia Argentina **85** C3 45 50S 67 30W
Como, Lake Italy **51** B6/7 46 00N 9 00E
COMOROS 67 E3
Conakry Guinea **66** A3 9 30N 13 43W
Concepción Chile **85** B4 36 50S 73 03W
Conejara *i.* Balearic Islands **50** G3 39 11N 2 58E
CONGO 66 D2
CONGO DEMOCRATIC REPUBLIC 67 C4
Congo *r.* Africa **67** B4 3 00S 16 00E
Coniston Water *l.* England **34** B3 54 20N 3 05W
Connecticut *state* U.S.A. **79** M5 41 00N 73 00W
Consett England **34** D3 54 51N 1 49W
Constance, Lake Europe **49** E2 47 40N 9 30E
Constanta Romania **42** M4 44 12N 28 40E
Constantine Algeria **66** C6 36 22N 6 40E
Conwy Wales **36** D3 53 17N 3 50W
Conwy *r.* Wales **36** D3 53 20N 3 55W
Cook Islands Pacific Ocean **4** 19 30S 159 50W
Cook, Mount New Zealand **73** C2 43 36S 170 09E
Cookstown Northern Ireland **32** C2 54 39N 6 45W
Cookstown *district* Northern Ireland **32** C2 54 35N 6 55W
Cook Strait New Zealand **73** C2 41 24S 174 36E
Cooktown Australia **72** E4 15 28S 145 15E
Cooper Creek Australia **72** E3 26 10S 142 20E
Copenhagen Denmark **42** J5 55 43N 12 34E
Coquet *r.* England **33** H3 55 20N 1 50W
Coral Sea Pacific Ocean **72** F4 15 00S 154 00E
Corby England **38** D2 52 49N 0 32W
Córdoba Argentina **85** C4 31 25S 64 11W
Córdoba Spain **50** C2 37 53N 4 46W
Corfu Greece **42** K3 39 00N 19 00E
Cornwall *co.* England **40** B3/C3 50 25N 4 50W
Corpus Christi U.S.A. **79** K3 27 47N 97 26W
Corrientes Argentina **85** D5 27 30S 58 48W
Corsewall Point Scotland **32** D3 55 00N 5 10W
Corsica *i.* France **51** B5 42 00N 9 00E
Cosenza Italy **51** F3 39 17N 16 16E
Costa Brava *geog. reg.* Spain **50** G4/5 41 40N 3 50E
Costa del Sol *geog. reg.* Spain **50** C2/D2 36 40N 4 40W
COSTA RICA 79 L1
CÔTE D'IVOIRE 66 B3
Cotonou Benin **66** C3 6 24N 2 31E
Cotopaxi *vol.* Ecuador **84** B7 0 40S 78 28W
Cotswold Hills England **38** B2/C2 51 40N 2 10W
Cottbus Germany **49** H4 51 43N 14 21E
Coupar Angus Scotland **31** F1 56 33N 3 17W
Coutainville France **41** F2 49 03N 1 34W
Coutances France **48** C4 49 03N 1 29W
Coventry England **37** F2 52 25N 1 30W
Cowes England **38** C1 50 45N 1 18W
Craigavon Northern Ireland **32** C2 54 28N 6 25W
Craigavon *district* Northern Ireland **32** C2 54 30N 6 30W
Craighouse Scotland **32** D3 55 51N 5 57W
Craignure Scotland **30** D2 56 28N 5 42W
Crail Scotland **33** G4 56 16N 2 38W
Craiova Romania **42** L4 44 18N 23 47E
Cramlington England **33** H3 55 05N 1 35W
Crawley England **38** D2 51 07N 0 12W
Crediton England **40** D3 50 47N 3 39W

Cree *r.* Scotland **33** E3 55 00N 4 30W
Creeslough Republic of Ireland **32** B3 55 07N 7 55W
Cremona Italy **51** C6 45 08N 10 01E
Crete *i.* Greece **42** M3 35 00N 25 00E
Crewe England **34** C2 53 05N 2 27W
Crewkerne England **41** E3 50 53N 2 48W
Crianlarich Scotland **31** E1 56 23N 4 37W
Crieff Scotland **31** F1 56 23N 3 52W
Crimea *p.* Ukraine **43** N5 46 00N 34 00E
CROATIA 42 K5
Cromarty Scotland **31** E2 57 40N 4 02W
Cromarty Firth *est.* Scotland **31** E2 57 40N 4 20W
Cromer England **39** F3 52 56N 1 18E
Cross Fell *sum.* England **34** C3 54 43N 2 29W
Crossmaglen Northern Ireland **32** C2 54 05N 6 37W
Crotone Italy **51** F3 39 05N 17 08E
Croydon England **38** D2 51 23N 0 06W
Crumlin Northern Ireland **32** C2 54 37N 6 14W
Cruzeiro do Sul Brazil **84** B7 7 40S 72 39W
Cuanza *r.* Angola **67** B4 9 40S 15 00E
CUBA 79 M3
Cubango *r.* Southern Africa **67** B3 17 00S 18 00E
Cúcuta Colombia **84** B8 7 55N 73 31W
Cuenca Ecuador **84** B7 2 54S 79 00W
Cuiabá Brazil **84** D6 15 32S 56 05W
Cuillin Hills Scotland **30** C2 57 15N 6 15W
Culiacán Mexico **79** J3 24 50N 107 23W
Cullen Scotland **31** G2 57 41N 2 49W
Cullompton England **40** D3 50 52N 3 24W
Cumaná Venezuela **84** C9 10 29N 64 12W
Cumbernauld Scotland **33** F3 55 57N 4 00W
Cumbria *co.* England **34** B3/C3 54 30N 2 50W
Cumnock Scotland **33** E3 55 27N 4 16W
Cunene *r.* Angola/Namibia **67** B3 17 00S 15 00E
Cuneo Italy **51** A6 44 24N 7 33E
Cunnamulla Australia **72** E3 28 03S 145 43E
Cupar Scotland **33** F4 56 19N 3 01W
Curaçao *i.* Lesser Antilles **79** N2 12 20N 68 20W
Curitiba Brazil **85** E5 25 25S 49 25W
Cuttack India **58** D3 20 26N 85 56E
Cuzco Peru **84** B6 13 32S 1 57W
Cwmbran Wales **36** D1 51 39N 3 00W
CYPRUS 43 N2
CZECH REPUBLIC 42 K5
Częstochowa Poland **42** K6 50 49N 19 07E

D

Daer Reservoir Scotland **33** F3 55 25N 3 30W
Dakar Senegal **66** A4 14 38N 17 27W
Dalbeattie Scotland **33** F2 54 56N 3 49W
Dalian China **59** D3 38 53N 121 37E
Dallas U.S.A. **79** K4 32 47N 96 48W
Dalmally Scotland **31** E1 56 24N 4 58W
Dal *r.* Sweden **42** K8 60 30N 15 30E
Dalton-in-Furness England **34** B3 54 09N 3 11W
Daly *r.* Australia **72** D4 13 30S 130 30E
Damascus Syria **61** D4 33 30N 36 19E
Dammam Saudi Arabia **61** F3 26 25N 50 06E
Da Nang Vietnam **60** B4 16 04N 108 14E
Danube *r.* Europe **42** L4 44 00N 25 00E
Dar es Salaam Tanzania **67** D4 6 51S 39 18E
Darfur *mts.* Sudan **61** C2 12 40N 24 20E
Dargaville New Zealand **73** C3 35 56S 173 52E
Darling *r.* Australia **72** E2 31 00S 144 00E
Darlington England **34** D3 54 31N 1 34W
Darmstadt Germany **49** E3 49 52N 8 39E
Darnah Libya **42** L2 32 46N 22 39E
Dart *r.* England **40** D3 50 30N 3 50W
Dartford England **39** E2 51 27N 0 13E
Dartmoor *geog. reg.* England **40** D3 50 35N 3 50W
Dartmouth England **40** D3 50 21N 3 35W
Darvel Scotland **33** E3 55 37N 4 18W
Darwin Australia **72** D4 12 24S 130 52E
Daugava *r.* Belarus **42** M7 55 00N 29 00E
Daugavpils Latvia **42** M7 55 52N 26 31E
Dauphine *geog. reg.* France **48** F2 45 00N 5 00E
Davao The Philippines **60** D3 7 05N 125 38E
Daventry England **38** C3 52 16N 1 09W
Dawlish England **40** D3 50 35N 3 28W
Dawson Canada **78** F7 64 04N 139 24W
Deal England **39** F2 51 14N 1 24E
Debrecen Hungary **42** L5 47 30N 21 37E
Deccan *plat.* India **58** C2 18 00N 78 00E
Dee *r.* Aberdeenshire/Aberdeen City Scotland **31** G2 57 05N 2 10W
Dee *r.* Dumfries and Galloway Scotland **33** E2/F2 54 55N 4 00W
Dee *r.* England/Wales **36** D3 53 20N 3 10W
Deeps, The *b.* Scotland **29** D3 60 10N 1 25W
Delaware *state* U.S.A. **79** M4 39 00N 75 00W
Delhi India **58** C3 28 40N 77 14E
Demavend, Mount Iran **61** F4 35 56N 52 08E
Denbigh Wales **36** D3 53 11N 3 26W
Denbighshire *u.a.* Wales **36** D3 53 10N 3 10W
Denizli Turkey **42** M3 37 46N 29 05E
DENMARK 42 H7
Denver U.S.A. **79** J4 39 45N 105 00W
De Panne Belgium **39** G2 51 06N 2 35E
Derby Australia **72** C4 17 18S 123 37E
Derby England **37** F2 52 55N 1 30W
Derbyshire *co.* England **37** F3 52 55N 1 30W
Derg *r.* Northern Ireland **32** B2 54 40N 7 45E
Derwent *r.* Cumbria England **34** B3 54 40N 3 30W
Derwent *r.* Derbyshire England **37** F3 52 55N 1 40W
Derwent *r.* Northumberland/Durham/Tyne and Wear England **34** D3 54 50N 2 05W
Derwent *r.* North Yorkshire/York/East Riding of Yorkshire England **35** E2 53 50N 0 55W
Derwent Water *l.* England **34** B3 54 35N 3 09W
Des Moines U.S.A. **79** K5 41 35N 93 35W
Dessau Germany **49** G4 51 51N 12 15E
Detroit U.S.A. **79** L5 42 23N 83 05W
Deveron *r.* Scotland **31** G2 57 35N 2 40W
Devizes England **38** C2 51 22N 1 59W
Devon *co.* England **40** C3/D3 50 45N 3 50W
Devon Island Canada **78** L8 75 41N 88 00W
Dewsbury England **34** D2 53 42N 1 37W
Dezful Iran **61** E4 32 23N 48 28E
Dhaka Bangladesh **58** E3 23 42N 90 22E

Dibrugarh India 58 E3 27 29N 94 56E
Didcot England 38 C2 51 37N 1 15W
Dieppe France 48 D4 49 55N 1 05E
Dijon France 48 F3 47 20N 5 02E
Dili Indonesia 60 D2 8 33S 125 34E
Dingwall Scotland 31 E2 57 35N 4 29W
Diredawa Ethiopia 61 E1 9 35N 41 50E
Diss England 39 F3 52 23N 1 06W
Diyarbakir Turkey 43 Q3 37 55N 40 14E
Djelfa Algeria 42 G2 34 43N 3 14E
DJIBOUTI 61 E2
Djibouti Djibouti 61 E2 11 35N 43 11E
Dnieper r. Ukraine/Belarus 56 D3 51 00N 30 00E
Dniestr r. Europe 42 M5 48 00N 27 00E
Dnipropetrovsk Ukraine 56 D2 48 29N 35 00E
Dodoma Tanzania 67 D4 6 10S 35 40E
Doha Qatar 61 F3 25 15N 51 36E
Dolgellau Wales 36 D2 52 44N 3 53W
Dolomites mts. Italy 49 F2 46 00N 12 00E
DOMINICA 79 N2
DOMINICAN REPUBLIC 79 M2
Don r. Russia 56 E3 50 00N 40 30E
Don r. Scotland 31 G2 57 15N 2 10W
Donaghadee Northern Ireland 32 D2 54 39N 5 33W
Doncaster England 35 D2 53 32N 1 07W
Donegal Republic of Ireland 32 A2 54 39N 8 07W
Donegal co. Republic of Ireland 32 A2/B2 54 55N 8 00W
Donets r. Asia 43 P5 49 00N 39 00E
Donetsk Ukraine 56 D2 48 00N 37 50E
Dongting Hu l. China 59 C2 29 00N 113 30E
Doon r. Scotland 33 E3 55 20N 4 30W
Dorchester England 41 E3 50 43N 2 26W
Dordogne r. France 48 D2 45 00N 1 30E
Dordrecht Netherlands 49 C4 51 48N 4 40E
Dorking England 38 D2 51 14N 0 20W
Dornoch Scotland 31 E2 57 52N 4 02W
Dornoch Firth est. Scotland 31 E2 57 55N 3 55W
Dorset co. England 41 E3 50 50N 2 20W
Dortmund Germany 49 D4 51 32N 7 27E
Douai France 48 E5 50 22N 3 05E
Douala Cameroon 66 C3 4 04N 9 43E
Douglas Isle of Man British Isles 33 E2 54 09N 4 29W
Douro r. Spain/Portugal 50 B4 41 30N 6 30W
Dove r. England 37 F3 53 10N 1 50W
Dover England 39 F2 51 08N 1 19E
Dover, Strait of English Channel 39 F1/2 51 00N 1 20W
Down district Northern Ireland 32 D2 54 25N 5 55W
Downham Market England 39 E3 52 36N 0 23E
Downpatrick Northern Ireland 32 D2 54 20N 5 43W
Drakensberg mts. Republic of South Africa 67 C2 30 00S 28 00E
Drava r. Europe 49 G2 46 45N 13 30E
Dresden Germany 49 G4 51 03N 13 45E
Droitwich England 37 E2 52 16N 2 09W
Dromore Northern Ireland 32 C2 54 25N 6 09W
Drummore Scotland 32 E2 54 42N 4 54W
Drumnadrochit Scotland 31 E2 57 20N 4 30W
Dubai United Arab Emirates 61 F3 25 14N 55 17E
Dubbo Australia 72 E2 32 15S 148 38E
Dublin Dublin Republic of Ireland 36 A3 53 20N 6 15W
Dubrovnik Croatia 42 K4 42 40N 18 07E
Dudley England 37 E2 52 30N 2 05W
Dufftown Scotland 31 F2 57 26N 3 08W
Duisburg Germany 49 D4 51 26N 6 45E
Duluth U.S.A. 79 K5 46 45N 92 10W
Dumbarton Scotland 33 E3 55 57N 4 35W
Dumbarton and Clydebank u.a. Scotland 33 E3/4 56 03N 4 30W
Dumfries Scotland 33 F3 55 04N 3 37W
Dumfries and Galloway u.a. Scotland 33 E3/F3 55 10N 4 00W
Dunbar Scotland 33 G4 56 00N 2 31W
Dunblane Scotland 33 F4 56 12N 3 59W
Duncansby Head c. Scotland 29 B1 58 39N 3 02W
Dundalk Republic of Ireland 32 C2 54 01N 6 25W
Dundee Scotland 31 G1 56 28N 3 00W
Dundee City u.a. Scotland 31 F1/G1 56 30N 2 55W
Dunedin New Zealand 73 C1 45 53S 170 30E
Dunfermline Scotland 33 F4 56 04N 3 29W
Dungannon Northern Ireland 32 C2 54 31N 6 46W
Dungannon district Northern Ireland 32 B2/C2 54 30N 7 00W
Dungeness c. England 39 E1 50 55N 0 58E
Dungiven Northern Ireland 32 C2 54 55N 6 55W
Dunkerque France 39 G2 51 02N 2 23E
Dunkery Beacon sum. England 40 D4 51 11N 3 35W
Dunkirk France 48 E5 51 02N 2 23E
Dún Laoghaire Dublin Republic of Ireland 36 A3 53 17N 6 08W
Dunnett Head Scotland 29 B1 58 40N 3 25W
Dunoon Scotland 32 E3 55 57N 4 56W
Duns Scotland 33 G3 55 47N 2 20W
Dunstable England 38 D2 51 53N 0 32W
Dunvegan Scotland 30 C2 57 26N 6 35W
Durance r. France 48 F1 43 50N 5 15E
Durango Mexico 79 J3 24 01N 104 40W
Durban Republic of South Africa 67 D2 29 53S 31 00E
Durham England 34 D3 54 47N 1 34W
Durham co. England 34 C3/D3 54 40N 2 00W
Dursley England 37 E1 51 42N 2 21W
Dushanbe Tajikistan 56 G1 38 38N 68 51E
Düsseldorf Germany 49 D4 51 13N 6 47E
Dyce Scotland 31 G2 57 12N 2 11W
Dyfi r. Wales 36 D2 52 38N 3 50W

E

Ealing England 38 D2 51 31N 0 18W
Earn r. Scotland 31 F1 56 15N 3 40W
East Ayrshire u.a. Scotland 33 E3 55 35N 4 15W
Eastbourne England 39 E1 50 46N 0 17E
East Cape New Zealand 73 D3 37 41S 178 33E
East Dereham England 39 E3 52 41N 0 56E
East Dunbartonshire u.a. Scotland 33 E3 55 55N 4 15W
Eastern Rift Valley East Africa 67 D4/5 4 00N 36 00E
East Friesian Islands Netherlands 49 D5 53 00N 7 00E
East Kilbride Scotland 33 E3 55 46N 4 10W
Eastleigh England 38 C1 50 58N 1 22W

East London Republic of South Africa 67 C1 33 00S 27 54E
East Lothian u.a. Scotland 33 G3 55 56N 2 42W
East Renfrewshire u.a. Scotland 33 E3 55 45N 4 25E
East Riding of Yorkshire u.a. England 35 E2 53 54N 0 40W
East Sussex co. England 39 E1 50 55N 0 10E
Ebbw Vale Wales 36 D1 51 47N 3 12W
Ebro r. Spain 50 E4 42 00N 1 15W
Ech Cheliff Algeria 42 G3 36 05N 1 15E
ECUADOR 84 B7
Eday i. Scotland 29 C2 59 11N 2 47W
Eddrachillis Bay Scotland 30 D3 58 25N 5 15W
Eden r. Cumbria England 34 C3 54 45N 2 40W
Eden r. Surrey/Kent England 38 D2 51 10N 0 05E
Edinburgh Scotland 33 F3 55 57N 3 13W
Edirne Turkey 42 M4 41 40N 26 35E
Edmonton Canada 78 H6 53 34N 113 25W
Edward, Lake Zaïre/Uganda 67 C4 0 30S 29 00E
EGYPT 61 C3
Eigg i. Scotland 30 C1 56 55N 6 10W
Eindhoven Netherlands 49 C4 51 26N 5 30E
El Aaiun Western Sahara 66 A5 27 10N 13 11W
Elâzig Turkey 43 P3 38 41N 39 14E
Elba i. Italy 51 C5 42 00N 10 00E
Elbe r. Europe 49 F5 53 15N 10 00E
Elbrus, Mount Russia 43 Q4 43 21N 42 29E
Elche Spain 50 E3 38 16N 0 41W
Eleuthera i. The Bahamas 79 M3 25 05N 76 30W
El Faiyum Egypt 61 D3 29 19N 30 50E
El Fasher Sudan 61 C2 13 37N 25 22E
Elgin Scotland 31 F2 57 39N 3 20W
Elgol Scotland 30 C2 57 09N 6 06W
El Kharga Egypt 61 D3 25 27N 30 32E
Ellen r. England 34 B3 54 45N 3 25W
Ellesmere Island Canada 78 L8 77 30N 82 30W
Ellesmere Port England 34 C2 53 17N 2 54W
Ellon Scotland 31 G2 57 22N 2 05W
Ellsworth Land geog. reg. Antarctica 86 75 00S 80 00W
El Minya Egypt 61 D3 28 06N 30 45E
El Paso U.S.A. 79 J4 31 45N 106 30W
EL SALVADOR 79 L2
Elvas Portugal 50 B3 38 53N 7 10W
Ely England 39 E3 52 24N 0 16E
Emden Germany 49 D5 53 23N 7 13E
Emi Koussi mt. Chad 66 D4 19 52N 18 31E
Ems r. Germany 49 D5 53 00N 7 00E
Enard Bay Scotland 30 D3 58 10N 5 25W
Enfield England 38 D2 51 39N 0 05W
Engel's Russia 43 R6 51 30N 46 07E
Enggano i. Indonesia 60 B2 5 20S 102 20E
England country United Kingdom 28 53 00N 2 00W
English Channel United Kingdom/France 28 50 00N 2 00W
Enniskillen Northern Ireland 32 B2 54 21N 7 38W
Enschede Netherlands 49 D5 52 13N 6 55E
Entebbe Uganda 67 D5 0 04N 32 27E
Épinal France 48 G4 48 10N 6 28E
Epsom England 38 D2 51 20N 0 16W
EQUATORIAL GUINEA 66 D3
Erebus, Mount Antarctica 86 77 40S 167 20E
Erfurt Germany 49 F4 50 58N 11 02E
Erie, Lake Canada/U.S.A. 79 L5 42 15N 81 00W
Eriskay i. Scotland 30 B2 57 05N 7 10W
ERITREA 61 D2
Erlangen Germany 49 F4 49 36N 11 02E
Erne r. Northern Ireland/Republic of Ireland 32 B2 54 10N 7 30W
Errigal Mountain Republic of Ireland 32 A3 55 02N 8 07W
Erzurum Turkey 43 Q3 39 57N 41 17E
Esbjerg Denmark 42 H7 55 28N 8 28E
Esfahan Iran 61 F4 32 41N 51 41E
Esha Ness pt. Scotland 29 D3 60 29N 1 37W
Esk r. England 35 E3 54 30N 0 45W
Esk r. Scotland/England 33 F3 55 15N 3 05W
Eskisehir Turkey 43 N3 39 46N 30 30E
Esperance Australia 72 C2 33 51S 121 54E
Espoo Finland 42 L8 60 10N 24 40E
Esquel Argentina 85 B3 42 55S 71 20W
Essen Germany 49 D4 51 27N 6 57E
Essex co. England 39 E2 51 46N 0 30E
ESTONIA 42 M7
ETHIOPIA 61 E1
Ethiopian Highlands Africa 61 D1 8 00N 37 00E
Etna, Mount Italy 51 E2 37 45N 15 00E
Etosha Pan salt l. Namibia 67 B3 18 30S 16 30E
Eyre, Lake Australia 72 D3 28 43S 137 11E
Euphrates (Firat) r. Iraq/Syria/Turkey 61 D4/E4 35 00N 40 00E
Europa i. MOZAMBIQUE CHANNEL 67 E2 22 20S 40 20E
Everest, Mount China/Nepal 58 D3 27 59N 86 56E
Evesham England 37 F2 52 06N 1 56W
Evreux France 48 D4 49 03N 1 11E
Exe r. England 40 D4 51 10N 3 35W
Exeter England 40 D3 50 43N 3 31W
Exmoor geog. reg. England 40 D4 51 08N 3 40W
Exmouth England 40 D3 50 37N 3 25W
Eyemouth Scotland 33 G3 55 25N 2 06W
Eye Peninsula Scotland 30 C3 58 10N 6 10W

F

Faeroe Islands Atlantic Ocean 42 E8 62 00N 7 00W
Fairbanks U.S.A. 78 E7 64 50N 147 50W
Fair Head c. Northern Ireland 32 C3 55 15N 6 10W
Fair Isle i. Shetland Islands United Kingdom 29 D2 59 32N 1 38W
Faisalabad Pakistan 58 C4 31 25N 73 09E
Fakenham England 39 E3 52 50N 0 51E
Fal r. England 40 C3 50 15N 4 55W
Falkirk Scotland 33 F3 56 00N 3 48W
Falkirk u.a. Scotland 33 F3/4 56 05N 3 53W
Falkland Islands South Atlantic Ocean 85 D2 52 30S 60 00W
Falmouth England 40 B3 50 08N 5 04W
Falster i. Denmark 49 F6/G6 54 00N 12 00E
Fareham England 38 C1 50 51N 1 10W

Farewell, Cape Greenland 78 Q6 60 00N 44 00W
Farewell, Cape New Zealand 73 C2 40 30S 172 41E
Faringdon England 38 C2 51 40N 1 35W
Farnborough England 38 D2 51 17N 0 46W
Farnham England 38 D2 51 13N 0 49W
Faro Portugal 50 B2 37 01N 7 56W
Fawley England 38 C1 50 49N 1 20W
FEDERATED STATES OF MICRONESIA 5
Fehmarn i. Germany 49 F6 54 30N 11 00E
Feilding New Zealand 73 D2 40 14S 175 34E
Felixstowe England 39 F2 51 58N 1 20E
Fens, The geog. reg. England 35 E1/F1 52 45N 0 05E
Fergana Uzbekistan 56 H2 40 23N 71 19E
Fermanagh district Northern Ireland 32 B2 54 25N 7 45W
Ferrara Italy 51 C6 44 50N 11 38E
Fès Morocco 66 B6 34 05N 5 00W
Fethaland, Point of Scotland 29 D3 60 35N 1 18W
Fetlar i. Scotland 29 E3 60 37N 0 52W
Fife u.a. Scotland 33 F4/G4 56 10N 3 00W
Fiji 5
Filchner Ice Shelf Antarctica 86 80 00S 37 00W
Finke r. Australia 72 D3 25 00S 135 00E
FINLAND 42 M8
Finland, Gulf of Finland/Russia 42 L7 59 40N 23 30E
Finn r. Northern Ireland/Republic of Ireland 32 B2 54 50N 7 50W
Fionnphort Scotland 30 C1 56 19N 6 23W
Firat (Euphrates) r. Turkey/Syria/Iraq 43 P3 37 30N 38 00E
Firth of Clyde est. Scotland 32 E3 55 45N 5 00W
Firth of Forth est. Scotland 33 G4 56 05N 3 00W
Firth of Lorn est. Scotland 30 D1 56 15N 6 00W
Firth of Tay est. Scotland 31 F1 56 25N 3 00W
Fishguard Wales 36 C1 51 59N 4 59W
Fitzroy r. Australia 72 C4 17 00S 126 00E
Flamborough Head c. England 35 D3 54 06N 0 04W
Fleetwood England 34 B2 53 56N 3 01W
Flinders r. Australia 72 E3/4 20 00S 142 00E
Flinders Range Australia 72 D2 31 20S 138 45E
Flint Wales 36 D3 53 15N 3 07W
Flintshire u.a. Wales 36 D3 53 25N 3 10W
Florence Italy 51 C5 43 47N 11 15E
Flores i. Indonesia 60 D2 8 30S 121 00E
Flores Sea Indonesia 60 D2 7 00S 119 00E
Florianópolis Brazil 85 E5 27 35S 48 31W
Florida state U.S.A. 79 L3 28 00N 82 00W
Florida, Straits of sd. Cuba/U.S.A. 79 L3 24 00N 81 00W
Fly r. Papua New Guinea 72 E5 8 00S 142 00E
Fochabers Scotland 31 F2 57 37N 3 05W
Foggia Italy 51 E4 41 28N 15 33E
Folkestone England 39 F2 51 05N 1 11E
Fontainebleau France 48 E4 48 24N 2 42E
Forel, Mount Greenland 86 67 00N 37 00W
Forest of Bowland hills England 34 C2 54 00N 2 35W
Forfar Scotland 31 G1 56 38N 2 54W
Forli Italy 51 D6 44 13N 12 02E
Formby England 34 B2 53 34N 3 05W
Formentera i. Balearic Islands 50 F3 38 41N 1 30E
Fornells Balearic Islands 50 H3 40 04N 4 07E
Forres Scotland 31 F2 57 37N 3 38W
Fortaleza Brazil 84 F7 3 45S 38 35W
Fort Augustus Scotland 31 E2 57 09N 4 41W
Forth r. Scotland 33 E3 56 06N 4 18W
Fort McMurray Canada 79 J5 48 01N 106 28W
Fort Peck Reservoir U.S.A. 79 J5 48 01N 106 28W
Fort Simpson Canada 78 G7 61 46N 121 15W
Fort William Scotland 31 D2 56 49N 5 07W
Fort Worth U.S.A. 79 K4 32 45N 97 20W
Foula i. Scotland 29 C3 60 08N 2 05W
Foveaux Strait New Zealand 73 B1 46 42S 167 59E
Fowey England 40 C3 50 20N 4 38W
Fowey r. England 40 C3 50 25N 4 30W
Foyle r. Northern Ireland/Republic of Ireland 32 B2 54 58N 7 35W
FRANCE 48
Frankfurt Germany 49 E4 50 06N 8 41E
Franz Josef Land is. Russia 57 G8 80 00N 50 00E
Fraser r. Canada 78 G6 52 00N 122 00W
Fraserburgh Scotland 31 G2 57 42N 2 00W
Freetown Sierra Leone 66 A3 8 30N 13 17W
Freiburg Germany 49 D3 48 00N 7 52E
Fréjus France 48 G1 43 26N 6 44E
Fremantle Australia 72 B2 32 03S 115 46E
FRENCH GUIANA 84 D8
French Polynesia is. Pacific Ocean 4 21 00S 150 00W
Fresno U.S.A. 79 H4 36 41N 119 47W
Frome England 41 E4 51 14N 2 20W
Frome r. England 41 E3 50 40N 2 20W
Fuji, Mount Japan 59 M2 35 23N 138 42E
Fukui Japan 59 M2 36 04N 136 12E
Fukuoka Japan 59 L1 33 39N 130 21E
Fukushima Japan 59 N2 37 44N 140 28E
Fukuyama Japan 59 L1 34 29N 133 21E
Furnace Scotland 32 E4 56 09N 5 12W
Fushun China 59 D4 41 50N 123 54E
Fuzhou China 59 D2 26 09N 119 17E
Fyn i. Denmark 49 F6 55 30N 10 00E
FYROM see MACEDONIA, FORMER YUGOSLAV REPUBLIC OF

G

Gabès Tunisia 42 J2 33 52N 10 06E
GABON 66 D2
Gaborone Botswana 67 C2 24 45S 25 55E
Gafsa Tunisia 42 H2 34 28N 8 43E
Gainsborough England 35 E2 53 24N 0 48W
Gairloch Scotland 30 D2 57 42N 5 40W
Galapagos Islands Pacific Ocean 4 12 00S 87 00W
Galashiels Scotland 33 G3 55 37N 2 49W
Galati Romania 42 M5 45 27N 28 02E
Gallipoli Italy 51 G4 40 03N 17 59E
GAMBIA, THE 66 A4
Gander Canada 79 P5 49 00N 54 15W
Ganges r. India/Bangladesh 58 D3 24 00N 88 00E
Gap France 48 G2 44 33N 6 05E
Garelochhead Scotland 33 E4 56 05N 4 50W

Garonne r. France 48 D2 44 45N 0 15E
Gatehouse of Fleet Scotland 33 E2 54 53N 4 11W
Gateshead England 34 D3 54 58N 1 35W
Gaziantep Turkey 43 P3 37 04N 37 21E
Gdańsk Poland 42 K6 54 22N 18 41E
Gdynia Poland 42 K6 54 31N 18 30E
Geelong Australia 72 E2 38 08S 144 20E
Gelsenkirchen Germany 49 D4 51 30N 7 05E
Geneva Switzerland 49 D2 46 13N 6 09E
Geneva, Lake France/Switzerland 49 D2 46 20N 6 20E
Genoa Italy 51 B6 44 24N 8 56E
Georgetown Guyana 84 D8 6 46N 58 10W
George Town Malaysia 60 B3 5 25N 100 20E
GEORGIA 56 E2
Georgia state U.S.A. 79 L4 33 00N 83 00W
Gera Germany 49 G4 50 51N 12 11E
Geraldton Australia 72 B3 28 46S 114 36E
GERMANY 49 E4
Ghadàmis Libya 42 H2 30 08N 9 30E
GHANA 66 B3
Ghent Belgium 49 B4 51 02N 3 42E
Gibraltar territory U.K. 50 C1 36 09N 5 21W
Gibraltar, Strait of Spain/Morocco 50 C1 35 58N 5 30W
Gibson Desert Australia 72 C3 24 00S 122 00E
Giessen Germany 49 E4 50 35N 8 42E
Gifu Japan 59 M2 35 27N 136 46E
Gigha i. Scotland 32 D3 55 40N 5 45W
Gijón Spain 50 C5 43 32N 5 40W
Gillingham England 39 E2 51 24N 0 33E
Gironde r. France 48 C2 45 30N 1 00W
Girvan Scotland 32 E3 55 15N 4 51W
Gisborne New Zealand 73 D3 38 40S 178 01E
Giza Egypt 61 D4 30 01N 31 12E
Glasgow Scotland 33 E3 55 53N 4 15W
Glastonbury England 41 E4 51 09N 2 43W
Glazov Russia 43 S7 58 09N 52 42E
Glenluce Scotland 32 E2 54 53N 4 49W
Glenrothes Scotland 33 F4 56 12N 3 10W
Gloucester England 38 B2 51 53N 2 14W
Gloucestershire co. England 38 B2 51 50N 2 20W
Goat Fell mt. Scotland 32 D3 55 39N 5 11W
Gobi Desert Mongolia 57 L2 48 30N 100 00E
Godavari r. India 58 C2/D2 19 00N 80 00E
Godthåb see Nuuk
Goiânia Brazil 84 E6 16 43S 49 18W
Gold Coast tn. Australia 72 F3 28 04S 153 25E
Gomel' see Homyel'
Gongga Shan mt. China 59 B2 29 34N 101 53E
Good Hope, Cape of Republic of South Africa 67 B1 34 30S 19 00E
Goole England 35 E2 53 42N 0 52W
Gore New Zealand 73 B1 46 06S 168 56E
Gorkiy see Nizhniy Novgorod
Goroka Papua New Guinea 72 E5 6 02S 145 22E
Göteborg Sweden 42 J7 57 45N 12 00E
Gotland i. Sweden 42 K7 57 30N 18 40E
Göttingen Germany 49 E4 51 32N 9 57E
Governador Valadares Brazil 84 E6 18 51S 41 57W
Gower p. Wales 36 C1 51 35N 4 10W
Grafton Australia 72 F3 29 40S 152 58E
Grampian Mountains Scotland 31 E1/F1 56 45N 4 00W
Granada Spain 50 D2 37 10N 3 35W
Grand Bahama i. The Bahamas 79 M3 27 00N 78 00W
Grand Canyon U.S.A. 79 H4 36 04N 112 07W
Grand Rapids U.S.A. 79 L5 42 57N 86 40W
Grangemouth Scotland 33 F4 56 01N 3 44W
Grantham England 35 E1 52 55N 0 39W
Grantown-on-Spey Scotland 31 F2 57 20N 3 58W
Gravesend England 39 E2 51 27N 0 24E
Grays England 39 E2 51 29N 0 20E
Graz Austria 42 K5 47 05N 15 22E
Great Abaco i. The Bahamas 79 M3 26 40N 77 00W
Great Australian Bight b. Australia 72 C2 32 31S 130 00E
Great Barrier Island New Zealand 73 D3 36 13S 175 24E
Great Barrier Reef Australia 72 E4/F3 15 00S 146 00E
Great Bear Lake Canada 78 H7 66 00N 120 00W
Great Dividing Range mts. Australia 72 E2/F3 35 00N 148 00E
Great Driffield England 35 E3 54 01N 0 26W
Greater Antilles is. West Indies 79 M2/N2 19 00N 78 00W
Greater London co. England 38 D2 51 30N 0 10W
Greater Manchester co. England 34 C2 53 30N 2 15W
Great Inagua i. The Bahamas 79 M3 21 40N 73 00W
Great Karoo mts. Republic of South Africa 67 C1 32 30S 22 30E
Great Malvern England 37 E2 52 07N 2 19W
Great Ouse r. England 39 E3 52 40N 0 20E
Great St. Bernard Pass France/Italy 48 G2 45 50N 7 10E
Great Salt Lake U.S.A. 79 H5 41 10N 112 40W
Great Sandy Desert Australia 72 C3 21 00S 121 00E
Great Slave Lake Canada 78 H7 62 00N 114 00W
Great Stour r. England 39 F2 51 20N 1 10E
Great Torrington England 40 C3 50 57N 4 09W
Great Victoria Desert Australia 72 C3/D3 28 00S 129 00E
Great Wall China 59 B3 39 00N 109 00E
Great Whernside sum. England 34 D3 54 10N 1 59W
Great Yarmouth England 39 F3 52 37N 1 44E
GREECE 42 L3
GREENLAND 78 Q8
Greenock Scotland 33 E3 55 57N 4 45W
Greenwich England 38 D2 51 29N 0 00
GRENADA 79 N2
Grenoble France 48 F2 45 11N 5 43E
Greta r. England 34 C3 54 10N 2 36W
Greymouth New Zealand 73 C2 42 27S 171 12E
Greystones Wicklow Republic of Ireland 36 A3 53 09N 6 04W
Grimsby England 35 E2 53 35N 0 05W
Grodno see Hrodna
Groningen Netherlands 49 D5 53 13N 6 35E
Grosseto Italy 51 C5 42 46N 11 07E
Grossglockner mt. Austria 49 G2 47 05N 12 44E
Grozny Russia 56 E2 43 21N 45 42E
Guadalajara Mexico 79 J3 20 40N 103 20W
Guadalquivir r. Spain 50 C2 37 45N 5 30W
Guadalupe i. Mexico 79 H3 29 00N 118 24W

Guadeloupe *i.* Lesser Antilles **79** N2 16 30N 61 30W
Guadiana *r.* Spain/Portugal **50** C3 39 00N 5 30W
GUAM 5
Guangzhou *(Canton)* China **59** C2 23 08N 113 20E
Guantánamo Cuba **79** M3 20 09N 75 14W
Guarda Portugal **50** B4 40 32N 7 17W
GUATEMALA 79 K2
Guatemala Guatemala **79** K2 14 38N 90 22W
Guayaquil Ecuador **84** B7 2 13S 79 54W
Guernsey *i.* Channel Islands British Isles **41** E2 46 27N 2 35W
Guildford England **38** D2 51 14N 0 35W
GUINEA 66 A4
GUINEA-BISSAU 66 A4
Guinea, Gulf of Atlantic Ocean **66** C3 2 00N 2 30E
Guisborough England **35** D3 54 32N 1 04W
Guiyang China **59** B2 26 35N 106 40E
Gulf, The Middle East **61** F3 27 00N 51 00E
Guwahati India **58** E3 26 10N 91 45E
GUYANA 84 D8
Gwadar Pakistan **58** B3 25 07N 62 19E
Gwalior India **58** C3 26 12N 78 09E
Gyandzha Azerbaijan **56** E2 40 39N 46 20E
Györ Hungary **42** K5 47 41N 17 40E

H

Haarlem Netherlands **49** C5 52 23N 4 39E
Hachinohe Japan **59** N3 40 30N 141 30E
Haifa Israel **61** D4 32 49N 34 59E
Hail Saudi Arabia **61** E3 27 31N 41 45E
Hainan *i.* China **59** B1 18 50N 109 50E
Haiphong Vietnam **60** B5 20 50N 106 41E
HAITI 79 M2
Hakodate Japan **59** N3 41 46N 140 44E
Halesowen England **37** E2 52 26N 2 05W
Halifax Canada **79** N5 44 63 35W
Halifax England **34** D2 53 44N 1 52W
Halkirk Scotland **31** F3 58 30N 3 30W
Halle Germany **49** F4 51 28N 11 58E
Halmahera *i.* Indonesia **60** D3 0 30S 127 00E
Haltwhistle England **34** C3 54 58N 2 27W
Hamadan Iran **61** E4 34 46N 48 35E
Hamah Syria **43** P3 35 10N 36 45E
Hamamatsu Japan **59** M1 34 42N 137 42E
Hamburg Germany **49** E5 53 33N 10 00E
Hamersley Range Australia **72** B3 22 04S 117 37E
Hami China **58** E5 42 37N 93 32E
Hamilton Canada **79** M5 43 15N 79 50W
Hamilton New Zealand **73** D3 37 47S 175 17E
Hamilton Scotland **33** E3 55 47N 4 03W
Hamm Germany **49** D4 51 40N 7 49E
Hampshire *co.* England **38** C2 51 10N 1 15W
Hampshire Downs *hills* England **38** C2 51 15N 1 10W
Hangzhou China **59** D3 30 18N 120 07E
Hannover Germany **49** E5 52 23N 9 44E
Hanoi Vietnam **60** B5 21 01N 105 52E
Haradh Saudi Arabia **61** E3 24 12N 49 12E
Harare Zimbabwe **67** D3 17 50S 31 03E
Harbin China **59** D4 45 45N 126 41E
Hargeisa Somalia **67** E5 9 31N 44 02E
Harlech Wales **36** C2 52 52N 4 07W
Harlow England **39** E2 51 47N 0 08E
Haroldswick Scotland **29** E3 60 47N 0 50W
Harris, *i.* Scotland **30** B2 57 56N 6 55W
Harris, Sound of Scotland **30** B2 57 45N 7 10W
Harrogate England **34** D2 54 00N 1 33W
Harrow England **38** D2 51 34N 0 20W
Hartland Point England **40** C4 51 02N 4 31W
Hartlepool England **35** D3 54 41N 1 13W
Hartlepool *u.a.* England **35** D3 54 41N 1 13W
Harwich England **39** F2 51 57N 1 17E
Harz *mts.* Europe **49** F4 52 00N 10 00E
Haslemere England **38** D2 51 06N 0 43W
Hassi Messaoud Algeria **66** C6 31 52N 5 43E
Hastings England **39** E1 50 51N 0 36E
Hastings New Zealand **73** D3 39 39S 176 51E
Hatherleigh England **40** C3 50 49N 4 04W
Hauraki Gulf New Zealand **73** D3 36 38S 175 04E
Havana Cuba **79** L3 23 07N 82 25W
Havant England **38** D1 50 51N 0 59W
Haverfordwest Wales **36** C1 51 49N 4 58W
Haverhill England **39** E2 52 05N 0 26E
Havering England **39** E2 51 34N 4 58W
Hawaiian Islands Pacific Ocean **4** 20 00N 156 00W
Hawera New Zealand **73** C3 39 35S 174 17E
Hawick Scotland **33** G3 55 25N 2 47W
Hawke Bay New Zealand **73** D3 39 23S 177 12E
Hay-on-Wye Wales **36** D2 52 04N 3 07W
Hay River *tn.* Canada **78** H7 60 51N 115 42W
Haywards Heath England **38** D2 51 00N 0 06W
Hefei China **59** C3 31 55N 117 18E
Hegang China **59** E4 47 36N 130 30E
Heidelberg Germany **49** E3 49 25N 8 42E
Heilbronn Germany **49** E3 49 08N 9 14E
Helensburgh Scotland **33** E4 56 01N 4 44W
Hellín Spain **50** E3 38 31N 1 43W
Helmsdale Scotland **31** F3 58 07N 3 40W
Helmsdale *r.* Scotland **31** F3 58 10N 3 50W
Helsinki Finland **42** L8 60 08N 25 00E
Helston England **40** B3 50 05N 5 16W
Helvellyn *mt.* England **34** B3 54 32N 3 02W
Hemel Hempstead England **38** D2 51 46N 0 28W
Hemsworth England **35** D2 53 38N 1 21W
Hengelo Netherlands **49** D5 52 16N 6 46E
Henley-on-Thames England **38** D2 51 32N 0 56W
Herat Afghanistan **58** B4 34 20N 62 12E
Hereford England **37** E2 52 04N 2 43W
Hereford and Worcester *co.* England **37** E2 52 10N 3 00W
Herma Ness *c.* Scotland **29** E3 60 50N 0 54W
Hermosillo Mexico **79** H3 29 15N 110 59W
Hertford England **38** D2 51 48N 0 05W
Hertfordshire *co.* England **38** D2 51 50N 0 05W
Hexham England **34** C3 54 58N 2 06W
Heysham England **34** C3 54 02N 2 54W
Highland *u.a.* Scotland **30/31** D3/E2 57 00N 5 00W
High Veld *mts.* Republic of South Africa **67** C2 28 00S 28 00E
High Wycombe England **38** D2 51 38N 0 46W
Hilla Iraq **61** E4 32 28N 44 29E

Hillingdon England **38** D2 51 32N 0 27W
Hilversum Netherlands **49** C5 52 14N 5 10E
Himalayas *mts.* Asia **58** D3 28 00N 85 00E
Himeji Japan **59** L1 34 50N 134 40E
Hinckley England **37** F2 52 33N 1 21W
Hindu Kush *mts.* Afghanistan **58** B4 35 00N 70 00E
Hiroshima Japan **59** L1 34 23N 132 27E
Hitchin England **38** D2 51 57N 0 17W
Ho Chi Minh City *(Saigon)* Vietnam **60** B4 10 46N 106 43E
Hodeida Yemen Republic **61** E2 14 50N 42 58E
Höfn Iceland **42** K6 64 16N 15 10W
Hohhot China **59** C4 40 49N 117 37E
Hokkaido *i.* Japan **59** N3 43 30N 143 00E
Holderness *p.* England **35** E2 53 45N 0 05W
Holguín Cuba **79** M3 20 54N 76 15W
Hollywood U.S.A. **79** H4 34 05N 118 21W
Holsworthy England **40** C3 50 49N 4 21W
Holyhead Wales **36** C3 53 19N 4 38W
Holy Island Wales **36** C3 53 16N 4 39W
Holy Island England **33** H3 55 41N 1 48W
Homs Syria **61** D4 34 42N 36 40E
Homyel' *(Gomel')* Belarus **56** D3 52 25N 31 00E
HONDURAS 79 L2
Hong Kong *territory* U.K. **59** C2 23 00N 114 00E
Honiara Solomon Islands **72** F5 9 28S 159 57E
Honiton England **41** D3 50 48N 3 13W
Honshu *i.* Japan **59** M2 37 15N 139 00E
Horn, Cape Chile **85** C2 56 00S 67 15W
Horncastle England **35** E2 53 13N 0 07W
Hornsea England **35** E2 53 55N 0 10W
Horsham England **38** D2 51 04N 0 21W
Hospitalet Spain **50** G4 41 21N 2 06E
Hounslow England **38** D2 51 28N 0 21W
Houston U.S.A. **79** K3 29 45N 95 25W
Hove England **38** D1 50 49N 0 11W
Howe, Cape Australia **72** E2 37 29S 149 59E
Howth Republic of Ireland **36** A3 53 23N 6 04W
Hoy *i.* Scotland **29** B1 58 48N 3 20W
Hrodna *(Grodno)* Belarus **42** L6 53 40N 23 50E
Huainan China **59** C3 32 41N 117 06E
Huambo Angola **67** B3 12 44S 15 47E
Huancayo Peru **84** B6 12 05S 75 12W
Huang He *r.* China **59** C3 36 00N 116 00E
Hubli India **58** C2 15 20N 75 14E
Huddersfield England **34** D2 53 39N 1 47W
Hudson Bay Canada **78** L6/7 60 00N 89 00W
Hudson *r.* U.S.A. **79** M5 43 20N 73 50W
Hue Vietnam **60** B4 16 28N 107 35E
Huelva Spain **50** B2 37 15N 6 56W
Hufuf Saudi Arabia **61** E3 25 20N 49 34E
Hugh Town England **40** A2 49 55N 6 19W
Hull *r.* England **35** E2 53 50N 0 25W
Humber *r.* England **35** E2 53 40N 0 10W
HUNGARY 42 K5
Hungnam North Korea **59** D3 39 49N 127 40E
Hunstanton England **39** E3 52 57N 0 30E
Huntingdon England **38** D3 52 20N 0 12W
Huntly Scotland **31** G2 57 27N 2 47W
Huron, Lake Canada/U.S.A. **79** L5 45 00N 83 00W
Hyderabad India **58** C2 17 22N 78 26E
Hyderabad Pakistan **58** B3 25 22N 68 22E

I

Iași Romania **42** M5 47 09N 27 38E
Ibadan Nigeria **66** C3 7 23N 3 56E
Ibagué Colombia **84** B8 4 25N 75 20W
Ibiza Balearic Islands **50** F3 38 54N 1 26E
Ibiza *i.* Balearic Islands **50** F3 39 00N 1 20E
ICELAND 42 C9
Idaho *state* U.S.A. **79** H5 44 00N 115 00W
Ieper *(Ypres)* Belgium **39** G1 50 51N 2 53E
IJsselmeer *l.* Netherlands **49** C5 52 50N 5 15E
Ilchester England **41** E3 51 01N 2 41W
Ilebo Zaïre **67** C4 4 20S 20 35E
Ilfracombe England **40** C4 51 13N 4 08W
Ilhéus Brazil **84** F6 14 50S 39 06W
Ilkeston England **37** F2 52 59N 1 18W
Ilkley England **34** D2 53 55N 1 50W
Illinois *state* U.S.A. **79** L5 40 00N 89 00W
Ilmen, Lake Russia **42** N7 58 00N 31 30E
Ilminster England **41** E3 50 56N 2 55W
Iloilo The Philippines **60** D4 10 41N 122 33E
Immingham England **35** E2 53 36N 0 11W
Imphal India **58** E3 24 47N 93 55E
Inca Balearic Islands **50** G3 39 43N 2 54E
Inchon South Korea **59** D3 37 30N 126 38E
Indal *r.* Sweden **42** K8 63 00N 15 30E
INDIA 58 C3
Indiana *state* U.S.A. **79** L5 40 00N 86 00W
Indianapolis U.S.A. **79** L4 39 45N 86 10W
Indian Ocean **7**
INDONESIA 60 A3/D2
Indore India **58** C3 22 42N 75 54E
Ingleborough *sum.* England **34** C3 54 10N 2 23W
Ingolstadt Germany **49** F3 48 46N 11 27E
Inland Sea *sd.* Japan **59** L1 34 00N 132 30E
Inn *r.* Europe **49** G3 48 15N 13 00E
Inner Hebrides *is.* Scotland **30** C1/2 56 45N 6 45W
Innerleithen Scotland **33** F3 55 38N 3 05W
Inner Sound Scotland **30** D2 57 25N 5 55W
Innsbruck Austria **42** J5 47 17N 11 25E
Inuvik Canada **78** F7 68 16N 133 40W
Inveraray Scotland **32** D4 56 13N 5 05W
Inverbervie Scotland **31** G1 56 51N 2 17W
Invercargill New Zealand **73** B1 46 25S 168 22E
Inverclyde *u.a.* Scotland **33** E3 55 50N 4 45W
Invergarry Scotland **31** E2 57 02N 4 47W
Invergordon Scotland **31** E2 57 42N 4 10W
Inverkeithing Scotland **33** F4 56 02N 3 25W
Invermoriston Scotland **31** E2 57 13N 4 38W
Inverness Scotland **31** E2 57 27N 4 15W
Inveruie Scotland **31** G2 57 17N 2 23W
Ioannina Greece **42** L3 39 40N 20 51E
Iona *i.* Scotland **30** C1 56 19N 6 25W

Ionian Sea Mediterranean Sea **42** K3 38 00N 27 00E
Iowa *state* U.S.A. **79** K5 42 00N 94 00W
Ipoh Malaysia **60** B4 4 36N 101 05E
Ipswich England **39** F3 52 04N 1 10E
Iquique Chile **84** B5 20 15S 70 08W
Iquitos Peru **84** B7 3 51S 73 13W
Iraklion Greece **42** M3 35 20N 25 08E
IRAN 61 E4
IRAQ 61 E4
Irbid Jordan **43** P2 32 33N 35 51E
Irian Jaya *admin.* Indonesia **72** D5 3 00S 133 00E
Irish Sea British Isles **28** 53 30N 5 30W
Irkutsk Russia **57** L3 52 18N 104 15E
Irrawaddy *r.* Myanmar **58** E3 26 00N 97 30E
Irthing *r.* England **34** C3 55 00N 2 40W
Irtysh *r.* Russia **56** H3 57 30N 72 30E
Irvine Scotland **33** E3 55 37N 4 40W
Isafjördour Iceland **42** B6 66 05N 23 08W
Ishikari *r.* Japan **59** N3 43 30N 142 00E
Isigny-sur-Mer France **42** F2 49 18N 1 06W
Isla *r.* Scotland **31** F1 56 40N 3 15W
Islamabad Pakistan **58** C4 33 42N 73 10E
Island Magee *p.* Northern Ireland **32** D2 53 45N 5 45W
Islay *i.* Scotland **32** C3 55 48N 6 12W
Isle of Man British Isles **32** C4 54 15N 4 30W
Isle of Wight *u.a.* England **38** C1 50 40N 1 20W
ISRAEL 61 D4
Istanbul Turkey **42** M4 41 02N 28 57E
Istria *p.* Croatia **49** G1 45 10N 14 00E
Itabuna Brazil **84** F6 14 48S 39 18W
ITALY 51
Itchen *r.* England **38** C2 51 05N 1 15W
Ivanovo Russia **56** E3 57 00N 41 00E
Iwaki Japan **59** N2 37 03N 140 58E
Izhevsk Russia **43** S7 56 49N 53 11E
Izmir Turkey **42** M3 38 25N 27 10E
Izmit Turkey **43** M4 40 47N 29 55E
Izu Islands Japan **59** M1 34 20N 139 20E

J

Jabalpur India **58** C3 23 10N 79 59E
Jackson U.S.A. **79** K4 32 20N 90 11W
Jacksonville U.S.A. **79** L4 30 20N 81 40W
Jaffna Sri Lanka **58** D1 9 40N 80 01E
Jaipur India **58** C3 26 53N 75 50E
Jakarta Indonesia **60** B2 6 08S 106 45E
JAMAICA 79 M2
Jambi Indonesia **60** B2 1 34S 103 37E
James Bay Canada **78** L6 53 45N 81 00W
Jammu & Kashmir *state* Southern Asia **58** C4 29 40N 76 30E
Jamshedpur India **58** D3 22 47N 86 12E
JAPAN 59
Japan, Sea of Pacific Ocean **59** M3 39 00N 137 00E
Jauf Saudi Arabia **61** D3 29 49N 39 52E
Java *i.* Indonesia **60** B2/C2 7 00S 110 00E
Javalambre *mt.* Spain **50** E4 40 05N 1 02W
Java Peak Indonesia **72** D5 4 05S 137 09E
Java Sea Indonesia **60** C2 5 00S 112 00E
Jaya Peak Indonesia **72** D5 4 05S 137 09E
Jedburgh Scotland **33** G3 55 29N 2 34W
Jedda Saudi Arabia **61** D3 21 30N 39 10E
Jena Germany **49** F4 50 56N 11 35E
Jerez de la Frontera Spain **50** B2 36 41N 6 08W
Jersey *i.* Channel Islands British Isles **41** E2 49 13N 2 07W
Jerusalem Israel/Jordan **61** D4 31 47N 35 13E
Jiamusi China **59** E4 46 59N 130 29E
Jiayuguan China **59** A3 39 48 98 14E
Jilin China **59** D4 43 53N 126 35E
Jinan *(Tsinan)* China **59** C3 36 41N 117 00E
Jinsha Jiang *(Yangtze) r.* China **59** B2 27 30N 103 00E
Jisan Saudi Arabia **61** E2 16 56N 42 33E
Jixi China **59** E4 45 17N 131 00E
João Pessoa Brazil **84** F7 7 06S 34 53W
Johannesburg Republic of South Africa **67** C2 26 10S 28 02E
John o'Groats Scotland **31** F3 58 38N 3 05W
Johnstone Scotland **33** E3 55 50N 4 31W
Johor Baharu Malaysia **60** B3 1 27N 103 45E
Joinville Brazil **85** E6 26 20S 48 55W
Jönköping Sweden **42** J7 57 45N 14 10E
JORDAN 61 D4
Jos Plateau Nigeria **66** C3/4 9 30N 8 55E
Juan Fernández Islands Chile **85** B4 33 30S 80 00W
Juba Sudan **61** D1 4 50N 31 35E
Juba *r.* Somalia/Ethiopia **67** E5 5 00N 41 00E
Juiz de Fora Brazil **84** E5 21 47S 43 23W
Jungfrau *mt.* Switzerland **49** D2 46 33N 7 58E
Jura *i.* Scotland **32** D3/D4 55 55N 6 00W
Jura *mts.* France/Switzerland **48** F3 46 30N 6 00E
Jura, Sound of Scotland **32** D3/D4 56 00N 5 45W
Jutland *p.* Denmark **49** E6 55 00N 9 00E

K

Kabul Afghanistan **58** B4 34 30N 70 00E
Kabwe Zambia **67** C3 14 29S 28 25E
Kaduna Nigeria **66** C4 10 28N 7 25E
Kaesong South Korea **59** D3 37 59N 126 30E
Kagoshima Japan **59** L1 31 37N 130 32E
Kainji Reservoir Nigeria **66** C4 10 25N 4 56E
Kaipara Harbour New Zealand **73** C3 36 12S 174 06E
Kaiserslautern Germany **49** D3 49 27N 7 47E
Kalahari Desert Southern Africa **67** C2 23 30S 23 00E
Kalámai Greece **42** L3 37 02N 22 07E
Kalemie Zaïre **67** C4 5 57S 29 10E
Kalgoorlie Australia **72** C2 30 49S 121 29E
Kalinin see Tver
Kaliningrad Russia **42** K5 54 40N 20 30E
Kalmyshin Russia **43** R6 50 05N 45 24E
Kamchatka Peninsula Russia **57** R3 57 30N 160 00E
Kampala Uganda **67** D5 0 19N 32 35E
Kananga Zaïre **67** C4 5 53S 22 26E
Kanazawa Japan **59** M2 36 35N 136 38E
Kandahar Afghanistan **58** B4 31 35N 65 45E
Kandalaksha Russia **42** N9 67 09N 32 31E
Kandla India **58** C3 23 03N 70 11E
Kandy Sri Lanka **58** D1 7 17N 80 40E
Kankan Guinea **66** B4 10 22N 9 11W

Kano Nigeria **66** C4 12 00N 8 31E
Kanpur India **58** D3 26 27N 80 14E
Kansas *state* U.S.A. **79** K4 38 00N 98 00W
Kansas City U.S.A. **79** K4 39 02N 94 33W
Kao-hsiung Taiwan **59** D2 22 36N 120 17E
Kapuas *r.* Indonesia **60** C3 0 30N 112 00E
Karachi Pakistan **58** B3 24 52N 67 03E
Karaganda Kazakhstan **56** H2 49 53N 73 07E
Karbala Iraq **61** E4 32 37N 44 03E
Kariba, Lake Zambia/Zimbabwe **67** C3 17 00S 28 00E
Karlovac Croatia **51** E6 45 30N 15 34E
Karlsruhe Germany **49** E3 49 00N 8 24E
Karun *r.* Iran **61** E4 31 25N 48 12E
Kasai *r.* Angola/Zaïre **67** B4 4 00S 19 00E
Kashi China **59** A3 39 29N 76 02E
Kassala Sudan **61** D2 15 24N 36 30E
Kassel Germany **49** E4 51 18N 9 30E
Kasserine Tunisia **51** B1 35 13N 8 43E
Katherine Australia **72** D4 14 27S 132 15E
Kathmandu Nepal **58** D3 27 42N 85 19E
Katowice Poland **42** K6 50 15N 18 59E
Kaunas Lithuania **42** L6 54 52N 23 55E
Kayes Mali **66** A4 14 26N 11 28W
Kayseri Turkey **43** P3 38 42N 35 28E
KAZAKHSTAN 56 G2
Kazan' Russia **56** E3 55 45N 49 10E
Keady Northern Ireland **32** C2 54 15N 6 42W
Keighley England **34** D2 53 52N 1 54W
Keith Scotland **31** G2 57 32N 2 57W
Kelso Scotland **33** G3 55 36N 2 25W
Kemerovo Russia **56** J3 55 25N 86 05E
Kemi *r.* Finland **42** M9 67 00N 27 00E
Kendal England **34** C3 54 20N 2 45W
Kenilworth England **38** C2 51 30N 1 34W
Kenitra Morocco **66** B6 34 20N 6 34W
Kennet *r.* England **38** C2 51 30N 1 45W
Kent *co.* England **39** E2 51 15N 0 09E
KENYA 67 D5
Kenya, Mount Kenya **67** D4 0 10S 37 19E
Kerema Papua New Guinea **72** E5 7 59S 145 46E
Kerguelen *is.* Indian Ocean **5** 49 15N 69 10E
Kerman Iran **61** F4 30 18N 57 05E
Kermanshah Iran **61** E4 34 19N 47 04E
Kerrera *i.* Scotland **32** D1 56 24N 5 33W
Keswick England **34** B3 54 37N 3 08W
Kettering England **38** D3 52 24N 0 44W
Keynsham England **38** B2 51 26N 2 30W
Khabarovsk Russia **57** P2 48 32N 135 08E
Khaniá Greece **42** L3 35 31N 24 01E
Khanka, Lake Asia **57** P2 45 00N 132 30E
Kharkov Ukraine **56** D2 50 00N 36 15E
Khartoum Sudan **61** D2 15 33N 32 35E
Kherson Ukraine **56** D2 46 39N 32 38E
Khulna Bangladesh **58** D2 22 49N 89 34E
Khyber Pass Afghanistan/Pakistan **58** C4 34 06N 71 05E
Kidderminster England **37** E2 52 23N 2 14W
Kidsgrove England **37** E3 53 05N 2 14W
Kidwelly Wales **36** C1 51 45N 4 18W
Kiel Germany **49** F6 54 20N 10 08E
Kielder Water *res.* England **33** G3 55 10N 2 30W
Kiev Ukraine **56** D3 50 25N 30 30E
Kigali Rwanda **67** D4 1 56S 30 04E
Kigoma Tanzania **67** C4 4 52S 29 36E
Kikwit Zaïre **67** B4 5 02S 18 51E
Kilbrannan Sound Scotland **32** E3 55 30N 5 30W
Kilimanjaro, Mount Tanzania **67** D4 3 04S 37 22E
Kilkeel Northern Ireland **32** C2 54 04N 6 00W
Kilmacrenan Republic of Ireland **32** B3 55 02N 7 47W
Kilmaluag Scotland **30** C2 57 41N 6 17W
Kilmarnock Scotland **33** E3 55 36N 4 30W
Kilmory Scotland **32** D3 55 55N 5 41W
Kimberley Republic of South Africa **67** C2 28 45S 24 46E
Kinabalu, Mount Malaysia **60** C3 6 03N 116 32E
Kinbrace Scotland **31** F3 58 15N 3 56W
Kingsbridge England **40** D3 50 17N 3 46W
King's Lynn England **39** E3 52 45N 0 24E
Kingston Jamaica **79** M2 17 58N 76 48W
Kingston upon Hull England **35** E2 53 45N 0 20W
Kingston upon Thames England **38** D2 51 25N 0 18W
Kingswood England **38** B2 51 28N 2 30W
Kington England **36** D2 52 12N 3 01W
Kingussie Scotland **31** E2 57 05N 4 03W
Kinloch Scotland **30** C2 57 01N 6 17W
Kinross Scotland **31** F1 56 13N 3 27W
Kinshasa Zaïre **67** B4 4 18S 15 18E
Kintyre *p.* Scotland **32** D3 55 30N 5 35W
KIRGYZSTAN 56 H2
KIRIBATI 4/5
Kirikkale Turkey **43** N3 39 51N 33 32E
Kirkbean Scotland **33** F2 54 55N 3 35W
Kirkby England **34** C2 53 29N 2 54W
Kirkby Stephen England **34** C3 54 28N 2 20W
Kirkcaldy Scotland **33** F4 56 07N 3 10W
Kirkcudbright Scotland **33** E2 54 50N 4 03W
Kirkintilloch Scotland **33** E3 55 57N 4 10W
Kirk Michael Isle of Man British Isles **33** E2 54 17N 4 35W
Kirkpatrick, Mount Antarctica **86** 84 25S 165 30E
Kirkuk Iraq **61** E4 35 28N 44 26E
Kirkwall Scotland **29** C1 58 59N 2 58W
Kirov *(Vyatka)* Russia **56** E3 58 00N 49 38E
Kirovohrad Ukraine **43** N5 48 31N 32 15E
Kirriemuir Scotland **31** F1 56 41N 3 01W
Kisangani Zaïre **67** C5 0 33N 25 14E
Kishinev see Chisinau
Kisumu Kenya **67** D4 0 08S 34 47E
Kitakami *r.* Japan **59** N2 39 00N 141 20E
Kitakyushu Japan **59** L1 33 52N 130 49E
Kitwe Zambia **67** C3 12 50S 28 04E
Kitzbühel Austria **51** D7 47 27N 12 23E
Kivu, Lake Zaïre/Rwanda **67** C4 2 00S 29 00E
Kizil Irmak *r.* Turkey **43** N4 40 30N 34 00E
Klagenfurt Austria **49** H2 46 38N 14 20E
Klaipeda Lithuania **42** K7 55 43N 21 07E
Klar *r.* Sweden **42** J8 61 00N 13 00E
Knaresborough England **35** D3 54 00N 1 27W
Knighton England **36** D2 52 21N 3 03W

Kobe Japan 59 M1 34 40N 135 12E
Koblenz Germany 49 D4 50 21N 7 36E
Kochi Japan 59 L1 33 33N 133 32E
Kodiak Island U.S.A. 78 D6 57 20N 153 40W
Kokand Uzbekistan 56 H2 40 33N 70 55E
Kolhapur India 58 C2 16 40N 74 20E
Kolyma r. Russia 57 R4 68 00N 152 00E
Komsomolsk-on-Amur Russia 57 P3 50 32N 136 59E
Konya Turkey 43 N3 37 51N 32 30E
Koriyama Japan 59 N2 37 23N 140 22E
Kosciusko, Mount Australia 72 E2 36 27S 148 17E
Košice Slovakia 42 L5 48 44N 21 15E
Kota Baharu Malaysia 60 B3 6 08N 102 14E
Kota Kinabalu Malaysia 60 C3 5 59N 116 04E
Kotlas Russia 43 R8 61 15N 46 35E
Kragujevac Serbia Yugoslavia 42 L4 44 01N 20 55E
Kra, Isthmus of Myanmar/Thailand 60 A4 10 20N 99 00E
Kranj Slovenia 51 E7 46 15N 14 20E
Krasnodar Russia 43 Q4 45 02N 39 00E
Krasnovodsk Turkmenistan 56 F2 40 01N 53 00E
Krasnoyarsk Russia 57 K3 56 05N 92 46E
Kratie Cambodia 60 B4 12 30N 106 03E
Krefeld Germany 49 D4 51 20N 6 32E
Kremenchuk Ukraine 43 N5 49 03N 33 25E
Krishna r. India 58 C2 16 00N 79 00E
Krivoy Rog see Kryvy Rih
Krung Thep see Bangkok
Kryvy Rih (Krivoy Rog) Ukraine 56 D2 47 55N 33 24E
Kuala Lumpur Malaysia 60 B3 3 09N 101 42E
Kuala Terengganu Malaysia 60 B3 5 20N 103 09E
Kuantan Malaysia 60 B3 3 48N 103 19E
Kuching Malaysia 60 C3 1 35N 110 21E
Kuh-e-Hazaran mt. Iran 61 F3 29 35N 57 20E
Kumamoto Japan 59 L1 32 50N 130 42E
Kumasi Ghana 66 B3 6 45N 1 35W
Kunlun Shan mts. China 58 D4 36 30N 85 00E
Kunming China 59 B2 25 04N 102 41E
Kupang Indonesia 60 D1 10 13S 123 38E
Kurgan Russia 56 G3 55 30N 65 20E
Kuril Islands Russia 57 R2 50 00N 155 00E
Kursk Russia 56 D3 51 45N 36 14E
Kushiro Japan 59 N3 42 58N 144 24E
Kutaisi Georgia 43 Q4 42 15N 42 44E
KUWAIT 61 E3
Kuwait Kuwait 61 E3 29 20N 48 00E
Kuybyshev see Samara
Kwangju South Korea 59 D3 35 07N 126 52E
Kyle of Lochalsh Scotland 30 D2 57 17N 5 43W
Kyoga, Lake Uganda 67 D5 2 00N 34 00E
Kyoto Japan 59 M2 35 02N 135 45E
Kyushu i. Japan 59 L1 32 20N 131 00E

L

Laccadive Islands see Lakshadweep
La Coruña Spain 50 A5 43 22N 8 24W
Ladoga, Lake Russia 56 D4 61 00N 30 00E
Lae Papua New Guinea 72 E5 6 45S 147 00E
Lagos Nigeria 66 C3 6 27N 3 28E
La Grande Rivière r. Canada 78 L6 53 34N 74 36W
Lahore Pakistan 58 C4 31 35N 74 18E
Lairg Scotland 31 E3 58 01N 4 25W
Lake District geog. reg. England 34 B3/C3 54 30N 3 00W
Lakshadweep (Laccadive Islands) India 58 C2 9 30N 73 00E
Lambert Glacier Antarctica 86 73 00S 70 00E
Lambourn r. England 38 C2 51 30N 1 30W
Lammermuir Hills Scotland 33 G3 55 50N 2 45W
Lampedusa i. Italy 51 D1 35 00N 12 00E
Lampeter Wales 36 C2 52 07N 4 05W
Lanark Scotland 33 F3 55 41N 3 48W
Lancang Jiang (Mekong) r. China/Myanmar/ Laos/Cambodia 59 A3 32 00N 98 00E
Lancashire co. England 34 C2 53 50N 2 30W
Lancaster England 34 C3 54 03N 2 48W
Land's End c. England 40 B3 50 03N 5 44W
Langholm Scotland 33 G3 55 09N 3 00W
Languedoc geog. reg. France 48 E1/E2 44 00N 4 00E
Lanzhou China 59 B3 36 01N 103 45E
LAOS 60 B4
La Paz Bolivia 84 C6 16 30S 68 10W
La Plata Argentina 85 D4 34 52S 57 55W
La Puebla Balearic Islands 50 G3 39 46N 3 01E
Largs Scotland 33 E3 55 48N 4 52W
Lárisa Greece 42 L3 39 38N 22 25E
Larne Northern Ireland 32 D2 54 51N 5 49W
Larne district Northern Ireland 32 D2 54 50N 5 50W
La Rochelle France 48 C3 46 10N 1 10W
Larsen Ice Shelf Antarctica 86 67 00S 62 00W
La Sagra mt. Spain 50 D2 37 57N 2 34W
Las Palmas Canary Islands 66 A5 28 08N 15 27W
La Spezia Italy 51 B6 44 07N 9 48E
Las Vegas U.S.A. 79 H4 36 10N 115 10W
Latakia Syria 61 D4 35 31N 35 47E
Latina Italy 51 D4 41 28N 12 53E
LATVIA 42 M7
Launceston Australia 72 E1 41 27S 147 09E
Launceston England 40 C3 50 38N 4 21W
Laurencekirk Scotland 31 G1 56 50N 2 29W
Lausanne Switzerland 49 D2 46 32N 6 39E
Laval France 48 C4 48 04N 0 45W
Leader Water r. Scotland 33 G3 55 45N 2 50W
LEBANON 61 D4
Ledbury England 37 E2 52 02N 2 25W
Leeds England 34 D2 53 50N 1 35W
Leeuwin, Cape Australia 72 B2 34 21S 115 08E
le Havre France 48 D4 49 30N 0 06E
Leicester England 37 F2 52 38N 1 05W
Leicestershire co. England 37 F2/G2 52 30N 1 00W
Leiden Netherlands 49 C5 52 10N 4 30E
Leighton Buzzard England 38 D2 51 55N 0 41W
Leipzig Germany 49 G4 51 20N 12 25E
Leith Hill England 38 D2 51 11N 0 23W
Leitrim co. Republic of Ireland 32 A2 54 05N 8 00W
le Mans France 48 D4 48 00N 0 12E
Lena r. Russia 57 N4 64 30N 127 00E
Leningrad see St. Petersburg
Lens France 48 E5 50 26N 2 50E

Leominster England 37 E2 52 14N 2 45W
León Mexico 79 J3 21 10N 101 42W
León Spain 50 C5 42 35N 5 34W
Le Puy France 48 E2 45 03N 3 53E
Lérida Spain 50 F4 41 37N 0 38E
Lerwick Scotland 29 D3 60 09N 1 09W
LESOTHO 67 C2
Lessay France 41 F2 49 13N 1 32W
Lesser Antilles is. West Indies 79 N2 18 00N 65 00W
Letchworth England 38 D2 51 58N 0 14W
le Touquet-Paris-Plage France 39 F1 50 13N 1 36E
Letterkenny Donegal Republic of Ireland 32 B2 54 57N 7 44W
Leverkusen Germany 49 D4 51 02N 6 59E
Levin New Zealand 73 D2 40 37S 175 17E
Lewes England 38 E1 50 52N 0 01E
Lewis i. Scotland 30 C3 58 15N 6 30W
Leyburn England 34 D3 54 19N 1 49W
Leyland England 34 C2 53 42N 2 42W
Leyte i. The Philippines 60 D4 11 00N 125 00E
Lhasa China 58 E3 29 08N 87 43E
Lianyungang China 59 C3 34 37N 119 10E
Liao He r. China 59 D4 42 30N 122 00E
Liard r. Canada 78 G7 61 00N 122 00W
LIBERIA 66 B3
Libreville Gabon 66 C3 0 30N 9 25E
LIBYA 66 D5
Libyan Desert North Africa 61 C3 25 00N 25 00E
Lichfield England 37 F2 52 42N 1 48W
Liddel Water r. England/Scotland 33 G3 55 15N 2 50W
LIECHTENSTEIN 49 E2
Liège Belgium 49 C4 50 38N 5 35E
Liepāja Latvia 42 L7 56 30N 21 00E
Likasi Zaïre 67 C3 10 58S 26 47E
Lille France 48 E5 50 39N 3 05E
Lillers France 39 G1 50 34N 2 29E
Lilongwe Malawi 67 D3 13 58S 33 49E
Lima Peru 84 B6 12 06S 8 40W
Limassol Cyprus 43 N2 34 04N 33 02E
Limavady Northern Ireland 32 C3 55 03N 6 57W
Limavady district Northern Ireland 32 B2/C2 54 50N 7 00W
Limoges France 48 D2 45 50N 1 15E
Limpopo r. Southern Africa 67 C2 22 30S 28 00E
Lincoln England 35 E2 53 14N 0 33W
Lincolnshire co. England 35 E2 53 14N 0 20W
Lincoln Wolds hills England 35 E2 53 25N 0 05W
Lingga i. Indonesia 60 B2 0 10S 104 40E
Linköping Sweden 42 K7 58 25N 15 35E
Linlithgow Scotland 33 F3 55 59N 3 37W
Linz Austria 42 J5 48 19N 14 18E
Lipetsk Russia 56 D3 52 37N 39 36E
Lisbon Portugal 50 A3 38 44N 9 08W
Lisburn Northern Ireland 32 C2 54 31N 6 03W
Lisburn district Northern Ireland 32 C2 54 30N 6 10W
Lisieux France 48 D4 49 09N 0 14E
Liskeard England 40 C3 50 28N 4 28W
Lismore Scotland 30 D1 56 30N 5 30W
LITHUANIA 42 L7
Littlehampton England 38 D1 50 48N 0 33W
Little Minch sd. Scotland 30 C2 57 45N 6 30W
Little Ouse r. England 39 E3 52 30N 0 30E
Little Rock U.S.A. 79 K4 34 42N 92 17W
Liuzhou China 59 B2 24 17N 109 15E
Liverpool England 34 C2 53 25N 2 55W
Livingston Scotland 33 F3 55 53N 3 32W
Livorno Italy 51 C5 43 33N 10 18E
Lizard England 40 B2 49 57N 5 13W
Lizard Point England 40 B2 49 56N 5 13W
Ljubljana Slovenia 51 E7 46 04N 14 30E
Llandeilo Wales 36 D1 51 53N 3 59W
Llandovery Wales 36 D1 51 59N 3 48W
Llandrindod Wells Wales 36 D2 52 15N 3 23W
Llandudno Wales 36 D3 53 19N 3 49W
Llanelli Wales 36 C1 51 42N 4 10W
Llangollen Wales 36 D2 52 58N 3 10W
Llanidloes Wales 36 D2 52 27N 3 32W
Lleyn Peninsula Wales 36 C2 52 53N 4 30W
Lobito Angola 67 B3 12 20S 13 34E
Lochaline tn. Scotland 30 D1 56 32N 5 47W
Loch Arkaig l. Scotland 30 D1 56 59N 5 10W
Loch Awe l. Scotland 30/31 D1 56 15N 5 17W
Loch Doon l. Scotland 33 E3 55 26N 4 38W
Loch Earn l. Scotland 31 E1 56 23N 4 10W
Loch Eishort est. Scotland 30 D2 57 08N 6 00W
Loch Ericht l. Scotland 31 E1 56 48N 4 25W
Loch Etive l. Scotland 30/31 D1 56 30N 5 10W
Lochgilphead tn. Scotland 30 D4 56 03N 5 26W
Loch Katrine l. Scotland 33 E4 56 16N 4 30W
Loch Ken l. Scotland 33 E3 55 02N 4 07W
Loch Leven l. Scotland 31 F1 56 15N 3 23W
Loch Linnhe b. Scotland 30 D1 56 35N 5 25W
Loch Lochy l. Scotland 31 E1 56 58N 4 55W
Loch Lomond l. Scotland 33 E4 56 10N 4 35W
Loch Long l. Scotland 32/33 E4 56 10N 4 50W
Lochmaben tn. Scotland 33 F3 55 08N 3 27W
Lochmaddy tn. Scotland 30 B2 57 36N 7 08W
Loch Nan Clar l. Scotland 31 E3 58 30N 4 00W
Loch Maree l. Scotland 30 D2 57 40N 5 30W
Lochnagar mt. Scotland 31 F1 56 57N 3 16W
Loch Ness l. Scotland 31 E2 57 02N 4 30W
Loch Rannoch l. Scotland 31 E1 56 41N 4 18W
Lochranza tn. Scotland 30 D3 55 42N 5 18W
Loch Shiel l. Scotland 30 D1 56 45N 5 35W
Loch Shin l. Scotland 31 E3 58 05N 4 30W
Loch Snizort b. Scotland 30 C2 57 30N 6 30W
Loch Tay l. Scotland 31 E1 56 31N 4 10W
Loch Torridon b. Scotland 30 D2 57 35N 5 46W
Lockerbie Scotland 33 F3 55 07N 3 22W
Logan, Mount Canada 78 E7 60 34N 140 25W
Logroño Spain 50 D5 42 28N 2 26W
Loire r. France 48 D3 47 30N 1 00E
Lolland i. Denmark 49 F6 54 45N 12 20E
Lombok i. Indonesia 60 C2 8 30S 116 30E
Lomé Togo 66 C3 6 10N 1 21E

London England 38 D2 51 30N 0 10W
Londonderry Northern Ireland 32 B2 54 59N 7 19W
Londonderry district Northern Ireland 32 B2 54 55N 7 20W
Londrina Brazil 84 D5 23 18S 51 13W
Long Eaton England 37 F2 52 54N 1 15W
Long Island The Bahamas 79 M3 23 20N 75 00W
Long Mynd sum. England 37 E2 52 32N 2 52W
Longreach Australia 72 E3 23 26S 144 15E
Longs Peak U.S.A. 79 J5 40 20N 105 50W
Looe England 40 C3 50 21N 4 27W
Lorient France 48 B3 47 45N 3 21W
Los Angeles U.S.A. 79 H4 34 00N 118 15W
Lossiemouth Scotland 31 F2 57 43N 3 18W
Lostwithiel England 40 C3 50 25N 4 40W
Lot r. France 48 E2 44 30N 2 15E
Lough Allen l. Republic of Ireland 32 A2 54 15N 8 00W
Lough Beg l. Northern Ireland 32 C2 54 48N 6 16W
Loughborough England 37 F2 52 47N 1 11W
Lough Derg l. Republic of Ireland 32 B2 52 55N 8 15W
Lough Foyle est. Northern Ireland/Republic of Ireland 32 B3 55 10N 7 10W
Lough Macnean Lower l. Northern Ireland 32 B2 54 17N 7 50W
Lough Macnean Upper l. Northern Ireland/ Republic of Ireland 32 B2 54 18N 7 55W
Lough Melvin l. Northern Ireland/Republic of Ireland 32 A2 54 25N 8 05W
Lough Neagh l. Northern Ireland 32 C2 54 35N 6 30W
Lough Oughter l. Republic of Ireland 32 B2 54 00N 7 30W
Lough Swilly b. Republic of Ireland 32 B3 55 20N 7 35W
Louisiana state U.S.A. 79 K4 32 00N 92 00W
Louisville U.S.A. 79 L4 38 13N 85 48W
Lourdes France 48 C1 43 06N 0 02W
Louth England 35 E2 53 22N 0 01W
Louth co. Republic of Ireland 32 C1/2 53 55N 6 25W
Lower California n. Mexico 79 H3 27 30N 113 00W
Lower Lough Erne l. Northern Ireland 32 B2 54 25N 7 45W
Lowestoft England 39 F3 52 29N 1 45E
Lowther Hills Scotland 33 F3 55 25N 3 45W
Lualaba r. Zaïre 67 C4 4 00S 26 30E
Luanda Angola 67 B4 8 50S 13 15E
Luang Prabang Laos 60 B4 19 53N 102 10E
Lubango Angola 67 B3 14 55S 13 30E
Lübeck Germany 49 F5 53 52N 10 40E
Lublin Poland 42 L6 51 18N 22 35E
Lubumbashi Zaïre 67 C3 11 41S 27 29E
Luce Bay Scotland 32/33 E2 54 47N 4 50W
Lucerne Switzerland 49 E2 47 03N 8 17E
Lucknow India 58 D3 26 50N 80 54E
Lüderitz Namibia 67 B2 26 38S 15 10E
Ludhiana India 58 C4 30 56N 75 52E
Ludlow England 37 E2 52 22N 2 43W
Ludwigshafen Germany 49 E3 49 29N 8 27E
Lugano Switzerland 49 E2 46 01N 8 57E
Luhans'k Ukraine 56 D2 48 35N 39 20E
Luleå Sweden 42 L9 65 35N 22 10E
Lundy i. England 40 C4 51 11N 4 40W
Lune r. England 34 C3 54 10N 2 40W
Luoyang China 59 C3 34 47N 112 26E
Lurgan Northern Ireland 32 C2 54 28N 6 20W
Lusaka Zambia 67 C3 15 26S 28 20E
Luton England 38 D2 51 53N 0 25W
LUXEMBOURG 49 C3/D3
Luxembourg Luxembourg 49 D3 49 37N 6 08E
Luxor Egypt 61 D3 25 41N 32 24E
Luzon i. The Philippines 60 D4 15 00N 122 00E
L'viv Ukraine 56 C2 49 50N 24 00E
Lybster Scotland 31 F3 58 18N 3 13W
Lyme Bay England 41 E3 50 40N 2 55W
Lyme Regis England 41 E3 50 44N 2 57W
Lymington England 38 C1 50 46N 1 33W
Lynn Lake tn. Canada 78 J6 56 51N 101 01W
Lynton England 40 D4 51 15N 3 50W
Lyons France 48 F2 45 46N 4 50E
Lys r. France 39 G1 50 40N 2 10E
Lytham St. Anne's England 34 B2 53 45N 3 01W

M

Maas r. Netherlands 49 C4 51 50N 5 45E
Maastricht Netherlands 49 C4 50 51N 5 42E
Mablethorpe England 35 F2 53 21N 0 15E
Macao territory Portugal 59 C2 22 10N 113 40E
Macapá Brazil 84 D8 0 04N 51 04W
Macclesfield England 34 C2 53 16N 2 07W
Macdonnell Ranges Australia 72 D3 23 45S 128 42E
Macduff Scotland 31 G2 57 40N 2 29W
MACEDONIA, FORMER YUGOSLAV REPUBLIC OF (FYROM) 42 L4
Maceió Brazil 84 F7 9 40S 35 44W
Machynlleth Wales 36 D2 52 35N 3 51W
Mackay, Lake Australia 72 C3 22 25S 128 42E
Mackenzie r. Canada 78 G7 64 00N 123 00 W
Mackenzie Mountains Canada 78 G7 66 00N 132 00W
McKinley, Mount U.S.A. 78 F7 62 02N 151 01W
Mâcon France 48 F3 46 18N 4 50E
MADAGASCAR 67 E2/3
Madang Papua New Guinea 72 E5 5 14S 145 45E
Madeira r. Brazil 84 C7 6 00S 61 30W
Madeira Islands Atlantic Ocean 53 32 45N 17 00W
Madras India 58 D2 13 05N 80 18E
Madrid Spain 50 D4 40 25N 3 43W
Madura i. Indonesia 60 C2 7 00S 113 00E
Madurai India 58 C1 9 55N 78 07E
Maebashi Japan 59 M2 36 24N 139 04E
Magadan Russia 57 R3 59 38N 150 50E
Magdalena r. Colombia 84 B8 3 00N 75 40W
Magdeburg Germany 49 F5 52 08N 11 37E
Maggiore, Lake Italy 51 B6/7 46 00N 8 00E
Maghera Northern Ireland 32 C2 54 51N 6 40W
Magherafelt Northern Ireland 32 C2 54 45N 6 36W
Magherafelt district Northern Ireland 32 C2 54 45N 6 50W
Magnitogorsk Russia 56 F3 53 28N 59 06E
Mahajanga Madagascar 67 E3 15 40S 46 20E
Mahakam r. Indonesia 60 C3 0 30N 116 00E

Mahilyow (Mogilev) Belarus 56 D3 53 54N 30 20E
Mahón Balearic Islands 50 H3 39 54N 4 15E
Maidenhead England 38 D2 51 32N 0 44W
Maidstone England 39 E2 51 17N 0 32E
Maiduguri Nigeria 66 D4 11 53N 13 16E
Main r. Germany 49 F4 50 00N 8 18E
Main r. Northern Ireland 32 C2 54 50N 6 25W
Maine state U.S.A. 79 N5 45 00N 70 00W
Mainland i. Orkney Islands Scotland 29 B1/B2 59 00N 3 15W
Mainland i. Shetland Islands Scotland 29 D3 60 15N 1 20W
Mainz Germany 49 D3 50 00N 8 16E
Majorca i. Balearic Islands 50 G3 39 50N 2 30E
Makassar Strait Indonesia 60 C2 0 00 119 00E
Makeyevka Ukraine 56 E2 48 01N 38 00E
Makhachkala Russia 56 E2 42 59N 47 30E
Malabo Equatorial Guinea 66 C3 3 45N 8 48E
Malacca, Strait of Indonesia 60 B3 4 00N 100 00E
Málaga Spain 50 C2 36 43N 4 25W
Malahide Dublin Republic of Ireland 36 A3 53 27N 6 09W
Malakal Sudan 61 D1 9 31N 31 40E
Malang Indonesia 60 C2 7 59S 112 45E
Malanje Angola 67 B4 9 32S 16 20E
Malatya Turkey 43 P3 38 22N 38 18E
MALAWI 67 D3
Malawi, Lake see Nyasa, Lake
Malaya admin. Malaysia 60 B3 5 00N 102 00E
MALAYSIA 60 B3/C3
MALDIVES 58 C1
MALI 66 B4
Malin Head c. Republic of Ireland 32 B3 55 30N 7 20W
Mallaig Scotland 30 D2 57 00N 5 50W
Malmesbury England 38 B2 51 36N 2 06W
Malmö Sweden 42 J7 55 35N 13 00E
MALTA 51 E1
Malton England 35 E3 54 08N 0 48W
Manacor Balearic Islands 50 G3 39 35N 3 12E
Manado Indonesia 60 D3 1 32N 124 55E
Managua Nicaragua 79 L2 12 06N 86 18W
Manaus Brazil 84 D7 3 06S 60 00W
Manawatu r. New Zealand 73 D2 40 30S 176 00E
Manchester England 34 C2 53 30N 2 15W
Mandalay Myanmar 58 E3 21 57N 96 04E
Manfredonia Italy 51 E4 41 37N 15 55E
Mangalore India 58 C2 12 54N 74 51E
Mangotsfield England 38 B2 51 29N 2 31W
Manila The Philippines 60 D4 14 37N 120 58E
Manitoba province Canada 78 K6 55 00N 98 00W
Manizales Colombia 84 B8 5 03N 75 32W
Mannheim Germany 49 E3 49 30N 8 28E
Mansfield England 35 D2 53 09N 1 11W
Manzanares Spain 50 D3 39 00N 3 23W
Maputo Mozambique 67 D2 25 58S 32 35E
Maracaibo Venezuela 84 B9 10 44N 71 37W
Maracaibo, Lake Venezuela 84 B8 9 50N 71 30W
Marañon r. Peru 84 B7 7 00S 77 40W
Marbella Spain 50 C2 36 31N 4 53W
Marble Bar Australia 72 B3 21 15S 119 43E
Marden England 39 E2 51 11N 0 30E
Margarita i. Venezuela 79 N2 11 30N 64 00W
Margate England 39 F2 51 24N 1 24E
Maribor Slovenia 51 E7 46 34N 15 38E
Marie Byrd Land geog. reg. Antarctica 86 77 00S 130 00W
Mariscal Estigarribia Paraguay 84 C5 22 03S 60 35W
Maripol Ukraine 56 D2 47 05N 37 34E
Market Drayton England 37 E2 52 54N 2 29W
Market Harborough England 37 G2 52 29N 0 55W
Market Rasen England 35 E2 53 24N 0 21W
Markham, Mount Antarctica 86 82 45S 160 25E
Marlborough England 38 C2 51 26N 1 43W
Marlow England 38 D2 51 35N 0 48W
Marne r. France 48 E4 49 00N 4 30E
Marrakesh Morocco 66 B6 31 49N 8 00W
Marsala Italy 51 D2 37 48N 12 27E
Marseille France 48 F1 43 18N 5 22E
MARSHALL ISLANDS 5
Martinique i. Lesser Antilles 79 N2 14 30N 61 00W
Maryland state U.S.A. 79 M4 39 00N 77 00W
Maryport England 34 B3 54 43N 3 30W
Maseru Lesotho 67 C2 29 19S 27 29E
Mashhad Iran 61 F4 36 16N 59 34E
Massachusetts state U.S.A. 79 M5 42 00N 72 00W
Massawa Eritrea 61 D1 15 42N 39 25E
Massif Central mts. France 48 E2 45 00N 3 30E
Masterton New Zealand 73 D2 40 57S 175 39E
Matadi Zaïre 67 B4 5 50S 13 32E
Matamoros Mexico 79 K3 25 33N 103 51W
Matlock England 35 D2 53 08N 1 32W
Mato Grosso geog. reg. Brazil 84 D6 14 00S 56 00W
Matsue Japan 59 L2 35 29N 133 04E
Matsuyama Japan 59 L1 33 50N 132 47E
Matterhorn mt. Switzerland 49 D1 45 59N 7 39E
MAURITANIA 66 A5
MAURITIUS 5
Maybole Scotland 33 E3 55 21N 4 41W
Maykop Russia 43 Q4 44 37N 40 48E
Mazatlán Mexico 79 J3 23 11N 106 25W
Mbandaka Zaïre 66 D3 0 03N 18 28E
Mbeya Tanzania 67 D4 8 54S 33 29E
Mbuji-Mayi Zaïre 67 C4 6 10S 23 39E
Mecca Saudi Arabia 61 D3 21 26N 39 49E
Medan Indonesia 60 A3 3 35N 98 39E
Medellín Colombia 84 B8 6 15N 75 36W
Medina Saudi Arabia 61 D3 24 30N 39 35E
Mediterranean Sea Africa/Europe 42/43 35 00N 15 00E
Medway r. England 39 E2 51 24N 0 31E
Meekatharra Australia 72 B3 26 35S 118 30E
Meerut India 58 C3 29 00N 77 42E
Mega Ethiopia 61 D1 4 02N 38 19E
Meharry, Mount Australia 72 B3 22 58S 118 35E
Meig r. Scotland 31 E2 57 40N 4 50W
Meknes Morocco 66 B6 33 53N 5 37W
Mekong (Lancang Jiang) r. Cambodia/Laos/ Myanmar/China 59 B1 15 00N 105 00E
Melbourne Australia 72 E2 37 49S 144 58E

Melrose Scotland **33** G3 55 36N 2 44W
Melton Mowbray England **37** G2 52 46N 0 53W
Melville Island Canada **78** H8 75 30N 112 00W
Memphis U.S.A. **79** K4 35 10N 90 00W
Menam r. Thailand **60** B4 15 00N 100 00E
Mendip Hills England **41** E4 51 18N 2 45W
Mendoza Argentina **85** C4 32 48S 68 52W
Mentawai Islands Indonesia **60** A2 2 00N 99 00E
Menzies, Mount Antarctica **86** 73 30S 62 00E
Meon r. England **38** C1 50 55N 1 10W
Mere England **38** B2 51 06N 2 16W
Mérida Mexico **79** L3 20 59N 89 39W
Mersey r. England **34** C2 53 20N 2 55W
Merseyside co. England **34** C2 53 30N 3 20W
Mersin Turkey **43** N3 36 47N 34 37E
Merthyr Tydfil Wales **36** D1 51 46N 3 23W
Merthyr Tydfil u.a. Wales **36** D1 51 48N 3 20W
Merton England **39** D2 51 25N 0 12W
Messina Italy **51** E3 38 13N 15 33E
Metz France **48** G4 49 07N 6 11E
Meuse r. Belgium/France **48** G4 50 30N 5 00E
Mexicali Mexico **79** H4 32 36N 115 30W
MEXICO 79 H4/K2
Mexico City Mexico **79** K2 19 25N 99 10W
Mexico, Gulf of Mexico **79** L3 25 00N 90 00W
Miami U.S.A. **79** L3 25 45N 80 15W
Michigan state U.S.A. **79** L5 45 00N 85 00W
Michigan, Lake Canada/U.S.A. **79** L5 45 00N 87 00W
Mickle Fell sum. England **34** C3 54 38N 2 18W
Middlesbrough England **35** D3 54 35N 1 14W
Middlesbrough u.a. England **35** D3 54 33N 1 04W
Midlothian u.a. Scotland **33** F3 55 50N 3 05W
Milan Italy **51** B6 45 28N 9 12E
Mildenhall England **39** E3 52 21N 0 30E
Mildura Australia **72** E2 34 12S 142 09E
Milford Haven Wales **36** B1 51 44N 5 02W
Milford Sound New Zealand **73** D1 44 41S 167 56E
Milton Keynes England **38** D3 52 02N 0 42W
Milton Ness c. Scotland **31** G1 56 40N 2 20W
Milwaukee U.S.A. **79** L5 43 03N 87 56W
Minch, The sd. Scotland **30** C3/D3 58 00N 6 00W
Mindanao i. The Philippines **60** D3 8 00N 125 00E
Mindoro i. The Philippines **60** D4 13 00N 121 00E
Minehead England **40** D3 51 13N 3 29W
Mingulay i. Scotland **30** B1 56 49N 7 38W
Minneapolis U.S.A. **79** K5 45 00N 93 15W
Minnesota state U.S.A. **79** K5 47 00N 95 00W
Minorca i. Balearic Islands **50** H3 39 45N 4 15E
Minsk Belarus **56** C3 53 51N 27 30E
Miskolc Hungary **42** L5 48 07N 20 47E
Misool i. Indonesia **60** E2 1 50S 129 55E
Mississippi r. U.S.A. **79** K4 33 00N 90 30W
Mississippi state U.S.A. **79** K4 32 00N 90 00W
Missouri r. U.S.A. **79** K4 38 00N 109 00W
Missouri state U.S.A. **79** K4 38 00N 93 00W
Misurata Libya **66** D6 32 23N 15 06E
Miyazaki Japan **59** L1 31 56N 131 27E
Mobile U.S.A. **79** L4 30 40N 88 05W
Mobutu, Lake Uganda/Zaïre **67** D5 2 00N 31 00E
Módena Italy **51** C6 44 39N 10 55E
Moffat Scotland **33** F3 55 20N 3 27W
Mogadishu Somalia **67** E5 2 02N 45 21E
Mogilev see Mahilyow
Mold Wales **36** D3 53 10N 3 08W
Moldau r. Czech Republic **49** H3 49 30N 14 15E
MOLDOVA 42 M5
Moluccas is. Indonesia **60** D3/E2 4 00S 127 00E
Molucca Sea Indonesia **60** D3 0 00S 125 30E
Mombasa Kenya **67** D4 4 04S 39 40E
MONACO 48 G1
Monadhliath Mountains Scotland **31** E2 57 10N 4 00W
Monaghan Monaghan Republic of Ireland **32** C2 54 15N 6 58W
Monaghan co. Republic of Ireland **32** B2/C2 54 10N 7 00W
Monforte Spain **50** B5 42 32N 7 30W
MONGOLIA 57 L2
Monmouth Wales **37** E1 51 50N 2 43W
Monmouthshire u.a. Wales **37** E1 51 47N 2 55W
Monopoli Italy **51** F4 40 57N 17 18E
Monrovia Liberia **66** A3 6 20N 10 46W
Montana state U.S.A. **79** H5 47 00N 111 00W
Montauban France **48** D2 44 01N 1 20E
Montbéliard France **48** G3 47 31N 6 48E
Mont Blanc mt. France/Italy **48** G2 45 50N 6 52E
Monte Carlo Monaco **48** G1 43 44N 7 25E
Montenegro d. Yugoslavia **42** K4 42 30N 19 00E
Monterrey Mexico **79** J3 25 40N 100 20W
Montes Claros tn. Brazil **84** E6 16 45S 43 52W
Montevideo Uruguay **85** D4 34 55S 56 10W
Montgomery Wales **36** D2 52 34N 3 10W
Montluçon France **48** E3 46 20N 2 36E
Montpellier France **48** E1 43 36N 3 53E
Montréal Canada **79** M5 45 30N 73 36W
Montreux Switzerland **49** D2 46 27N 6 55E
Montrose Scotland **31** G1 56 43N 2 29W
Monza Italy **51** B6 45 35N 9 16E
Moosonee Canada **79** L6 51 18N 80 39W
Moray u.a. Scotland **31** F2 57 20N 3 10W
Moray Firth est. Scotland **31** F2 57 45N 3 45W
Morecambe England **34** C3 54 04N 2 53W
Morecambe Bay England **34** B3/C3 54 00N 3 00W
Morelia Mexico **79** J2 19 40N 101 11W
Moreton-in-Marsh England **38** C2 51 59N 1 42W
Morioka Japan **59** N2 39 43N 141 08E
Morlaix France **48** B4 48 35N 3 50W
MOROCCO 66 B6
Moroni Comoros **67** E3 11 40S 43 16E
Morotai i. Indonesia **60** D3 2 10N 128 30E
Morven mt. Scotland **31** F3 58 14N 3 42W
Moscow Russia **56** D3 55 45N 37 42E
Mosel r. Germany/France **48** G3 50 00N 7 00E
Móstoles Spain **50** D4 40 19N 3 53W
Mosul Iraq **61** E4 36 21N 43 08E
Motherwell Scotland **33** E3 55 48N 3 59W
Moulmein Myanmar **58** E2 16 30N 97 39E
Mount Hagen tn. Papua New Guinea **72** E5 5 54S 114 13E
Mount Isa tn. Australia **72** D3 20 44S 139 29E
Mount Magnet tn. Australia **72** B3 28 02S 117 50E

Mounts Bay England **40** B3 50 05N 5 30W
Moyale Kenya **66** D5 3 31N 39 04E
Moyle district Northern Ireland **32** C3 55 10N 6 10W
MOZAMBIQUE 67 D3
Mozambique Mozambique **67** E3 15 03S 40 45E
Mozambique Channel Mozambique/Madagascar **67** E3 18 00S 42 00E
Muck i. Scotland **30** C1 56 50N 6 15W
Muckle Roe i. Scotland **29** D3 60 22N 1 26W
Mudanjiang China **59** D4 44 36N 129 42E
Mukalla Yemen Republic **61** E2 14 34N 49 09E
Mulhouse France **48** G3 47 45N 7 21E
Mull i. Scotland **30** C1/D1 56 25N 6 00W
Mull Head c. Scotland **29** C2 59 20N 2 58W
Mullion England **40** B3 50 01N 5 14W
Mull of Galloway c. Scotland **32** E2 54 38N 4 50W
Mull of Kintyre c. Scotland **32** C3 55 17N 5 55W
Mull of Oa c. Scotland **32** C3 55 35N 6 20W
Mull, Sound of Scotland **30** D1 56 30N 6 00W
Multan Pakistan **58** C4 30 10N 71 36E
München Gladbach Germany **49** D4 51 12N 6 25E
Munich Germany **49** F3 48 08N 11 35E
Münster Germany **49** D4 51 58N 7 37E
Mur r. Europe **49** H2 47 00N 14 00E
Murchison r. Australia **72** B3 26 00S 117 00E
Murcia Spain **50** E2 37 59N 1 08W
Murmansk Russia **56** D4 68 59N 33 08E
Muroran Japan **59** N3 42 21N 140 59E
Murray r. Australia **72** E2 35 40S 144 00E
Murrumbidgee r. Australia **72** E2 35 00S 145 00E
Muscat Oman **61** F3 23 37N 58 38E
Musi r. Indonesia **60** B2 2 30S 104 00E
Musselburgh Scotland **33** F3 55 57N 3 04W
Mwanza Tanzania **67** D4 2 31S 32 56E
Mweru, Lake Zaïre/Zambia **67** C4 8 30S 28 30E
MYANMAR (BURMA) 58 E3
Mykolayiv (Nikolayev) Ukraine **56** D2 46 57N 32 00E
Mynydd Eppynt hills Wales **36** D2 52 02N 3 35W
Mynydd Preseli hills Wales **36** C1 51 58N 4 45W
Mysore India **58** C2 12 18N 76 37E

N

Naberezhnye Chelny Russia **56** F3 55 42N 52 19E
Nabeul Tunisia **42** H3 36 30N 10 44E
Nador Morocco **50** D1 35 10N 3 00W
Nagano Japan **59** M2 36 39N 138 10E
Nagasaki Japan **59** K1 32 45N 129 52E
Nagoya Japan **59** M2 35 08N 136 53E
Nagpur India **58** C3 21 10N 79 12E
Nairn Scotland **31** F2 57 35N 3 53W
Nairn r. Scotland **31** E2 57 28N 4 10W
Nairobi Kenya **67** D4 1 17S 36 50E
Najran Saudi Arabia **61** E2 17 37N 44 40E
Nalchik Russia **43** S7 43 30N 43 31E
Namangan Uzbekistan **56** H2 40 59N 71 41E
Namib Desert Namibia **67** B2 22 00S 14 00E
NAMIBIA 67 B2
Nampo North Korea **59** D3 38 51N 125 10E
Nampula Mozambique **66** D3 15 09S 39 14E
Namur Belgium **49** C4 50 28N 4 52E
Nanchang China **59** C2 28 33N 115 58E
Nancy France **48** G4 48 42N 6 12E
Nanjing China **59** C3 32 03N 118 47E
Nanning China **59** B2 22 50N 108 19E
Nan Shan mts. China **59** A3 38 00N 99 00E
Nantes France **48** C3 47 14N 1 35W
Napier New Zealand **73** D3 39 30S 176 54E
Naples Italy **51** E4 40 50N 14 15E
Napo r. Ecuador/Peru **84** B7 1 30S 74 30W
Narbonne France **48** E1 43 11N 3 00E
Narmada r. India **58** C2 22 00N 78 00E
Narvik Norway **42** K9 68 26N 17 25E
Nassau The Bahamas **79** M3 25 05N 77 20W
Nasser, Lake Egypt **61** D3 22 35N 31 40E
Natal Brazil **84** F7 5 46S 35 15W
Natuna Islands Indonesia **60** B3 3 40N 108 00E
NAURU 5
Ndjamena Chad **66** D4 12 10N 14 59E
Ndola Zambia **67** C3 13 00S 28 39E
Neath Wales **36** D1 51 40N 3 48W
Neath and Port Talbot u.a. Wales **36** D1 51 40N 3 45W
Nebraska state U.S.A. **79** J5 42 00N 102 00W
Negro r. Argentina **85** C4 39 39S 67 30W
Negro r. Bolivia/Brazil **84** C7 1 00S 62 20W
Negros i. The Philippines **60** D3 10 00N 123 00E
Neiva Colombia **84** B8 2 58N 75 15W
Nelson England **34** C2 53 51N 2 13W
Nelson New Zealand **73** C2 41 30S 172 30E
Nelson r. Canada **78** K6 57 00N 94 00W
Nemuro Japan **59** P3 43 22N 145 36E
Nene r. England **39** E3 52 45N 0 10E
Nen Jiang r. China **59** D4 45 00N 124 00E
NEPAL 58 D3
NETHERLANDS 49 C5/D5
Nevada state U.S.A. **79** H4 39 00N 118 00W
Nevers France **48** E3 47 00N 3 09E
Nevis i. St. Kitts & Nevis **79** N2 17 00N 62 30W
Newark U.S.A. **79** M5 40 43N 74 11W
Newark-on-Trent England **37** G3 53 05N 0 49W
New Britain i. Papua New Guinea **72** F5 4 45S 150 30E
New Brunswick province Canada **79** N5 47 30N 66 00W
Newburgh Scotland **33** F4 57 18N 2 00W
Newbury England **38** C2 51 25N 1 20W
New Caledonia i. Pacific Ocean **5** 22 00S 165 00E
Newcastle Australia **72** F2 32 57S 151 43E
Newcastle Northern Ireland **32** D2 54 13N 5 54W
Newcastle Emlyn Wales **36** C2 52 02N 4 28W
Newcastle-under-Lyme England **34** C2 53 00N 2 14W
Newcastle upon Tyne England **34** D3 54 59N 1 35W
New Cumnock Scotland **33** E3 55 24N 4 12W
Newfoundland i. Canada **79** P5 53 51N 56 56W
Newfoundland province Canada **78** P6 56 00N 60 00W
New Galloway Scotland **33** E3 55 05N 4 10W
New Hampshire state U.S.A. **79** M5 44 00N 72 00W
New Ireland i. Papua New Guinea **72** F5 3 15S 152 30E
New Jersey state U.S.A. **79** M4 40 00N 75 00W
Newman Australia **72** B3 23 22S 119 43E

Newmarket England **39** E3 52 15N 0 25E
New Mexico state U.S.A. **79** J4 35 00N 107 00W
New Orleans U.S.A. **79** K3 30 00N 90 03W
New Plymouth New Zealand **73** C3 39 04S 174 04E
Newport Isle of Wight England **38** C1 50 42N 1 18W
Newport Shropshire England **37** E2 52 47N 2 22W
Newport Wales **36** D1 51 35N 3 00W
Newport u.a. Wales **36** D1/E1 51 33N 3 00W
Newquay England **40** B3 50 25N 5 05W
New Quay Wales **36** C2 52 13N 4 22W
Newry Northern Ireland **32** C2 54 11N 6 20W
Newry and Mourne district Northern Ireland **32** C2 54 10N 6 20W
New Siberian Islands Russia **57** Q5 75 00N 145 00E
New South Wales state Australia **72** E2 32 00S 145 00E
Newton Abbot England **40** D2 50 32N 3 36W
Newton Aycliffe England **34** D3 54 37N 1 34W
Newtonmore Scotland **31** E2 57 04N 4 08W
Newton Stewart Scotland **33** E2 54 57N 4 29W
Newtown Wales **36** D2 52 32N 3 19W
Newtownabbey Northern Ireland **32** D2 54 40N 5 54W
Newtownabbey district Northern Ireland **32** D2 54 45N 5 55W
Newtownards Northern Ireland **32** D2 54 36N 5 41W
Newtownhamilton Northern Ireland **32** C2 54 12N 6 35W
Newtownstewart Northern Ireland **32** B2 54 43N 7 24W
New York U.S.A. **79** M5 40 40N 73 50W
New York state U.S.A. **79** M5 43 00N 76 00W
NEW ZEALAND 73
Ngaoundéré Cameroon **66** D3 7 20N 13 35E
Nguru Nigeria **66** D4 12 53N 10 30E
Nha-Trang Vietnam **60** B4 12 15N 109 10E
Niamey Niger **66** C4 13 32N 2 05E
Nias i. Indonesia **60** A3 1 00N 97 30E
NICARAGUA 79 L2
Nicaragua, Lake Nicaragua **79** L2 11 50N 86 00W
Nice France **48** G1 43 42N 7 16E
Nicobar Islands India **58** E1 8 30N 94 00E
Nicosia Cyprus **43** N3 35 11N 33 23E
Nidd r. England **35** D3 54 01N 1 40W
Nieuwpoort Belgium **39** G2 51 08N 2 45E
NIGER 66 C4
Niger r. Africa **66** B4 11 00N 5 00W
NIGERIA 66 C3
Niigata Japan **59** M2 37 58N 139 02E
Nijmegen Netherlands **49** C4 51 50N 5 52E
Nikolayev see Mykolayiv
Nile r. Sudan/Egypt **61** D3 28 00N 31 00E
Nimba, Mount Guinea/Liberia **66** B3 7 39N 8 30W
Nimes France **48** F1 43 50N 4 21E
Niort France **48** C3 46 19N 0 27W
Niš Serbia Yugoslavia **42** L4 43 20N 21 54E
Niteroi Brazil **84** E5 22 54S 43 06W
Nith r. Scotland **33** F3 55 35N 3 50W
Nizhnekamsk Russia **43** S7 55 38N 51 49E
Nizhniy Novgorod (Gorkiy) Russia **56** E3 56 20N 44 00E
Nizhniy Tagil Russia **56** F3 58 00N 59 58E
Norfolk U.S.A. **79** M4 36 54N 76 18W
Norfolk co. England **39** E3/F3 52 45N 1 00E
Norfolk Broads geog. reg. England **39** F3 52 45N 1 30E
Norilsk Russia **57** J4 69 21N 88 02E
Normandy geog. reg. France **48** C4/D4 49 00N 0 00
Norrköping Sweden **42** K7 58 35N 16 10E
Northallerton England **35** D3 54 20N 1 26W
Northampton England **38** D3 52 14N 0 54W
Northamptonshire co. England **38** C3/D3 52 20N 1 00W
North Ayrshire u.a. Scotland **32/33** D3/E3 55 30N 5 05W
North Berwick Scotland **33** G4 56 04N 2 44W
North Cape New Zealand **73** C4 34 25S 173 03E
North Carolina state U.S.A. **79** M4 36 00N 80 00W
North Channel British Isles **32** D2/3 55 20N 5 50W
North Dakota state U.S.A. **79** J5 47 00N 102 00W
North Down district Northern Ireland **32** D2 54 35N 5 50W
North Downs hills England **38/39** D2/E2 51 15N 0 30E
North Dvina r. Russia **56** E4 63 00N 43 00E
North East Lincolnshire u.a. England **35** E2 53 30N 0 10W
Northern Ireland province United Kingdom **32** B2 54 40N 7 00W
NORTHERN MARIANAS 5
Northern Territory Australia **72** D4 19 00S 132 00E
North Esk r. Scotland **31** G1 56 50N 2 50W
North Foreland c. England **39** F2 51 23N 1 27E
North Friesian Islands Germany **49** E6 54 00N 8 00E
North Island New Zealand **73** D3 39 00N 176 00E
NORTH KOREA 59 D4
North Lanarkshire u.a. Scotland **33** F3 55 50N 3 55W
North Lincolnshire u.a. England **35** E2 53 40N 0 40W
North Pole Arctic Ocean **86** 90 00N
North Ronaldsay i. Scotland **29** C2 59 23N 2 26W
North Sea Atlantic Ocean **42** G7 57 00N 4 00E
North Shields England **35** D4 55 01N 1 26W
North Uist i. Scotland **30** B2 57 04N 7 15W
Northumberland co. England **33** G3/H3 55 10N 2 00W
Northwest Highlands Scotland **30/31** D2/E3 58 00N 5 00W
North West Somerset u.a. England **38** B2 51 25N 2 50W
Northwest Territories territory Canada **78** G7/L7 64 00N 120 00W
Northwich England **34** C2 53 16N 2 32W
North York Moors England **35** E3 55 22N 0 45W
North Yorkshire co. England **34/35** D3/E3 54 05N 1 20W
Norton England **35** E3 54 08N 0 48W
NORWAY 42 H7/M9
Norwich England **39** F3 52 38N 1 18E
Nottingham England **37** F2 52 58N 1 10W
Nottinghamshire co. England **37** F3/G3 53 20N 1 00W
Nouadhibou Mauritania **66** A5 20 54N 17 01W
Nouakchott Mauritania **66** A4 18 09N 15 58W
Novara Italy **51** B6 45 27N 8 37E
Nova Scotia province Canada **79** N5 45 30N 63 00W

Novaya Zemlya is. Russia **56** F5 74 00N 55 00E
Novgorod Russia **42** N7 58 30N 31 20E
Novi Sad Serbia Yugoslavia **42** K5 45 15N 19 51E
Novokuznetsk Russia **57** J3 53 45N 87 12E
Novosibirsk Russia **56** J3 55 04N 83 05E
Nuevo Laredo Mexico **79** K3 27 39N 99 30W
Nu Jiang (Salween) r. China/Myanmar **58** E4 31 30N 94 00E
Nullarbor Plain Australia **72** C2 30 30S 129 00E
Nuneaton England **37** F2 52 32N 1 28W
Nunivak i. U.S.A. **78** C6 60 00N 166 00W
Nuremberg Germany **49** F3 49 27N 11 05E
Nuuk (Godthåb) Greenland **78** P7 64 10N 51 40W
Nyala Sudan **61** C2 12 01N 24 50E
Nyasa, Lake (Lake Malawi) Malawi/Mozambique **67** D3 12 00S 35 00E

O

Oahe, Lake U.S.A. **79** J5 45 00N 100 00W
Oamaru New Zealand **73** C1 45 06S 170 58E
Ob r. Russia **56** G4 64 00N 65 00E
Oban Scotland **30** D1 56 25N 5 29W
Oberammergau Germany **49** F2 47 35N 11 07E
Obihiro Japan **59** N3 42 56N 143 10E
Obi Islands i. Indonesia **60** D2 1 30S 127 30E
Ochil Hills Scotland **33** F4 56 15N 3 30W
Odense Denmark **42** J7 55 24N 10 25E
Oder r. Europe **49** H5 53 00N 14 30E
Odessa Ukraine **56** D2 46 30N 30 46E
Ogbomosho Nigeria **66** B3 8 05N 4 11E
Ohio r. U.S.A. **79** L4 39 00N 86 00W
Ohio state U.S.A. **79** L5 40 00N 83 00W
Oiapoque Brazil **84** E4 3 54N 51 46W
Oise r. France **48** E4 49 30N 3 00E
Oita Japan **59** L1 33 15N 131 36E
Oka r. Russia **42** Q7 54 00N 42 00E
Okavango Swamp Botswana **67** C3 19 00S 23 00E
Okayama Japan **59** L1 34 40N 133 54E
Okehampton England **40** C2 50 44N 4 00W
Okhotsk, Sea of Russia **57** Q3 56 00N 145 00E
Oki Islands Japan **59** L2 36 05N 133 00E
Oklahoma state U.S.A. **79** K4 36 00N 98 00W
Oklahoma City U.S.A. **79** K4 35 28N 97 33W
Öland i. Sweden **42** K7 56 45N 51 50E
Olbia Italy **51** B4 40 56N 9 30E
Oldenburg Germany **49** E5 53 08N 8 13E
Oldham England **34** C2 53 33N 2 07W
Oldmeldrum Scotland **31** G2 57 20N 2 20W
Olongapo The Philippines **60** D4 14 49N 120 17E
Omagh Northern Ireland **32** B2 54 36N 7 18W
Omagh district Northern Ireland **32** B2 54 30N 7 30W
Omaha U.S.A. **79** K5 41 15N 96 00W
OMAN 61 F3
Oman, Gulf of Iran/Oman **61** F3 24 30N 58 30E
Omdurman Sudan **61** D2 15 37N 32 29E
Omsk Russia **56** H3 55 00N 73 22E
Onega, Lake i. Russia **56** D4 62 00N 40 00E
Onitsha Nigeria **66** C3 6 10N 6 47E
Ontario province Canada **79** L6 50 00N 85 00W
Ontario, Lake Canada/U.S.A. **79** M5 43 45N 78 00W
Oostende Belgium **39** G2 51 13N 2 55E
Oporto Portugal **50** A4 41 09N 8 37W
Oran Algeria **66** B6 35 45N 0 38W
Orange France **48** F2 44 08N 4 48E
Orange r. Southern Africa **67** B2 29 00S 19 00E
Ord r. Australia **72** C4 15 00S 128 00E
Örebro Sweden **42** K7 59 17N 15 13E
Oregon state U.S.A. **79** G5 44 00N 120 00W
Orel Russia **56** D3 52 58N 36 04E
Orenburg Russia **56** F3 51 50N 55 00E
Orford Ness c. England **39** F2 52 05N 1 34E
Orinoco r. Venezuela/Colombia **84** C8 6 40N 64 30W
Oristano Italy **51** B3 39 54N 8 36E
Orkney Islands u.a. Scotland **29** B1/C2 59 00N 3 00W
Orléans France **48** D3 47 54N 1 54E
Orne r. France **41** G1/2 49 00N 1 30W
Oronsay i. Scotland **32** C4 56 00N 6 15W
Orsk Russia **56** F3 51 13N 58 35E
Ortles mt. Italy **49** F2 46 31N 10 33E
Oruro Bolivia **84** C6 17 59S 67 08W
Osaka Japan **59** M1 34 40N 135 30E
Osh Kirgyzstan **56** H2 40 37N 72 49E
Osijek Croatia **42** K5 45 33N 18 41E
Oslo Norway **42** J7 59 56N 10 45E
Osnabrück Germany **49** E5 52 17N 8 03E
Osorno Chile **85** B3 40 35S 73 14W
Ostende Belgium **49** B4 51 13N 2 55E
Ostrava Czech Republic **42** K5 49 50N 18 15E
Oswestry England **36** D2 52 52N 3 03W
Otranto Italy **51** G4 40 08N 18 30E
Ottawa r. Canada **79** M5 46 00N 77 00W
Ouagadougou Burkina **66** B4 12 20N 1 40W
Oubangui r. Central Africa **67** C5 4 00N 21 00E
Oujda Morocco **66** B6 34 41N 1 45W
Oulu Finland **42** M9 65 02N 25 27E
Oundle England **38** D3 52 29N 0 29W
Ouse r. England **35** D2 53 40N 1 05W
Outer Hebrides is. Scotland **30** B1/C3 58 00N 7 00W
Out Skerries is. Scotland **29** E3 60 25N 0 46W
Oviedo Spain **50** C5 43 21N 7 18W
Oxford England **38** C2 51 46N 1 15W
Oxfordshire co. England **38** C2 51 50N 1 25W

P

Pabbay i. Scotland **30** B2 57 47N 7 14W
Pacific Ocean 79 J2
Padang Indonesia **60** B2 1 00S 100 21E
Paderborn Germany **49** E4 51 43N 8 44E
Padstow England **40** C3 50 33N 4 56W
Padua Italy **51** C6 45 24N 11 53E
Paisley Scotland **33** E3 55 50N 4 26W
Pakanbaru Indonesia **60** B3 0 33N 101 30E
PAKISTAN 58 B3
Palau Islands Pacific Ocean **60** E3 7 30N 134 30E
Palawan i. The Philippines **60** C3 10 00N 119 00E
Palembang Indonesia **60** B2 2 59S 104 45E
Palermo Italy **51** D3 38 08N 13 23E

Palma Balearic Islands 50 G3 39 35N 2 39E
Palmerston North New Zealand 73 D2 40 22S 175 37E
Pamirs mts. Asia 58 C4 38 00N 74 00E
Pamplona Spain 50 E5 42 49N 1 39W
PANAMA 79 L1
Panamá Panama 79 M1 8 57N 19 30W
Panama Canal Panama 79 L1 9 00N 80 00W
Panay i. The Philippines 60 D4 11 00N 122 00E
Pantelleria i. Italy 51 D2 36 00N 12 00E
Papa Stour i. Scotland 29 D3 60 20N 1 42W
Papa Westray i. Scotland 29 C2 59 22N 2 54W
PAPUA NEW GUINEA 72 E5
PARAGUAY 84 D5
Paraguay r. South America 84 D5 21 20S 58 20W
Paramaribo Suriname 84 D8 5 52N 55 14W
Paraná Argentina 85 C4 31 45S 60 30W
Paraná r. South America 85 D5 30 00S 59 50W
Paris France 48 E4 48 52N 2 20E
Parma Italy 51 C6 44 48N 10 19E
Parnaíba Brazil 84 E7 2 58S 41 46W
Parrett r. England 41 E4 51 05N 2 55W
Parry Islands Canada 78 J8 75 15N 109 00W
Pasto Colombia 84 B8 1 12N 77 17W
Patagonia geog. reg. Argentina 85 C3 44 00S 70 00W
Patna India 58 D3 25 37N 85 12E
Patras Greece 42 L3 38 14N 21 44E
Pau France 48 C1 43 18N 0 22W
Peace r. Canada 78 H6 57 30N 117 00W
Pechora Russia 43 T9 65 14N 57 18E
Pechora r. Russia 43 S9 66 00N 53 00E
Pécs Hungary 42 K5 46 04N 18 15E
Peebles Scotland 33 F3 55 39N 3 12W
Peel Isle of Man British Isles 33 E2 54 14N 4 42W
Peel Fell sum. Scotland/England 33 G5 55 17N 2 35W
Pegasus Bay New Zealand 73 C2 43 22S 172 55E
Pegu Myanmar 58 E2 17 18N 96 31E
Peking see Beijing
Peloponnese geog. reg. Greece 42 L3 37 00N 22 00E
Pelotas Brazil 85 D4 31 45S 52 20W
Pematangsiantar Indonesia 60 A3 2 59N 99 01E
Pembroke Wales 36 C1 51 41N 4 55W
Pembrokeshire u.a. Wales 36 B1/C1 51 50N 5 00W
Peñalara mt. Spain 50 D4 40 51N 3 58W
Penicuik Scotland 33 F3 55 50N 3 14W
Pennines hills England 34 C3 54 40N 2 10W
Pennsylvania state U.S.A. 79 M5 41 00N 78 00W
Penrith England 34 C3 54 40N 2 44W
Penryn England 40 B3 50 09N 5 06W
Pentland Firth sd. Scotland 29 F3 58 45N 3 10W
Pentland Hills Scotland 33 F3 55 45N 3 30W
Penza Russia 56 E3 53 11N 45 00E
Penzance England 40 B3 50 07N 5 33W
Perm Russia 56 F3 58 01N 56 10E
Perpignan France 48 E1 42 42N 2 54E
Perth Australia 72 B3 31 57S 115 52E
Perth Scotland 31 F1 56 42N 3 28W
Perthshire and Kinross u.a. Scotland 31 E1/F1 56 45N 3 50W
PERU 84 B6
Perugia Italy 51 D5 43 07N 12 23E
Pescara Italy 51 E5 42 27N 14 13E
Peshawar Pakistan 58 C4 34 01N 71 33E
Peterhead Scotland 31 H2 57 30N 1 46W
Peterlee England 35 D3 54 46N 1 19W
Petersfield England 38 C2 51 00N 0 56W
Petropavlovsk Kazakhstan 56 G3 54 53N 69 13E
Petropavlovsk-Kamchatskiy Russia 57 R3 53 03N 158 43E
Petrozavodsk Russia 42 N8 61 46N 34 19E
Pforzheim Germany 49 E3 48 53N 8 41E
Philadelphia U.S.A. 79 M4 40 00N 75 10W
PHILIPPINES 60 D3/4
Phnom Penh Cambodia 60 B4 11 35N 104 55E
Phoenix U.S.A. 79 H4 33 30N 112 03W
Piacenza Italy 51 B6 45 03N 9 41E
Pickering England 35 E3 54 14N 0 46W
Pickering, Vale of England 35 E3 54 10N 0 45W
Pietermaritzburg Republic of South Africa 67 D2 29 36S 30 24E
Pilcomayo r. South America 84 C5 24 00S 61 00W
Pinsk Belarus 42 M6 52 08N 26 01E
Piraeus Greece 42 L3 37 57N 23 42E
Pisa Italy 51 C5 43 43N 10 24E
Pitcairn Islands Pacific Ocean 4 25 04S 130 06W
Pitlochry Scotland 31 F1 56 43N 3 45W
Piura Peru 84 A7 5 15S 80 38W
Plenty, Bay of New Zealand 73 D3 37 48S 177 12E
Pleven Bulgaria 42 L4 43 25N 24 64E
Ploiesti Romania 42 M4 44 57N 26 01E
Plovdiv Bulgaria 42 L4 42 08N 24 45E
Plymouth England 41 F3 50 23N 4 10W
Plynlimon mt. Wales 36 D2 52 28N 3 47W
Plzeň Czech Republic 42 J5 49 45N 13 25E
Po r. Italy 51 C6/D6 45 00N 12 00E
Pobeda Peak Kirgyzstan 56 J2 42 25N 80 15E
Pointe Noire r. Congo 66 D2 4 46S 11 53E
Poitiers France 48 D3 46 35N 0 20E
POLAND 42 K6
Ponta Grossa Brazil 85 D5 25 07S 50 09W
Pontardulais Wales 36 C1 51 43N 4 02W
Pontefract England 35 D2 53 42N 1 18W
Pontianak Indonesia 60 B2 0 05S 109 16E
Pontypool Wales 36 D1 51 43N 3 02W
Pontypridd Wales 36 D1 51 37N 3 22W
Poole England 41 F3 50 43N 1 59W
Poolewe Scotland 30 D2 57 45N 5 37W
Poopo, Lake Bolivia 84 C6 18 30S 67 20W
Popocatepetl vol. Mexico 79 K2 19 02N 98 38W
Porbandar India 58 B3 21 04N 69 40E
Portadown Northern Ireland 32 C2 54 26N 6 27W
Port Askaig Scotland 32 C3 55 51N 6 07W
Port Augusta Australia 72 C2 32 30S 137 48E
Port Ellen Scotland 32 C3 55 39N 6 12W
Port Gentil Gabon 66 C2 0 40S 8 50E
Port Glasgow Scotland 33 E3 55 56N 4 41W
Port Harcourt Nigeria 66 C3 4 43N 7 05E

Port Hedland Australia 72 B3 20 18S 118 35E
Porthmadog Wales 36 C2 52 55N 4 08W
Portknockie Scotland 31 G2 57 42N 2 52W
Portland U.S.A. 78 G5 45 32N 122 40W
Portland Bill c. England 41 E3 50 31N 2 27W
Port Lincoln Australia 72 D2 34 44S 135 52E
Port Moresby Papua New Guinea 72 E5 9 30S 147 07E
Portnahaven Scotland 32 C3 55 41N 6 31W
Port of Ness Scotland 30 C3 58 29N 6 13W
Port of Spain Trinidad and Tobago 79 N2 10 38N 61 31W
Porto Novo Benin 66 C3 6 30N 2 47E
Pôrto Velho Brazil 84 C7 8 45S 63 54W
Portpatrick Scotland 32 D2 54 51N 5 07W
Port Pirie Australia 72 D2 33 10S 138 02E
Portree Scotland 30 C2 57 24N 6 12W
Portrush Northern Ireland 32 C3 55 12N 6 40W
Portsmouth England 38 C1 50 48N 1 05W
Portsoy Scotland 31 G2 57 41N 2 41W
Portstewart Northern Ireland 32 C3 55 11N 6 43W
Port Sudan Sudan 61 D2 19 38N 37 07E
Port Talbot Wales 36 D1 51 36N 3 47W
PORTUGAL 50 A3
Potenza Italy 51 E4 40 38N 15 48E
Potsdam Germany 49 G5 52 24N 13 04E
Powys u.a. Wales 36 D2 52 10N 3 30W
Poyang Hu l. China 59 C2 29 00N 116 30E
Poznań Poland 42 K6 52 25N 16 53E
Prague Czech Republic 42 J6 50 06N 14 26E
Prato Italy 51 C5 43 53N 11 06E
Preston England 34 C2 53 46N 2 42W
Prestwick Scotland 33 E3 55 30N 4 37W
Pretoria Republic of South Africa 67 C2 25 45S 28 12E
Prijedor Bosnia-Herzegovina 51 F6 45 00N 16 41E
Prince Edward Island province Canada 79 N5 46 30N 63 00W
Prince Rupert Canada 78 F6 54 09N 130 20W
Príncipe i. Gulf of Guinea 66 C3 1 37N 7 27E
Pripet r. Belarus 42 M6 52 00N 28 00E
Priština Serbia Yugoslavia 42 L4 42 39N 21 20E
Provence geog. reg. France 48 F1/G1 44 00N 6 00E
Providence U.S.A. 79 M5 41 50N 71 28W
Providence, Cape New Zealand 73 B1 46 01S 166 28E
Prudhoe Bay tn. U.S.A. 78 E7 70 05N 148 20W
Pskov Russia 42 M7 57 48N 28 26E
Pucallpa Peru 84 B7 8 21S 74 33W
Puebla Mexico 79 K2 19 03N 98 10W
Puerto Montt Chile 85 B3 41 28S 73 00W
PUERTO RICO 79 N2
Puig Mayor mt. Balearic Islands 50 G3 39 49N 2 47E
Pukekohe New Zealand 73 C3 37 12S 174 54E
Pune India 58 C2 18 34N 73 58E
Punta Arenas Chile 85 B2 53 10S 70 56W
Pusan South Korea 59 D3 35 05N 129 02E
Puy de Sancy mt. France 48 E2 45 32N 2 48E
Pwllheli Wales 36 C2 52 53N 4 25W
Pyongyang North Korea 59 D3 39 00N 125 47E
Pyrénées mts. France/Spain 50 F5 42 50N 0 30E

Q

Qaidam Basin see Qaidam Pendi
Qaidam Pendi (Qaidam Basin) China 59 A4 37 30N 94 00E
QATAR 61 F3
Qattara Depression Egypt 61 C3 24 00N 27 30E
Qazvin Iran 61 E4 36 16N 50 00E
Qingdao China 59 D3 36 04N 120 22E
Qinghai Hu l. China 59 B3 37 00N 100 00E
Qiqihar China 59 D4 47 23N 124 00E
Qizil r. Iran 61 E4 36 00N 48 00E
Qom Iran 61 F4 34 39N 50 57E
Quantock Hills England 41 D4 51 05N 3 15W
Québec Canada 79 M5 46 50N 71 15W
Québec province Canada 79 M6 51 00N 75 00W
Queen Charlotte Islands Canada 78 F6 53 30N 131 50W
Queen Elizabeth Islands Canada 78 J8 77 30N 105 00W
Queen Maud Land geog. reg. Antarctica 86 73 00S 10 00E
Queensland state Australia 72 E3 22 00S 143 00E
Queenstown New Zealand 73 B1 45 02S 168 40E
Quetta Pakistan 58 B4 30 12N 67 00E
Quezon City The Philippines 60 D4 14 39N 121 02E
Qui Nhon Vietnam 60 B4 13 47N 109 11E
Quito Ecuador 84 B7 0 14S 78 30W

R

Raasay i. Scotland 30 C2 57 25N 6 05W
Rabat-Salé Morocco 66 B6 34 02N 6 51W
Radom Poland 42 L6 51 26N 21 10E
Rainier, Mount U.S.A. 78 G5 46 25N 121 45W
Raipur India 58 D3 21 16N 81 42E
Rajang r. Malaysia 60 C3 2 00N 114 00E
Rakaia r. New Zealand 73 C2 43 00S 172 00E
Ramsey Isle of Man British Isles 33 E2 54 19N 4 23W
Ramsgate England 39 F2 51 20N 1 25E
Randalstown Northern Ireland 32 C2 54 45N 6 19W
Rangitaiki r. New Zealand 73 D3 38 45S 177 00E
Rangoon (Yangdon) Myanmar 58 E2 16 47N 96 10E
Ras Dashan mt. Ethiopia 61 D2 13 15N 38 27E
Rasht Iran 61 E4 37 18N 49 38E
Rathlin Island Northern Ireland 32 C3 55 20N 6 10W
Rathlin Sound Northern Ireland 32 C3 55 20N 6 25W
Rattray Scotland 31 F1 56 36N 3 20W
Ravenna Italy 51 D6 44 25N 12 12E
Rawalpindi Pakistan 58 C4 33 36N 73 04E
Reading England 38 D2 51 28N 0 59W
Recife Brazil 84 F7 8 06S 34 53W
Recklinghausen Germany 49 D4 51 37N 7 11E
Redbridge England 39 E2 51 34N 0 05E
Redcar England 35 D3 54 37N 1 04W
Redcar and Cleveland u.a. England 35 D3/E3 54 30N 1 00W
Redditch England 37 F2 52 19N 1 56W
Rede r. England 33 G3 55 15N 2 20W

Redhill tn. England 38 D2 51 14N 0 11W
Redruth England 40 B3 50 13N 5 14W
Red Sea Middle East 61 D3 27 00N 35 00E
Regensburg Germany 49 G3 49 01N 12 07E
Reggio di Calabria Italy 51 E3 38 06N 15 39E
Reggio nell'Emilia Italy 51 C6 44 42N 10 37E
Regina Canada 78 J6 50 30N 104 38W
Reigate England 38 D2 51 14N 0 13W
Reims France 48 F4 49 15N 4 02E
Remscheid Germany 49 D4 51 10N 7 11E
Renfrewshire u.a. Scotland 33 E3 55 50N 4 40W
Rennes France 48 C4 48 06N 1 40W
Reno U.S.A. 79 H4 39 32N 119 49W
REPUBLIC OF IRELAND 28
REPUBLIC OF SOUTH AFRICA 67 C2
Resistencia Argentina 85 D5 27 28S 59 00W
Reutlingen Germany 49 E3 48 30N 9 13E
Reykjavík Iceland 42 B8 64 09N 21 58W
Rhayader Wales 36 D2 52 18N 3 30W
Rhine r. Europe 49 D4 50 30N 7 30E
Rhode Island state U.S.A. 79 M5 41 00N 71 00W
Rhodes i. Greece 42 M3 36 00N 28 00E
Rhondda Wales 36 D1 51 40N 3 30W
Rhondda Cynon Taff u.a. Wales 36 D1 51 40N 3 30W
Rhône r. Switzerland/France 48 F2 45 00N 4 50E
Rhum i. Scotland 30 C1/2 57 00N 6 20W
Rhyl Wales 36 D3 53 19N 3 29W
Ribble r. England 34 C2 53 58N 2 17W
Ribeirão Preto Brazil 84 E5 21 09S 47 48W
Richmond England 34 D3 54 24N 1 44W
Richmond U.S.A. 79 M4 37 34N 77 27W
Richmond upon Thames England 38 D2 51 28N 0 19W
Riga Latvia 42 L7 56 53N 24 08E
Rijeka Croatia 42 J5 45 20N 14 27E
Rimini Italy 51 D6 44 03N 12 34E
Ringwood England 41 F3 50 51N 1 47W
Rio Branco tn. Brazil 84 C7 9 59S 67 49W
Rio de Janeiro tn. Brazil 84 E5 22 53S 43 17W
Rio Grande r. Mexico/U.S.A. 79 J3 29 30N 105 00W
Rio Grande tn. Brazil 85 D4 32 03S 52 08W
Ripon England 34 D3 54 08N 1 31W
River Plate Estuary Uruguay/Argentina 85 D4 35 00S 57 00W
Rivne (Rovno) Ukraine 42 M6 50 39N 26 10E
Riyadh Saudi Arabia 61 E3 24 39N 46 46E
Roanne France 48 F3 46 02N 4 05E
Robson, Mount Canada 78 H6 53 08N 118 18W
Rochdale England 34 C2 53 38N 2 09W
Rochester England 39 E2 51 24N 0 30E
Rochester U.S.A. 79 M5 43 12N 77 37W
Rockhampton Australia 72 F3 23 22S 150 30E
Rocky Mountains Canada/U.S.A. 78/79 F7/J4 46 00N 110 00W
Roebourne Australia 72 B3 20 45S 117 08E
ROMANIA 42 L5
Rome Italy 51 D4 41 53N 12 30E
Romsey England 38 C1 50 59N 1 30W
Ronne Ice Shelf Antarctica 86 77 00S 60 00W
Rora Head Scotland 29 B1 58 52N 3 26W
Roraima mt. Guyana 84 C8 5 14N 60 44W
Rosario Argentina 85 C4 33 00S 60 40W
Rosehearty Scotland 31 G2 57 42N 2 07W
Rosenheim Germany 51 D7 47 51N 12 09E
Rossano Italy 51 F3 39 35N 16 38E
Ross Ice Shelf Antarctica 86 80 00S 180 00
Ross of Mull p. Scotland 30 C1 56 20N 6 10W
Ross-on-Wye England 37 E1 51 55N 2 35W
Ross Sea Antarctica 86 75 00S 180 00
Rostock Germany 49 G6 54 06N 12 09E
Rostov-on-Don Russia 56 D2 47 15N 39 45E
Rotherham England 35 D2 53 26N 1 20W
Rothes Scotland 31 F2 57 31N 3 13W
Rothesay Scotland 32 D3 55 51N 5 03W
Rotorua New Zealand 73 D3 38 08S 176 14E
Rotterdam Netherlands 49 C4 51 54N 4 28E
Rouen France 48 D4 49 26N 1 05E
Rousay i. Scotland 29 B2 59 10N 3 00W
Rovno see Rivne
Royal Leamington Spa England 37 F2 52 18N 1 31W
Royal Tunbridge Wells England 39 E2 51 08N 0 16E
Royston England 38 D3 52 03N 0 01W
Ruapehu mt. New Zealand 73 D3 39 18S 175 34E
Rubha Hunish c. Scotland 30 C2 57 40N 6 20W
Rugby England 37 F2 52 23N 1 15W
Rugeley England 37 F2 52 46N 1 55W
Rügen i. Germany 49 G6 54 00N 14 00E
Rukwa, Lake Tanzania 67 D4 8 00S 33 00E
Runcorn England 34 C2 53 20N 2 44W
Ruse Bulgaria 42 M4 43 50N 25 59E
RUSSIA see RUSSIAN FEDERATION
RUSSIAN FEDERATION (RUSSIA) 56/57
Rutland Water r. England 38 D3 52 40N 0 37W
Ruvuma r. Tanzania/Mozambique 67 D3 11 00S 39 00E
Ruwenzori, Mount Uganda/Zaïre 67 C5 0 23N 29 54E
RWANDA 67 C4
Ryazan Russia 56 D3 54 37N 39 43E
Rybinsk Russia 56 D3 58 03N 38 50E
Rybinsk Reservoir Russia 43 P7 59 00N 38 00E
Ryde England 38 C1 50 44N 1 10W
Rye England 39 E1 50 57N 0 44E
Ryukyu Islands Japan 59 D2 27 30N 127 30E

S

Saale r. Germany 49 F4 51 15N 12 00E
Saar r. Germany/France 49 D3 49 15N 6 58E
Saarbrücken Germany 49 D3 49 15N 6 58E
Sabadell Spain 50 G4 41 33N 2 07E
Sabah admin. Malaysia 60 C3 5 00N 115 00E
Sabhā Libya 66 D5 27 02N 14 26E
Sacramento U.S.A. 78 G4 38 32N 121 30W
Sado i. Japan 59 M2 38 20N 138 30E
Saffron Walden England 39 E3 52 01N 0 15E
Safi Morocco 66 B6 32 20N 9 17W
Sahara Desert North Africa 66 A5/E5 22 50N 0 00
Saigon see Ho Chi Minh City
St. Abb's Head c. Scotland 33 G3 55 55N 2 09W
St. Agnes England 40 B3 50 18N 5 13W
St. Albans England 38 D2 51 46N 0 21W
St. Albans Head c. England 41 E3 50 34N 2 04W

St. Andrews Scotland 33 G4 56 20N 2 48W
St. Anton Austria 49 F2 47 09N 10 17E
St. Austell England 40 C3 50 20N 4 48W
St. Bees Head England 34 B3 54 31N 3 39W
St. Bride's Bay Wales 36 B1 51 50N 5 15W
St. Brieuc France 48 B4 48 31N 2 45W
St. Catherine's Point England 38 C1 50 34N 1 18W
St. David's Wales 36 B1 51 54N 5 16W
St. David's Head Wales 36 B1 51 55N 5 19W
St-Denis France 48 E4 48 57N 2 22E
St. Dizier France 48 F4 48 38N 4 58E
Saintes France 48 C2 45 44N 0 38W
St-Étienne France 48 F2 45 26N 4 23E
St. Gallen Switzerland 51 B7 47 25N 9 23E
St. George's Channel British Isles 36 A1/B2 52 00N 6 00W
St. Germain France 48 E4 48 55N 2 08E
St. Gotthard Pass Switzerland 49 E2 46 34N 8 31E
St. Helena i. Atlantic Ocean 5 15 58S 5 43W
St. Helens England 34 C2 53 28N 2 44W
St. Helier Jersey Channel Islands 41 E2 49 12N 2 07W
St. Ives Cambridgeshire England 38 D3 52 20N 0 05W
St. Ives Cornwall England 40 B3 50 12N 5 29W
Saint John Canada 79 N5 45 16N 66 03W
St. John's Canada 79 P5 47 34N 52 43W
St. John's Point Northern Ireland 32 C2 54 15N 5 40W
St. John's Town of Dalry Scotland 33 E3 55 07N 4 10W
St. Just England 40 A3 50 07N 5 41W
St. Kilda i. Scotland 30 A2 57 49N 8 34W
St. Kitts-NEVIS 79 N2
St. Lawrence i. Alaska 78 C7 63 15N 169 50W
St. Lawrence r. Canada/U.S.A 79 M5 47 30N 70 00W
St. Lawrence, Gulf of Canada 79 N5 49 00N 62 30W
St-Lô France 48 C4 49 07N 1 05W
St. Louis Senegal 66 A4 16 01N 16 30W
St. Louis U.S.A. 79 K4 38 40N 90 15W
ST. LUCIA 79 N2
St. Magnus Bay Scotland 29 D3 60 25N 1 35W
St. Malo France 48 C4 48 39N 2 00W
St. Martin's i. England 40 A2 49 58N 6 17W
St. Mary's i. England 40 A2 49 55N 6 18W
St. Mary's Loch l. Scotland 33 F3 55 29N 3 12W
St. Matthew i. Alaska 78 B7 60 30N 172 30W
St. Moritz Switzerland 49 E2 46 30N 9 51E
St-Nazaire France 48 B3 47 17N 2 12W
St. Neots England 38 D3 52 14N 0 17W
St-Omer France 39 G1 50 45N 2 15E
St. Paul U.S.A. 79 K5 45 00N 93 10W
St. Peter-Port Guernsey Channel Islands 41 E2 49 27N 3 32W
St. Petersburg (Leningrad) Russia 56 D3 59 55N 30 25E
Saint Pierre & Miquelon is. Atlantic Ocean 79 P5 47 00N 56 00W
St-Quentin France 48 E4 49 51N 3 17E
St-Tropez France 48 G1 43 16N 6 39E
ST. VINCENT AND THE GRENADINES 79 N2
Saiwun Yemen Republic 61 15 59N 48 44E
Sakhalin i. Russia 57 Q3 50 00N 143 00E
Salado r. Argentina 85 C5 28 30S 62 30W
Salalah Oman 61 F2 17 00N 54 04E
Salamanca Spain 50 C4 40 58N 5 40W
Salcombe England 40 D2 50 13N 3 47W
Sale England 34 C2 53 26N 2 19W
Salem India 58 C2 11 38N 78 08E
Salerno Italy 51 E4 40 40N 14 46E
Salford England 34 C2 53 30N 2 16W
Salisbury England 38 C2 51 05N 1 48W
Salisbury Plain England 38 C2 51 10N 1 55W
Salta Argentina 84 C5 24 46S 65 28W
Saltash England 40 C3 50 24N 4 12W
Saltcoats Scotland 33 E3 55 38N 4 47W
Saltillo Mexico 79 J3 25 30N 101 00W
Salt Lake City U.S.A. 79 H5 40 45N 111 55W
Salvador Brazil 84 F6 12 58S 38 29W
Salween (Nu Jiang) r. Asia 58 E3 21 00N 99 00E
Salween r. see Nu Jiang
Salzburg Austria 42 J5 47 48N 13 03E
Salzgitter Germany 49 F5 52 13N 10 20E
Samar i. The Philippines 60 D4 12 00N 125 00E
Samara (Kuybyshev) Russia 56 F3 53 10N 50 10E
Samarinda Indonesia 60 C2 0 30S 117 09E
Samarkand Uzbekistan 56 G1 39 40N 66 57E
Sambre r. France 48 E5 50 15N 3 50E
SAMOA 4/5
Samsun Turkey 43 P4 41 17N 36 22E
San'a Yemen Republic 61 E2 15 23N 44 14E
Sanaga r. Cameroon 66 D3 5 00N 14 00E
San Antonio r. U.S.A. 79 K3 29 00N 97 00W
San Antonio Abad Balearic Islands 50 F3 38 59N 1 19E
San Benito Islands Mexico 79 H3 28 00N 115 00W
San Cristobal Venezuela 84 B8 7 46N 72 15W
Sandakan Malaysia 60 C3 5 52N 118 04E
Sanday i. Scotland 29 C2 59 15N 2 30W
San Diego U.S.A. 79 H4 32 45N 117 10W
Sandown England 38 C1 50 39N 1 09W
San Francisco U.S.A. 78 G4 37 45N 122 27W
San Francisco Javier Balearic Islands 50 F3 38 43N 1 26E
San José Costa Rica 79 L1 9 59N 84 04W
San Juan Argentina 85 C4 31 33S 68 31W
San Juan Puerto Rico 79 N2 18 29N 66 08W
San Luis Potosí Mexico 79 J3 22 10N 101 00W
SAN MARINO 51 D5
San Miguel de Tucumán Argentina 85 C5 26 47S 65 15W
San Pedro Sula Honduras 79 L2 15 26N 88 01W
Sanquhar Scotland 33 F3 55 22N 3 56W
San Salvador El Salvador 79 L2 13 40N 89 10W
San Sebastián Spain 50 E5 43 19N 1 59W
Santa Clara Cuba 79 M3 22 25N 79 58W
Santa Cruz Bolivia 84 C6 17 50S 63 10W
Santa Marta Colombia 84 B9 11 18N 74 10W
Santander Spain 50 D5 43 28N 3 48W
Santañy Balearic Islands 50 G3 39 22N 3 07E
Santarém Brazil 84 D7 2 26S 54 41W
Santarém Portugal 50 A3 39 14N 8 40W
Santiago Chile 85 B4 33 30S 70 40W
Santiago r. Mexico 79 J3 104 00W 21 30N

Santiago de Cuba Cuba 79 M3 20 00N 75 49W
Santiago del Estero Argentina 85 C5 27 47S 64 15W
Santo Domingo Dominican Republic 79 N2 18 30N 69 57W
Santos Brazil 84 E5 23 56S 46 22W
São Francisco r. Brazil 84 E6 13 40S 44 00W
São Luís Brazil 84 E7 2 34S 44 16W
Saône r. France 48 F3 47 30N 5 30E
São Paulo Brazil 84 E5 23 33S 46 39W
São Tomé i. Gulf of Guinea 66 C3 0 25N 6 35E
SÃO TOMÉ AND PRÍNCIPE 66 C3
Sapporo Japan 59 N3 43 05N 141 21E
Sarajevo Bosnia-Herzegovina 42 K4 43 52N 18 26E
Saratov Russia 56 E3 51 30N 45 55E
Sarawak admin. Malaysia 60 C3 1 00N 111 00E
Sardinia i. Italy 51 B4 40 00N 9 00E
Sarh Chad 66 D3 9 08N 18 22E
Sark i. Channel Islands British Isles 41 E2 49 26N 2 22W
Saskatchewan province Canada 78 J6 55 00N 105 00W
Saskatchewan r. Canada 78 J6 53 30N 105 00W
Saskatoon Canada 78 J6 52 10N 106 40W
Sassari Italy 51 B4 40 43N 8 34E
SAUDI ARABIA 61 E3
Saumur France 48 C3 47 16N 0 05W
Sava r. Europe 51 F6 45 45N 16 15E
Savannah U.S.A. 79 L4 32 04N 81 07W
Sawel mt. Northern Ireland 32 B2 54 49N 7 02W
Scafell Pike mt. England 34 B3 54 27N 3 14W
Scalasaig Scotland 32 C4 56 04N 6 12W
Scalloway Scotland 29 D3 60 08N 1 17W
Scalpay i. Highland Scotland 30 D2 57 15N 6 00W
Scalpay i. Western Isles Scotland 30 C2 57 15N 6 00W
Scapa Scotland 29 C1 58 58N 2 59W
Scapa Flow sd. Scotland 29 B1 58 55N 3 00W
Scarba i. Scotland 32 D4 56 45N 5 50W
Scarborough England 35 E3 54 17N 0 24W
Scarp i. Scotland 30 B3 58 02N 7 08W
Schefferville Canada 78 N6 54 50N 67 00W
Schelde r. Netherlands 49 B4/C4 51 00N 4 00E
Schwerin Germany 49 F6 53 38N 11 25E
Scilly, Isles of England 40 A2 49 56N 6 20W
Scotland country United Kingdom 28 56 10N 4 00W
Scottish Borders u.a. Scotland 33 F3/G3 55 30N 3 00W
Scunthorpe England 35 E2 53 35N 0 39W
Seascale England 34 B3 54 24N 3 29W
Seaton England 41 D3 50 43N 3 05W
Seattle U.S.A. 78 G5 47 35N 122 20W
Sedan France 48 F4 49 42N 4 57E
Seine r. France 48 D4 49 15N 1 15E
Sekondi Takoradi Ghana 66 B4 4 59N 1 43W
Selby England 35 D2 53 48N 1 04W
Selkirk Scotland 33 G3 55 33N 2 50W
Selsey Bill p. England 38 D1 50 43N 0 48W
Selvas geog. reg. South America 84 C7 7 00S 65 00W
Semarang Indonesia 60 C2 6 58S 110 29E
Semipalatinsk Kazakhstan 56 J3 50 26N 80 16E
Sendai Japan 59 N2 38 16N 140 52E
SENEGAL 66 A4
Senegal r. Senegal/Mauritania 66 A4 16 00N 15 00W
Sennar Sudan 61 D2 13 31N 33 38E
Sennen England 40 B3 50 03N 5 42W
Seoul South Korea 59 D3 37 32N 127 00E
Sept Îles tn. Canada 79 N6 50 10N 66 00W
Seram i. Indonesia 60 D2 3 30S 129 30E
Seram Sea Indonesia 60 D2 2 30S 130 00E
Serbia admin. Yugoslavia 42 L4 44 50N 21 00E
Seremban Malaysia 60 B3 2 43N 102 57E
Serov Russia 56 G3 59 42N 60 32E
Sétif Algeria 42 H3 36 11N 5 24E
Setúbal Portugal 50 A3 38 31N 8 54W
Sevastopol Ukraine 56 D2 44 36N 33 31E
Sevenoaks England 39 E2 51 16N 0 12E
Severn r. England 37 E1 51 30N 2 30W
Severnaya Zemlya is. Russia 57 K5 80 00N 95 00E
Severodvinsk Russia 43 P8 64 35N 39 50E
Seville Spain 50 C2 37 24N 5 59W
Seward U.S.A. 78 E7 60 05N 149 34W
SEYCHELLES 5
Sfax Tunisia 66 D6 34 45N 10 43E
Sgurr Mór mt. Scotland 31 D2 57 42N 5 03W
Shaftesbury England 41 E4 51 01N 2 12W
Shakhty Russia 43 Q5 47 43N 40 16E
Shanghai China 59 D3 31 06N 121 22E
Shanklin England 38 C1 50 38N 1 10W
Shannon r. Republic of Ireland 32 B2 54 15N 8 00W
Shapinsay i. Scotland 29 C2 59 03N 2 51W
Sheerness England 39 E2 51 27N 0 45E
Sheffield England 35 D2 53 23N 1 30W
Shenyang China 59 D4 41 50N 123 26E
Shepton Mallet England 41 E4 51 12N 2 33W
Sherborne England 41 E3 50 57N 2 31W
Sherbrooke Canada 79 M5 45 24N 71 54W
Sheringham England 39 F3 52 57N 1 12E
Shetland Islands u.a. Scotland 29 D3 60 00N 1 15W
Shiant Islands Scotland 30 C2 57 55N 6 20W
Shiel r. Scotland 30 D2 57 09N 5 20W
Shijiazhuang China 59 C3 38 04N 114 28E
Shikoku i. Japan 59 L1 33 40N 134 00E
Shilka r. Russia 57 M3 52 00N 118 00E
Shimonoseki Japan 59 L1 33 59N 130 58E
Shiraz Iran 61 F3 29 38N 52 34E
Shizuoka Japan 59 M1 34 59N 138 24E
Shkodër Albania 42 K4 42 03N 19 01E
Shrewsbury England 37 E2 52 43N 2 45W
Shropshire co. England 37 E2 52 35N 2 35W
Shymkent Kazakhstan 56 G2 42 16N 69 05E
Šiauliai Lithuania 42 L7 55 51N 23 20E
Siberian Lowland Russia 56 H4 60 00N 75 00E
Sibu Malaysia 60 C3 2 19N 111 50E
Sichuan Basin see Sichuan Pendi
Sichuan Pendi (Sichuan Basin) China 59 B3 32 00N 107 00E
Sicily i. Italy 51 E2 37 00N 14 00E
Sidi-Bel-Abbès Algeria 42 F3 35 15N 0 39W
Sidlaw Hills Scotland 31 F1/G1 56 30N 3 10W
Sidmouth England 41 D3 50 41N 3 15W
Siegen Germany 49 E4 50 52N 8 02E
Siena Italy 51 C5 43 19N 11 19E

SIERRA LEONE 66 A3
Sierra Madre mts. Mexico 79 J3 26 00N 108 00W
Sierra Nevada mts. Spain 50 D2 37 00N 3 20W
Sierra Nevada mts. U.S.A. 79 H4 37 00N 119 00W
Simbirsk see Ul'yanovsk
Simferopol Ukraine 56 D2 44 57N 34 05E
Simplon Pass Europe 49 E2 46 15N 8 03E
Simpson Desert Australia 72 D3 25 00S 137 00E
Sinai, Mount Egypt 61 D3 28 32N 33 59E
SINGAPORE 60 B3
Singkep i. Indonesia 60 B2 0 20S 104 30E
Sinuiju North Korea 59 D4 40 04N 124 25E
Siracusa Italy 51 E2 37 04N 15 19E
Sirte Libya 42 K2 31 13N 16 35E
Sivas Turkey 43 P3 39 44N 37 01E
Skegness England 35 F2 53 10N 0 21E
Skellefte r. Sweden 42 K9 65 30N 19 30E
Skelmersdale England 34 C2 53 55N 2 48W
Skiddaw mt. England 34 B3 54 40N 3 08W
Skikda Algeria 42 H3 36 53N 6 54E
Skipton England 34 C2 53 58N 2 01W
Skopje FYROM 42 L4 42 00N 21 28E
Skye i. Scotland 30 C2 57 20N 6 15W
Sleaford England 35 E1 53 00N 0 24W
Sleat, Sound of Scotland 30 D2 57 00N 5 55W
Slieve Donard mt. Northern Ireland 32 D2 54 11N 5 55W
Slieve Snaght sum. Republic of Ireland 32 B3 55 12N 7 20W
Slough England 38 D2 51 31N 0 36W
SLOVAKIA 42 K5
SLOVENIA 51 E7
Smallwood Reservoir Canada 78 N6 54 10N 63 50W
Smolensk Russia 56 D3 54 49N 32 04E
Snaefell mt. Isle of Man British Isles 33 E2 54 16N 4 28W
Snake r. U.S.A. 79 H5 43 00N 114 00W
Snowdon mt. Wales 36 C2 53 04N 4 05W
Snowy Mountains Australia 72 E2 36 24S 148 28E
Soar r. England 37 F2 52 40N 1 10W
Soay i. Scotland 30 C2 57 08N 6 14W
Sochi Russia 43 P4 43 35N 39 46E
Socotra i. Yemen Republic 61 F2 12 05N 54 10E
Sofia Bulgaria 42 L4 42 40N 23 18E
Sokoto Nigeria 66 C4 13 02N 5 15E
Solapur India 58 C2 17 43N 75 56E
Solihull England 37 F2 52 25N 1 45W
Solikamsk Russia 43 T7 59 40N 56 45E
Sóller Balearic Islands 50 G3 39 46N 2 42E
SOLOMON ISLANDS 72 F5
Solway Firth est. Scotland/England 34 B3 54 40N 3 40W
SOMALIA 67 E5
Somerset co. England 41 D4/E4 51 10N 3 00W
Somme r. France 48 E4 49 45N 2 30E
Songhua Hu res. China 59 D4 43 30N 126 51E
Songhua Jiang r. China 59 D4 46 30N 129 00E
Songkhla Thailand 60 B3 7 12N 100 35E
Song-koi r. China/Vietnam 58 B2 23 00N 102 00E
Southampton England 38 C1 50 55N 1 25W
Southampton Island Canada 78 L7 64 50N 85 00W
South Australia state Australia 72 D3 27 00S 135 00E
South Ayrshire u.a. Scotland 32/33 D2/E3 55 20N 4 40W
South Barrule hill Isle of Man British Isles 33 E2 54 09N 4 40W
South Benfleet England 39 E2 51 33N 0 34E
South Carolina state U.S.A. 79 L4 34 00N 81 00W
South China Sea Pacific Ocean 60 C4 15 00N 110 00E
South Dakota state U.S.A. 79 J5 44 00N 101 00W
South Downs hills England 38/39 D1/E1 50 50N 0 45W
Southend England 38 C1 50 55N 1 29W
Southend-on-Sea England 39 E2 51 33N 0 43E
Southern Alps mts. New Zealand 73 C2 43 07S 171 13E
Southern Ocean 86
Southern Uplands Scotland 33 E3/G3 55 30N 3 30W
South Esk r. Scotland 31 G1 56 40N 2 40W
South Georgia i. South Atlantic Ocean 85 F2 54 00S 36 00W
South Gloucestershire u.a. England 38 B2 51 30N 2 30W
South Island New Zealand 73 C2 42 30S 172 00E
SOUTH KOREA 59 D3
South Lanarkshire u.a. Scotland 33 E3/F3 55 35N 3 55W
South Molton England 40 D4 51 01N 3 50W
South Orkney Islands Southern Ocean 85 E1 60 00S 45 00W
South Pole Antarctica 86 90 00S
Southport England 34 B2 53 39N 3 01W
South Ronaldsay i. Scotland 29 C1 58 47N 2 56W
South Shields England 35 D3 55 00N 1 25W
South Uist i. Scotland 30 B2 57 20N 7 15W
Southwest Cape New Zealand 73 B1 48 00S 168 00E
Southwold England 39 F3 52 20N 1 40E
South Yorkshire co. England 34/35 D2 53 30N 1 30W
Sovetskaya Gavan Russia 57 Q2 48 57N 140 16E
SPAIN 50 C3
Spalding England 35 E1 52 47N 0 10W
Spencer Gulf Australia 72 D2 34 16S 136 53E
Spennymoor tn. England 34 D3 54 42N 1 35W
Spey r. Scotland 31 F2 57 40N 3 10W
Spilsby England 35 F2 53 11N 0 05E
Spitsbergen i. Arctic Ocean 86 79 00N 15 00E
Split Croatia 42 K4 43 31N 16 28E
Spokane U.S.A. 78 H5 47 40N 117 25W
Spurn Head England 35 F2 53 36N 0 07E
SRI LANKA 58 D1
Srinagar Jammu & Kashmir 58 C4 34 08N 74 50E
Stafford England 37 E2 52 48N 2 07W
Staffordshire co. England 37 E2/F2 52 50N 2 00W
Staines England 38 D2 51 26N 0 30W
Stamford England 35 E1 52 39N 0 29W
Stanley Falkland Islands 85 E2 51 45S 57 56W
Stara Zagora Bulgaria 42 M4 42 25N 25 37E
Start Bay England 40 D3 50 16N 3 35W
Start Point England 40 D3 50 13N 3 38W
Stavanger Norway 42 H7 58 58N 5 45E

Stavropol Russia 43 Q5 45 03N 41 59E
Sterlitamak Russia 43 T6 53 40N 55 59E
Stevenage England 38 D2 51 55N 0 14W
Stewart Island New Zealand 73 B1 46 55S 167 55E
Stinchar r. Scotland 33 E3 55 10N 4 45W
Stirling Scotland 33 F4 56 07N 3 57W
Stirling u.a. Scotland 33 E4 56 10N 4 15W
Stockbridge England 38 C2 51 07N 1 29W
Stockholm Sweden 42 K7 59 20N 18 05E
Stockport England 34 C2 53 25N 2 10W
Stockton-on-Tees England 35 D3 54 34N 1 19W
Stockton-on-Tees u.a. England 35 D3 54 33N 1 24W
Stoke-on-Trent England 37 E3 53 00N 2 10W
Stonehaven Scotland 31 G1 56 38N 2 13W
Stornoway Scotland 30 C3 58 12N 6 23W
Storr, The mt. Scotland 30 C2 57 30N 6 11W
Stour r. Dorset England 41 E3 50 50N 2 10W
Stour r. Suffolk/Essex England 39 E2/F2 51 55N 0 55E
Stourbridge England 37 E2 52 27N 2 09W
Stourport-on-Severn England 37 E2 52 21N 2 16W
Stowmarket England 39 F2 52 11N 1 00E
Stow-on-the-Wold England 38 C2 51 56N 1 44W
Strabane Northern Ireland 32 B2 54 49N 7 27W
Strabane district Northern Ireland 32 B2 54 45N 7 30W
Stralsund Germany 49 G6 54 18N 13 06E
Strangford Lough inlet Northern Ireland 32 D2 54 25N 5 45W
Stranraer Scotland 32 D2 54 55N 5 02W
Strasbourg France 48 G4 48 35N 7 45E
Stratford-upon-Avon England 37 F2 52 12N 1 41W
Strathy Point Scotland 31 E3 58 35N 4 02W
Stroma i. Scotland 31 F3 58 40N 3 08W
Stromness Scotland 29 B1 58 57N 3 18W
Stronsay i. Scotland 29 C2 59 07N 2 37W
Stronsay Firth sd Scotland 29 C2 59 00N 2 55W
Stroud England 38 B2 51 45N 2 12W
Strumble Head c. Wales 36 B2 52 02N 5 04W
Sturt Desert Australia 72 E2 27 00S 139 00E
Stuttgart Germany 49 E3 48 47N 9 12E
Sucre Bolivia 84 C6 19 05S 65 15W
SUDAN 61 C2
Sudbury Canada 79 L5 46 30N 81 01W
Sudbury England 39 E3 52 02N 0 44E
Suez Egypt 61 D3 29 59N 32 33E
Suez Canal Egypt 61 D4 31 30N 32 20E
Suffolk co. England 39 E3/F3 52 10N 1 00E
Sukhumi Georgia 43 Q4 43 01N 41 01E
Sula Islands Indonesia 60 D2 1 50S 124 50E
Sulawesi i. Indonesia 60 D2 2 00S 120 00E
Sullom Voe inlet Scotland 29 D3 60 27N 1 20W
Sulu Sea The Philippines/Malaysia 60 D3 8 00N 120 00E
Sumatra i. Indonesia 60 A3/B2 0 00 100 00E
Sumba i. Indonesia 60 C2 10 00S 120 00E
Sumbawa i. Indonesia 60 C2 8 00S 118 00E
Sumburgh Head Scotland 29 D2 59 51N 1 16W
Sumy Ukraine 43 N6 50 55N 34 49E
Sunda Strait Indonesia 60 B2 5 50S 105 30E
Sunderland England 35 D3 54 55N 1 23W
Sundsvall Sweden 42 K8 62 22N 17 20E
Superior, Lake Canada/U.S.A. 79 L5 48 00N 88 00W
Surabaya Indonesia 60 C2 7 14S 112 45E
Surakarta Indonesia 60 C2 7 32S 110 50E
Surat India 58 C2 21 10N 72 54E
SURINAME 84 D8
Surrey co. England 38 D2 51 25N 0 14W
Sutton England 38 D2 51 22N 0 12W
Sutton Coldfield England 37 F2 52 34N 1 48W
Sutton in Ashfield England 37 F3 53 08N 1 15W
Suzhou China 59 D3 31 21N 120 40E
Sverdlovsk see Yekaterinburg
Sverdrup Islands Canada 78 K8 79 00N 96 00W
Swaffham England 39 E3 52 39N 0 41E
Swale r. England 34 D3 54 30N 2 00W
Swanage England 41 F3 50 37N 1 58W
Swansea Wales 36 D1 51 38N 3 57W
Swansea u.a. Wales 36 C1 51 40N 4 05W
SWAZILAND 67 D2
SWEDEN 42 J7/L9
Swilly r. Republic of Ireland 32 B3 55 00N 7 30W
Swindon England 38 C2 51 34N 1 47W
SWITZERLAND 49 D2/E2
Sydney Australia 72 F2 33 52S 151 13E
Sydney Canada 79 N5 46 10N 60 10W
Syktyvkar Russia 43 S8 61 42N 50 45E
Symbister Scotland 29 D3 60 21N 1 02W
Syr Darya r. Asia 56 G2 45 00N 66 00E
SYRIA 61 D4
Szczecin Poland 42 J6 53 25N 14 32E
Szeged Hungary 42 L5 46 15N 20 09E

T

Tabora Tanzania 67 D4 5 01S 32 48E
Tabriz Iran 61 E4 38 05N 46 18E
Tabuk Saudi Arabia 61 D3 28 33N 36 36E
Tacoma U.S.A. 78 G5 47 16N 122 30W
Tadcaster England 35 D2 53 53N 1 16W
Taegu South Korea 59 D3 35 52N 128 36E
Taejon South Korea 59 D3 36 20N 127 26E
Tagus r. Spain/Portugal 50 B3 39 30N 7 00W
Tahat, Mount Algeria 66 C5 23 18N 5 33E
Taif Saudi Arabia 61 E3 21 15N 40 21E
Tai Hu l. China 59 D3 31 15N 120 10E
Tain Scotland 31 E2 57 48N 4 04W
Taipei Taiwan 59 D2 25 03N 121 30E
TAIWAN 59 D2
Taiyuan China 59 C3 37 50N 112 30E
Ta'izz Yemen Republic 61 E2 13 35N 44 02E
TAJIKISTAN 56 H1
Takamatsu Japan 59 L1 34 20N 134 01E
Takazze r. Africa 61 D2 14 00N 38 00E
Talaud Islands Indonesia 60 D3 4 00N 127 00E
Talca Chile 85 B3 35 28S 71 40W
Talcahuano Chile 85 B3 36 40S 73 10W
Tamanrasset Algeria 66 C5 22 50N 5 28E
Tamar r. England 40 C3 50 35N 4 15W
Tambov Russia 43 Q6 52 44N 41 28E
Tampa U.S.A. 79 L3 27 58N 82 38W
Tampere Finland 42 L8 61 32N 23 45E

Tampico Mexico 79 K3 22 18N 97 52W
Tamworth England 37 F2 52 39N 1 40W
Tana, Lake Ethiopia 61 D2 12 20N 37 20E
Tanga Tanzania 67 D4 5 07S 39 05E
Tanganyika, Lake East Africa 67 C4 7 00S 30 00E
Tangier Morocco 66 B6 35 48N 5 45W
Tangshan China 59 C3 39 37N 118 05E
Tanimbar Islands Indonesia 60 E2 7 30S 131 30E
Tanjungkarang Indonesia 60 B2 5 28S 105 16E
TANZANIA 67 D4
Tapajós r. Brazil 84 D7 9 10S 56 20W
Taransay i. Scotland 30 B2 57 55N 7 00W
Táranto Italy 51 F4 40 28N 17 15E
Tarbat Ness c. Scotland 31 F2 57 50N 3 45W
Tarbert Argyll and Bute Scotland 32 D3 55 52N 5 26W
Tarbert Western Isles Scotland 30 C2 57 54N 6 49W
Tarbes France 48 D1 43 14N 0 05E
Tarbet Scotland 33 E4 56 12N 4 43W
Tarim Basin see Tarim Pendi
Tarim He r. China 58 C4 38 00N 77 00E
Tarim Pendi (Tarim Basin) China 58 D4/5 39 00N 84 00E
Tarn r. France 48 E1 44 00N 2 15E
Tarragona Spain 50 F4 41 07N 1 15E
Tartu Estonia 42 M7 58 20N 26 44E
Tashkent Uzbekistan 56 G2 41 16N 69 13E
Tasman Bay New Zealand 73 C2 41 00S 173 14E
Tasmania state Australia 72 E1 42 00S 143 00E
Tasman Sea Pacific Ocean 7 39 00S 155 00E
Taunton England 41 D4 51 01N 3 06W
Taupo New Zealand 73 D3 38 42S 176 05E
Taupo, Lake New Zealand 73 D3 37 41S 176 10E
Tauranga New Zealand 73 D3 37 41S 176 10E
Tavistock England 40 C3 50 33N 4 08W
Tavy r. England 40 C3 50 36N 4 05W
Taw r. England 40 C4/D3 51 00N 4 00W
Tay r. Scotland 31 F1 56 30N 3 30W
Tbilisi Georgia 56 E2 41 43N 44 48E
Te Anau, Lake New Zealand 73 B1 45 13S 167 45E
Tébessa Algeria 42 H3 35 21N 8 06E
Tees r. England 35 D3 54 30N 1 25W
Tegucigalpa Honduras 79 L2 14 05N 87 14W
Tehran Iran 61 F4 35 40N 51 26E
Teifi r. Wales 36 C2 52 03N 4 30W
Teign r. England 40 D3 50 45N 3 40W
Teignmouth England 40 D3 50 33N 3 30W
Tel Aviv-Jaffa Israel 61 N3 32 05N 34 46E
Telford England 37 E2 52 42N 2 28W
Teme r. England 37 E2 52 20N 2 30W
Temuco Chile 85 B3 38 45S 72 40W
Tenby Wales 36 C1 51 41N 4 43W
Tenerife i. Canary Islands 66 A5 28 15N 16 35W
Tennessee r. U.S.A. 79 L4 36 00N 89 00W
Tennessee state U.S.A. 79 L4 35 00N 87 00W
Teramo Italy 51 D5 42 40N 13 43E
Teresina Brazil 84 E7 5 09S 42 46W
Terni Italy 51 D5 42 34N 12 39E
Terracina Italy 51 D4 41 17N 13 15E
Test r. England 38 C2 51 10N 1 30W
Tétouan Morocco 66 B6 35 34N 5 22W
Teviot r. Scotland 33 G3 55 30N 2 45W
Tewkesbury England 38 B2 51 59N 2 09W
Texas state U.S.A. 79 K4 31 00N 100 00W
THAILAND 60 B4
Thailand, Gulf of Asia 60 B4 10 50N 101 00E
Thame England 38 D2 51 45N 0 59W
Thame r. England 38 D2 51 45N 1 00W
Thames r. England 39 E2 51 30N 0 05E
Thar Desert India 58 C3 27 30N 72 00E
The Hague Netherlands 49 C5 52 05N 4 16E
The Needles rocks England 38 C1 50 39N 1 35W
The Peak mt. England 37 F3 53 24N 1 51W
The Solent sd. England 38 C1 50 45N 1 25W
Thessalonica Greece 42 L4 40 38N 22 58E
Thetford England 39 E3 52 25N 0 45E
The Wrekin pk. England 37 E2 52 41N 2 32W
Thimphu Bhutan 58 D3 27 32N 89 43E
Thionville France 48 G4 49 22N 6 11E
Thirsk England 35 D3 54 14N 1 20W
Thornaby-on-Tees England 35 D3 54 34N 1 18W
Thornhill Scotland 33 F3 55 15N 3 46W
Three Kings Islands New Zealand 73 C4 34 10S 172 07E
Thunder Bay tn. Canada 79 L5 48 27N 89 12W
Thurrock England 39 E2 51 28N 0 20E
Thurso Scotland 31 F3 58 35N 3 32W
Thurso r. Scotland 31 F3 58 15N 3 35W
Tianjin China 59 C3 39 08N 117 12E
Tibetan Plateau Tibet 58 D4 33 00N 85 00E
Tibesti mts. Chad 66 D5 21 00N 17 00E
Tien Shan mts. China 58 C5/D5 41 00N 76 00E
Tierra del Fuego i. Chile/Argentina 85 C2 54 00S 67 30W
Tighnabruaich Scotland 32 D3 55 56N 5 14W
Tigris r. Iraq 61 E4 34 00N 43 00E
Tijuana Mexico 79 H4 32 29N 117 10W
Tilburg Netherlands 49 C4 51 34N 5 05E
Timaru New Zealand 73 C2 44 24S 171 15E
Timbuktu Mali 66 B4 16 49N 2 59W
Timişoara Romania 42 L5 45 45N 21 15E
Timor i. Indonesia 60 D2 9 00S 125 00E
Timor Sea Australia 72 C4 12 30S 127 00E
Tiranë Albania 42 K4 41 20N 19 50E
Tiraspol Moldova 42 M5 46 50N 29 38E
Tiree i. Scotland 30 C1 56 30N 6 55W
Tirgu Mures Romania 42 L5 46 33N 24 34E
Tisza r. Hungary/Yugoslavia 42 L5 47 00N 20 30E
Titicaca, Lake Peru/Bolivia 84 C6 16 00S 69 00W
Titograd Montenegro Yugoslavia 42 K4 42 28N 19 17E
Tiverton England 41 D3 50 55N 3 29W
Tivoli Italy 51 D4 41 58N 12 48E
Tizi Ouzou Algeria 50 H2 36 44N 4 05E
Tlemcen Algeria 42 F3 34 53N 1 21W
Toamasina Madagascar 67 E3 18 10S 49 23E
Tobago i. Trinidad and Tobago 84 C9 11 15N 60 40W
Tobermory Scotland 30 C1 56 37N 6 05W
Tobol r. Russia 56 G3 58 00N 66 00E
Tobruk Libya 66 E6 32 05N 23 59E
Tocantins r. Brazil 84 E7 8 40S 48 00W

TOGO 66 C3
Tokoroa New Zealand 73 D3 38 14S 175 52E
Tokyo Japan 59 M2 35 40N 139 45E
Toledo U.S.A. 79 L5 41 40N 83 35W
Toliara Madagascar 67 E2 23 20S 43 41E
Tol'yatti Russia 56 E3 53 32N 49 24E
Tomsk Russia 56 J3 56 30N 85 05E
Tonbridge England 39 E2 51 12N 0 16E
Tone r. England 41 D4/E4 51 00N 3 00W
Tone r. Japan 59 N2 36 00N 140 00E
TONGA 5
Toowoomba Australia 72 F3 27 34S 151 58E
Torbay England 40 D3 50 27N 3 30W
Tordesillas Spain 50 C4 41 30N 5 00W
Torfean u.a. Wales 36 D1 51 45N 3 03W
Torne r. Sweden 42 L9 67 30N 22 00E
Toronto Canada 79 M5 43 42N 79 46W
Torpoint tn. England 40 C3 50 22N 4 11W
Torre del Greco Italy 51 E4 40 46N 14 22E
Torrens, Lake Australia 72 D2 30 58S 137 52E
Torreón Mexico 79 J3 25 34N 103 25W
Torres Strait Australia 72 E5 9 30S 142 00E
Torridge r. England 40 C3 50 55N 4 15W
Tortosa Spain 50 F4 40 49N 0 31E
Toruń Poland 42 K6 53 01N 18 35E
Tory Island Republic of Ireland 32 A3 55 16N 8 14W
Tory Sound Republic of Ireland 32 A3 55 15N 8 05W
Totnes England 40 D3 50 25N 3 41W
Totton England 38 C1 50 56N 3 06W1 29W
Tottori Japan 59 M1 35 32N 134 12E
Toubkal, Mount Morocco 66 B6 31 03N 7 57W
Touggourt Algeria 66 C6 33 08N 6 04E
Toulon France 48 F1 43 07N 5 55E
Toulouse France 48 D1 43 33N 1 24E
Tours France 48 D3 47 23N 0 42E
Towcester England 38 D3 52 08N 1 00W
Townsville Australia 72 E4 19 17S 146 48E
Toyama Japan 59 M2 36 42N 137 14E
Trabzona Turkey 43 P4 41 00N 39 43E
Trent r. England 37 G3 53 30N 0 50W
Trento Italy 51 C7 46 04N 11 08E
Tresco i. England 40 A2 49 57N 6 20W
Trevose Head England 40 B3 50 33N 5 01W
Trier Germany 49 D3 49 45N 6 39E
Trieste Italy 51 D6 45 39N 13 47E
Trincomalee Sri Lanka 58 D1 8 34N 81 13E
TRINIDAD AND TOBAGO 79 N2
Tripoli Lebanon 61 D4 34 27N 35 50E
Tripoli Libya 66 D6 32 54N 13 11E
Tristan da Cunha i. Atlantic Ocean 5 37 15S 12 30W
Trivandrum India 58 C1 8 30N 76 57E
Tromsø Norway 42 K9 69 42N 19 00E
Trondheim Norway 42 J8 63 36N 10 23E
Troon Scotland 33 E3 55 32N 4 40W
Trowbridge England 38 B2 51 20N 2 13W
Troyes France 48 F4 48 18N 4 05E
Trujillo Peru 84 B7 8 06S 79 00W
Trujillo Spain 50 C3 39 28N 5 53W
Truro England 40 B3 50 16N 5 02W
Tsangpo see Yarlung Zangbo Jiang
Tselinograd see Akmola
Tsimlyansk Reservoir Russia 43 Q5 47 30N 43 00E
Tsinan see Jinan
Tsugaru Channel Japan 59 N3 41 30N 140 30E
Tucson U.S.A. 79 H4 32 15N 110 57W
Tula Russia 56 D3 54 11N 37 38E
Tulsa U.S.A. 79 K4 36 07N 95 58W
Tunis Tunisia 66 D6 36 50N 10 13E
TUNISIA 66 C6
Turfan Depression China 58 D5/E5 42 40N 89 30E
Turin Italy 51 A6 45 04N 7 40E
Turkana, Lake Ethiopia/Kenya 67 D5 4 00N 36 00E
TURKEY 43 N3
TURKMENISTAN 56 F1
Turks and Caicos Islands West Indies 79 M3 21 30N 72 00W
Turku Finland 42 L8 60 27N 22 15E
Turriff Scotland 31 G2 57 32N 2 28W
TUVALU 5
Túy Spain 50 A5 42 03N 8 39W
Tuz, Lake Turkey 43 N3 38 40N 33 35E
Tver (Kalinin) Russia 56 D3 56 49N 35 57E
Tweed r. Scotland/England 33 G3 55 45N 2 10W
Tynda Russia 57 N3 55 10N 124 35E
Tyndrum Scotland 33 E1 57 27N 4 44W
Tyne r. England 34 D3 54 58N 2 00W
Tyne and Wear co. England 35 D4 54 55N 1 24W
Tynemouth England 35 D4 55 01N 1 24W
Tyrrhenian Sea Europe 51 C4/D4 40 00N 12 00E
Tyumen Russia 56 G3 57 11N 65 29E
Tywi r. Wales 36 C1 51 45N 3 20W

U

Uberaba Brazil 84 E6 19 47S 47 57W
Uberlândia Brazil 84 E6 18 57S 48 17W
Ucayali r. Peru 84 B7 7 30S 75 00W
Udine Italy 51 D7 46 04N 13 14E
Uele r. Zaïre 67 C5 4 00N 26 00E
Ufa Russia 56 F3 54 45N 55 58E
UGANDA 67 D5
Ujung Pandang Indonesia 60 C2 5 09S 119 28E
Ukhta Russia 43 S8 63 33N 53 44E
UKRAINE 56 D2
Ulan Bator Mongolia 57 L2 47 54N 106 52E
Ulan-Ude Russia 57 L3 51 55N 107 40E
Ullapool Scotland 30 D2 57 54N 5 10W
Ullswater l. England 34 C3 54 35N 2 55W
Ullung Island South Korea 59 L2 37 30N 132 00E
Ulm Germany 49 F3 48 24N 10 00E
Ulva i. Scotland 30 C1 56 30N 6 15W
Ul'yanovsk (Simbirsk) Russia 56 E3 54 19N 48 22E
Umeå Sweden 42 L8 63 50N 20 15E
Unimak Island U.S.A. 78 C6 55 00N 164 00W
UNITED ARAB EMIRATES 61 F3
UNITED KINGDOM 42 F6
UNITED STATES OF AMERICA (U.S.A.) 79
Unst i. Scotland 29 E3 60 45N 0 55W

V

Vaal r. Republic of South Africa 67 C2 27 30S 25 00E
Vaasa Finland 42 L8 63 06N 21 36E
Vadodara India 58 C3 22 19N 73 14E
Vaduz Liechtenstein 49 E2 47 08N 9 32E
Valdepeñas Spain 50 D3 38 46N 3 24W
Valdivia Chile 85 B4 39 46S 73 15W
Valence France 48 F2 44 56N 4 54E
Valencia Spain 50 E3 39 29N 0 24W
Valencia Venezuela 84 C9 10 14N 67 59W
Valenciennes France 48 E5 50 22N 3 32E
Vale of Glamorgan u.a. Wales 36 D1 52 30N 3 30W
Valladolid Spain 50 C4 41 39N 4 45W
Valletta Malta 51 E1 35 54N 14 32E
Valognes France 41 F2 49 31N 1 28W
Valparaíso Chile 85 B4 33 05S 71 40W
Vancouver Canada 78 G5 49 13N 123 06W
Vancouver Island Canada 78 G4 48 55N 124 33W
Vänern, Lake Sweden 42 J7 59 00N 13 30E
Van, Lake Turkey 43 Q3 38 33N 42 46E
Vannes France 48 B3 47 40N 2 44W
VANUATU 5
Varanasi India 58 D3 25 20N 83 00E
Varaždin Croatia 51 F7 46 18N 16 21E
Varna Bulgaria 42 M4 43 12N 27 57E
Västerås Sweden 42 K7 59 36N 16 32E
VENEZUELA 84 C8
Venice Italy 51 D6 45 26N 12 20E
Veracruz Mexico 79 K2 19 11N 96 10W
Verdun France 48 F4 49 10N 5 24E
Verkhoyansk Russia 57 P4 67 35N 133 25E
Vermont state U.S.A. 79 M5 44 00N 73 00W
Verona Italy 51 C6 45 26N 11 00E
Versailles France 48 E4 48 48N 2 07E
Vesuvius mt. Italy 51 E4 40 49N 14 26E
Veurne Belgium 39 G2 51 04N 2 40E
Vicenza Italy 51 C6 45 33N 11 32E
Vichy France 48 E3 46 07N 3 25E
Victoria Canada 78 G5 48 26N 123 20W
Victoria r. Australia 72 D4 17 00S 131 00E
Victoria state Australia 72 E2 47 00S 143 00E
Victoria Falls Zambia/Zimbabwe 67 C3 17 55S 25 51E
Victoria Island Canada 78 H5 70 45N 115 00W
Victoria, Lake East Africa 67 D4 2 00S 33 00E
Vienna Austria 42 K5 48 13N 16 22E
Vienne France 48 F3 46 31N 4 53E
Vienne r. France 48 D3 47 13N 0 05E
Vientiane Laos 60 B4 17 59N 102 38E
Vierzon France 48 E3 47 14N 2 03E
VIETNAM 60 B4
Vigo Spain 50 A5 42 15N 8 44W
Vijayawada India 58 D2 16 34N 80 40E
Villach Austria 51 D7 46 37N 13 51E
Vilnius Lithuania 42 M6 54 40N 25 19E
Viña del Mar Chile 85 B4 33 02S 71 35W
Vinh Vietnam 60 B4 18 42N 105 41E
Vinnytsya Ukraine 56 C2 49 11N 28 30E
Vinson Massif mts. Antarctica 86 78 02S 22 00W
Vire r. France 41 E4 49 00N 1 05W
Virginia state U.S.A. 79 M4 38 00N 77 00W
Virgin Islands West Indies 79 N2 18 00N 64 30W
Visakhapatnam India 58 D2 17 42N 83 24E
Vistula r. Poland 42 K6 53 00N 19 00E
Vitória Brazil 84 E5 20 20S 40 18W
Vitoria Spain 50 D5 42 51N 2 40W
Vitsyebsk Belarus 56 D3 55 10N 30 14E
Vladikavkaz Russia 43 Q4 43 02N 44 43E
Vladimir Russia 56 E3 56 08N 40 25E
Vladivostok Russia 57 P2 43 09N 131 53E
Vlorë Albania 42 K4 40 29N 19 29E
Volga r. Russia 56 E3 51 30N 48 00E
Volgograd Russia 56 E2 48 45N 44 30E
Vologda Russia 56 D3 59 10N 39 55E
Volta, Lake Ghana 66 B3 7 30N 0 30W
Vorkuta Russia 56 G4 67 27N 64 00E
Voronezh Russia 56 D3 51 40N 39 13E
Vosges mts. France 48 G4 48 10N 6 50E
Vyatka see Kirov
Vyrnwy r. Wales 36 D2 52 45N 3 10W
Vyrnwy, Lake Wales 36 D2 52 47N 3 30W

W

Waal r. Netherlands 49 C4 51 50N 5 00E
Waddington, Mount Canada 78 G6 51 22N 125 14W
Wadebridge England 40 C3 50 32N 4 50W
Wadi Halfa Sudan 61 D3 21 55N 31 20E
Wad Medani Sudan 61 D2 14 24N 33 30E
Waiau r. New Zealand 73 B1 46 00S 167 30E
Waigeo i. Indonesia 60 E2 0 15S 130 45E
Waikato r. New Zealand 73 D3 37 30S 175 30E
Wairau r. New Zealand 73 C2 40 30S 173 00E
Waitaki r. New Zealand 73 C2 44 45S 170 30E
Wakatipu, Lake New Zealand 73 B1 45 06S 168 31E
Wakayama Japan 59 M1 34 12N 135 10E
Wakefield England 35 D2 53 42N 1 29W
Wakkanai Japan 59 N4 45 26N 141 43E
Walbury Hill England 38 C2 51 25N 1 35W
Wales country United Kingdom 36 D2 52 40N 3 30W

Wallasey England 34 B2 53 26N 3 03W
Walls Scotland 29 D3 60 14N 1 34W
Walsall England 37 F2 52 35N 1 58W
Waltham Forest England 38 D2 51 36N 0 00
Walton on the Naze England 39 F2 51 51N 1 16E
Walvis Bay tn. Namibia 67 B2 22 59S 14 31E
Wanaka, Lake New Zealand 73 B2 44 28S 169 09E
Wanganui New Zealand 73 D3 39 56S 175 03E
Wanganui r. New Zealand 73 D3 39 30S 175 00E
Wansbeck r. England 33 H3 55 10N 1 50W
Wantage England 38 C2 51 36N 1 25W
Ward Hill Scotland 29 B1 58 54N 3 20W
Ward's Stone hill England 34 C3 54 03N 2 38W
Wareham England 41 E3 50 41N 2 07W
Warley England 37 F2 52 30N 1 59W
Warminster England 38 B2 51 13N 2 12W
Warrenpoint tn. Northern Ireland 32 C2 54 06N 6 15W
Warrington England 34 C2 53 24N 2 37W
Warsaw Poland 42 L6 52 15N 21 00E
Warwick England 37 F2 52 17N 1 34W
Warwickshire co. England 37 F2 52 15N 1 40W
Washington England 34 D3 54 54N 1 31W
Washington state U.S.A. 79 G5 47 00N 120 00W
Washington D.C. U.S.A. 79 M4 38 55N 77 00W
Wash, The b. England 35 F2 53 00N 0 10E
Waterlooville England 38 C1 50 53N 1 02W
Water of Luce r. Scotland 32/33 E2 54 55N 4 55W
Watford England 38 D2 51 40N 0 25W
Wau Papua New Guinea 72 E5 7 22S 146 40E
Waveney r. England 39 F3 52 30N 1 30E
Weald, The geog. reg. England 39 E2 51 05N 0 25E
Wear r. England 34 C3 54 40N 2 05W
Weddell Sea Southern Ocean 86 71 00S 40 00W
Wei He r. China 59 B3 34 00N 106 00E
Welland r. England 38 D3 52 30N 0 40W
Wellingborough England 38 D3 52 19N 0 42W
Wellington England 41 D3 50 59N 3 15W
Wellington New Zealand 73 C2 41 17S 174 46E
Wells England 41 E4 51 13N 2 39W
Wells-next-the-Sea England 39 E3 52 58N 0 51E
Welshpool Wales 36 D2 52 40N 3 09W
Welwyn Garden City England 38 D2 51 48N 0 13W
Wenlock Edge hills England 37 E2 52 30N 2 45W
Wensum r. England 39 E3 52 45N 1 05E
Weser r. Germany 49 E5 52 30N 9 00E
West Bromwich England 37 F2 52 31N 1 59W
Westbury England 38 B2 51 16N 2 11W
Western Australia state Australia 72 C3 25 00S 123 00E
Western Ghats mts. India 58 C2 15 30N 74 00E
Western Isles u.a. Scotland 30 B2/C3 57 30N 7 00W
WESTERN SAHARA 66 A5
WESTERN SAMOA see SAMOA
West Friesian Islands Netherlands 49 C5 53 25N 5 15E
West Lothian u.a. Scotland 33 F3 55 50N 3 36W
West Midlands co. England 37 E2/F2 52 28N 1 40W
Weston-super-Mare England 38 B2 51 21N 2 59W
West Palm Beach tn. U.S.A. 79 L3 26 42N 80 05W
Westport New Zealand 73 C2 41 45S 171 36E
Westray i. Scotland 29 B2/C2 59 18N 3 00W
Westray Firth sd. Scotland 29 B2/C2 59 15N 3 00W
West Sussex co. England 38 D1 50 00N 0 25W
West Virginia state U.S.A. 79 L4 39 00N 81 00W
West Yorkshire co. England 34/35 D2 53 50N 1 30W
Wetherby England 35 D2 53 56N 1 23W
Weymouth England 41 E3 50 37N 2 25W
Whakatane New Zealand 73 D3 37 58S 176 59E
Whalsay i. Scotland 29 E3 60 22N 0 59W
Whangarei New Zealand 73 D3 35 43S 174 19E
Wharfe r. England 34 C3 54 10N 2 05W
Whernside sum. England 34 C3 54 14N 2 23W
Whitby England 35 E3 54 29N 0 37W
Whitchurch England 37 E2 52 58N 2 41W
Whiteadder Water r. Scotland/England 33 G3 55 50N 2 10W
Whitehaven England 34 B3 54 33N 3 35W
Whitehorse Canada 78 F7 60 41N 135 08W
White Nile r. Sudan 61 D2 11 00N 32 00E
White Sea Russia 42 P9 66 00N 37 30E
Whithorn Scotland 33 E2 54 44N 4 25W
Whitley Bay tn. England 33 H3 55 03N 1 25W
Whitney, Mount U.S.A. 79 H4 36 35N 118 17W
Whyalla Australia 72 D3 33 02S 137 35E
Wichita U.S.A. 79 K4 37 43N 97 20W
Wick Scotland 31 F3 58 26N 3 06W
Wicklow Wicklow Republic of Ireland 36 A2 52 59N 6 03W
Widnes England 34 C2 53 22N 2 44W
Wiesbaden Germany 49 E4 50 05N 8 15E
Wigan England 34 C2 53 33N 2 38W
Wigston England 37 F2 52 36N 1 05W
Wigton England 34 B3 54 49N 3 09W
Wigtown Scotland 32 E2 54 52N 4 26W
Wigtown Bay Scotland 33 E2 54 10N 4 20W
Wilhelmshaven Germany 49 E5 53 32N 8 07E
Wilkes Land geog. reg. Antarctica 86 68 00S 105 00E
Wiltshire co. England 38 B2/C2 51 30N 2 00W
Wimborne Minster England 41 F3 50 48N 1 59W
Wincanton England 41 E4 51 04N 2 25W
Winchester England 38 C2 51 04N 1 19W
Windermere England 34 C3 54 23N 2 54W
Windermere l. England 34 C3 54 20N 2 57W
Windhoek Namibia 67 B2 22 34S 17 06E
Windsor England 38 D2 51 29N 0 38W
Winnipeg Canada 79 K5 49 53N 97 10W
Winnipeg, Lake Canada 78 K6 53 00N 97 00W
Winsford England 34 C2 53 11N 2 31W
Winterthur Switzerland 49 E2 47 30N 8 45E
Wisbech England 39 E3 52 40N 0 10E
Wisconsin state U.S.A. 79 K5 45 00N 90 00W
Wishaw Scotland 33 F3 55 47N 3 56W
Witham r. England 35 E2 53 05N 0 10W
Witham England 38 C2 51 48N 0 38E
Witney England 38 C2 51 48N 1 29W
Wittenberg Germany 49 G5 51 53N 12 39E
Woking England 38 D2 51 20N 0 34W
Wokingham England 38 D2 51 25N 0 51W
Wolfsburg Germany 49 F5 52 27N 10 49E
Wollongong Australia 72 F2 34 25S 150 53E

Wolverhampton England 37 E2 52 36N 2 08W
Wonsan North Korea 59 D3 39 07N 127 26E
Woodbridge England 39 F3 52 06N 1 19E
Wooler England 33 G3 55 33N 2 01W
Worcester England 37 E2 52 11N 2 13W
Workington England 34 B3 54 39N 3 33W
Worksop England 37 F3 53 18N 1 07W
Worms Head Wales 36 C1 51 34N 4 20W
Worthing England 38 D1 50 48N 0 23W
Wrangel i. Russia 57 U5 61 30N 180 00
Wrath, Cape Scotland 31 D3 58 38N 5 01W
Wrexham Wales 36 D3 53 03N 3 00W
Wrexham u.a. Wales 36 D3 53 00N 3 00W
Wrocław Poland 42 K6 51 05N 17 00E
Wuhan China 59 C3 30 35N 114 19E
Wuppertal Germany 49 D4 51 15N 7 10E
Würzburg Germany 49 E3 49 48N 9 57E
Wye r. England/Wales 37 E1 51 40N 2 40W
Wymondham England 39 F3 52 34N 1 07E
Wyndham Australia 72 C4 15 28S 128 06E
Wyoming state U.S.A. 79 J5 43 00N 108 00W
Wyre r. England 34 C2 53 50N 2 50W

X

Xi r. China 60 C5 23 00N 112 00E
Xi'an China 59 B3 34 16N 108 54E
Xi Jiang r. China 59 C2 22 00N 111 00E
Xingu r. Brazil 84 D7 5 30S 52 40W
Xining China 59 B3 36 35N 101 55E
Xuzhou China 59 C3 34 17N 117 18E

Y

Yakutsk Russia 57 N4 62 10N 129 50E
Yamagata Japan 59 N2 38 16N 140 16E
Yamoussoukro Côte d'Ivoire 66 B3 6 50N 5 20W
Yangdon see Rangoon
Yangtze r. see Jinsha Jiang (upper course),
  Chang Jiang (lower course)
Yaoundé Cameroon 66 D3 3 51N 11 31E
Yarlung Zangbo Jiang (Tsangpo) r. China 58 D3 30 00N 90 00E
Yaroslavl Russia 56 D3 57 34N 39 52E
Yarrow Water r. Scotland 33 F3 55 35N 3 05W
Yazd Iran 61 F4 31 54N 54 22E
Yekaterinburg (Sverdlovsk) Russia 56 G3 56 52N 60 35E
Yell i. Shetland Islands United Kingdom 29 D3 60 35N 1 10W
Yellowknife Canada 78 H7 62 30N 114 29W
Yellow Sea China 59 D3 35 30N 122 30E
Yell Sound Scotland 29 D3 60 30N 1 15W
YEMEN REPUBLIC 61 E2
Yenisey r. Russia 57 J4 64 00N 88 00E
Yeo r. England 41 E4 51 00N 2 45W
Yeovil England 41 E3 50 57N 2 39W
Yerevan Armenia 43 Q4 40 10N 44 31E
Yes Tor sum. England 40 C3 50 42N 4 00W
Yogyakarta Indonesia 60 C2 7 48S 110 24E
Yokkaichi Japan 59 M1 34 58N 136 38E
Yokohama Japan 59 M2 35 27N 139 38E
York England 35 D2 53 58N 1 05W
York u.a. England 35 D2 53 56N 1 02W
York, Cape Australia 72 E4 10 41S 142 32E
Yorkshire Wolds hills England 35 E3 54 00N 0 45W
York, Vale of England 35 D3 54 10N 1 20W
Ypres see Ipres
Yucatan Channel Caribbean Sea 79 L3 21 00N 85 00W
Yucatan Peninsula Mexico 79 L2/3 19 00N 89 00W
YUGOSLAVIA 42 L4
Yukon r. Canada/U.S.A. 78 D7 65 00N 155 00W
Yukon Territory Canada 78 F7 62 00N 135 00W

Z

Zagreb Croatia 42 K5 45 48N 15 58E
Zagros Mountains Iran 61 E4/F3 32 45N 48 50E
Zahedan Iran 61 G3 29 32N 60 54E
Zahlé Lebanon 43 P2 33 50N 35 55E
ZAÏRE see CONGO DEMOCRATIC REPUBLIC
Zaïre r. see Congo
Zambezi r. Southern Africa 67 D3 17 00S 34 00E
ZAMBIA 67 C3
Zamboanga The Philippines 60 D3 6 55N 122 05E
Zanzibar Tanzania 67 D4 6 10S 39 12E
Zaporizhzhya Ukraine 43 P5 47 50N 35 10E
Zaragoza Spain 50 E4 41 39N 0 54W
Zaria Nigeria 66 C4 11 01N 7 44E
Zarqa Jordan 43 P2 32 04N 36 05E
Zaysan, Lake Kazakhstan 56 J2 48 00N 84 00E
Zealand i. Denmark 42 F6 55 00N 12 00E
Zeebrugge Belgium 49 B4 51 20N 3 13E
Zhambyl Kazakhstan 56 H2 42 50N 71 25E
Zhangjiakou China 59 C4 40 51N 114 59E
Zhangye China 59 B3 38.58N 100.30E
Zhanjiang China 59 C2 21 10N 110 20E
Zhengzhou China 59 C3 34 45N 113 38E
Zhytomyr Ukraine 42 M6 50 18N 28 40E
Zibo China 59 C3 36 51N 118 01E
Ziel, Mount Australia 72 D3 23 30S 132 24E
ZIMBABWE 67 C3
Zinder Niger 66 C4 13 46N 8 58E
Zonguldak Turkey 43 N4 41 26N 31 47E
Zürich Switzerland 49 E2 47 23N 8 33E
Zwickau Germany 49 G4 50 43N 12 30E